Convent
to
Catwalk

Hope you enjoy "walking"
from
Convent to Catwalk
with me!
Mary Jo Shaw

Contents

Readers Comments......................................vii

Acknowledgments......................................xiii

Religious Life Then and Now I

Mysterious Mysteries..................................4

Exodus..II

Full Day Eye-Openers................................21

First Letter Home 27

Challenging First Weeks..............................30

Visiting Twice The First Time.......................34

Summer Recollections 1956...........................39

The Lying Nun 48

Buddies, Misnomers and Shenanigans.................55

Postulancy, Investiture and Novitiate 67

Oil in a Day's Work..................................73

Profession Day 82

Powerful Throne 89

Little Organ in Abilene..............................94

Abilene Flashbacks...................................98

False Authority 102

Bus Flight to Lawton III

Just Say No. 114

Proposal for Danger. 118

I'm Not Me 121

Santa Rosa Daze. 127

Alone in Room 1109 134

Christmas Overdose. 141

Long Roads to Recovery 148

PLEASE God, Not My Music. 152

Show and Tell Habits 158

Changing Experiences. 162

Truth Serum and End of Life. 171

Walking Papers. 178

Another New Life. 182

Photos Convent 189

Before and After 213

Walking with Rules 220

On Live TV 228

Broadening Horizons 234

Geoffrey Beene 244

Fitting and Showing Big Beene. 250

New York Floor Model 260

Money's in My Name. 271

Raucous Dating Game 277

Designers and Excuses 282

Holiday Decisions 288

My Date with the Rose 293

Return or Not Return 298

Modeling Mexico 307

Parties, Proposals and Wedding One-Liners 314

Wedding Nightmare 323

Honeymoon's Alpha Police 329

London's First Shower 332

Modeling Mishaps 336

Photos Catwalk 339

Post Scripts 361

Glossary 365

READERS COMMENTS

"Mary Jo Shaw's attention to details in telling in telling her story makes it a winner! Convent to Catwalk is a fun read, yet informative. The book is so open and real, it sweeps you away. I experienced a captivation peek into the "old world" of becoming a nun, plus a fascinating glimpse into the world of fashion and modeling. It's a story expressing sincere and honest feeling of devotion for the Lord. I couldn't put the book down, and hated to see *the end.*"

—*Lu Neal, Bachelor of Science, retired K-12 educator.*

"Mary Jo has written an entertaining autobiography, filled with many amusing anecdotes. Her deep faith in God also shines through in the many difficult challenges she faced and overcame with the help of His grace."

—*Rev. Tim Ilgen, Pastor of Sacred Heart Parish, Lacey, WA.*

"Mary Jo, just read your book. Really well done. Congratulations!"

—*Sister Antoinette, former superior general of the Sisters of Divine Providence, San Antonio, TX.*

"Mary Jo not only writes well, but she has the gift of being aware of her inner life and her response to situations. Rare is the woman who has had experiences like hers, and fortunate are we that she shares with the reader both the events and what they meant for her."

—*Sister Mary Christine Morkovsky, CDP, teacher of philosophy, author of histories, keyboardist.*

"I promise—you will enjoy every single minute of Convent to Catwalk. It will touch your heart. Mary Jo doesn't *tell* her story: her descriptions and dialog *show* her story. Once you start reading, you don't want to put it down."

—*Jo Love Beach, a retired and still active educator, consultant in motivational techniques, and bilingual consultant.*

"I'm reading the book first. Then I have fun giving a *book report* during supper to Mom, Dad, and my little sister Emily. Right after grace, they ask what comes next. I don't want it to end."

—*Sarah, thirteen years old.*

"I just finished reading this memoir by Mary Jo Shaw. It takes something extraordinary to have excelled in two completely divergent careers, and to do so with such grace."

—*George Lanning, U.S. Navy electronic scientist, operations research analyst.*

"I so enjoyed your book. You revealed so much about your life and about you. What a gift to all of us! I only wish there were another chapter on the last 30+ years—and how those divergent experiences impacted your life—and you as we know you now. Thank you for sharing. Great job on all counts.!"

—*Linda Crabtree*

"Couldn't wait to get started reading your book, so that's exactly what I did after dinner – until 1 a.m. If I fall asleep in this afternoon's meetings, I'll just have to blame it all on you...it will indeed 'make Him loved.' I will treasure — and you."

—*Sara Bettencourt, volunteer in community organizations and projects, genealogist, historical researcher.*

"Convent to Catwalk is a different kind of book and a must-read. Its sincerity tells it like it is—straight forward, sincere, and gives a feeling of walking with Mary Jo, feeling her suffering in pain. Her descriptive scenes enveloped me."

—Arnold Anderson, Seattle postal worker, retired.

"Hey, Big Sister, I was lying in bed reading about the old pump organ, screaming out loud laughing at 4:30 a.m. hoping my neighbors would not call the police thinking something was wrong. So hysterical, and written so visually!!! Also, never knew our grandmothers, Ahmama and Nona, went to kindergarten together."

—I love you, Patti.

"You've certainly had an interesting life! When I got to the end, I found myself wondering what happened next. When is the sequel coming out?"

—Jane Hurst, administrative/computer world.

"Every time I open your book to read, I thank you!! Seems like I am with you."

—Charlotte Wiseman, educator, Write Your Life class facilitator.

"After work Thursday, I bought Mary Jo's Convent to Catwalk. I went home immediately and started reading. On Friday, I only stopped reading it to eat, bathe, and sleep, and finished on Saturday morning. What a wonderful book and delightful human being! Wish she would write a sequel."

—Nancy Vantusko, hair dresser.

"Fantastic! One of the most unusual stories, and so well written."

—Mary Jo Loftis

"Have enjoyed reading your book. What memory for detail! You gave me a better understanding of convent life and the world of modeling. I especially appreciated your candidness about dealing with depression. That took some courage. God bless."

—*Jeanette Willis*

"I spent all day yesterday reading your book. Can't read Convent to Catwalk fast enough. Phenomenal! I just can't put it down. I'm not getting ready for visitors arriving in a few days—can't get my nose out of that book! Super job"

—*Sarah Wright*

"I started reading your book and found it difficult to put down. Only took a few days to read. The middle part took a turn I had not expected. Well done."

—*Candy Berner, avid reader.*

"I felt I was with you and loved your style. It's truly a miracle that you physically lived through that particular year. You had little time to eat properly and had responsibilities beyond your experience. Second miracle was to survive with continued love for the convent and fellow nuns. It's just a beautiful, loving biography!"

—*Mary Ellen Friesen, retired from work, but not from life.*

"Love your book and your writing style and how you make it easy to visualize life of a noviate. As a Catholic and growing up being taught by nuns, there is always curiosity about their life and training."

—*Berenice Rolich*

"Author Mary Jo Shaw's life story is told straight from the heart in her debut autobiography Convent to Catwalk."

—*Charles J. Lee II*

"On a plane trip, I was reading Convent to Catwalk, and was laughing uncontrollably, then crying. A man across the aisle remarked how *into it* I was in the book. 'My sister wrote her memoir, I didn't know of many of the happy or challenging times in the convent.' The passenger took a picture of the cover so he could look it up in New York."

—*Jerri Kay, Mary Jo's sister and retired high fashion coordinator.*
Now a licensed interior decorator.

"Amazing book! Convent to Catwalk – how far removed one is from the other. It is extremely interesting to learn about aspects of each, and you progressed through their very different challenges...great read! Thank you for sharing your life experience."

—*Pam and Dave Clark*

"I finished reading your book and enjoyed every page (I had to finish it between cooking and cleaning for Thanksgiving—my family almost didn't get dinner!) Love your writing style. I appreciated reading your prayers as you worked or asked for guidance. It was a good reminder of how to approach difficult situations. Please consider a sequel! Your story was truly inspirational and entertaining...hard to put down. I feel like you are my friend now. Thank you for sharing."

—*Sandy Tremaine, CPCU, retired insurance adjustor*

"I bought five books to give away. While reading mine last night, we had lights go out in Spanaway, WA. I had to finish by FLASH-LIGHT. I just couldn't put it down!"

—*JLC*

ACKNOWLEDGMENTS

I wonder what I would be writing about, if it were not for my loving, dedicated, fun Sisters of Divine Providence. They formed and inspired me how to live spiritually, not only from my birth through the first half of this book, but they continue to influence me daily. Sisters mentioned by their real names or by fictional names made these stories come alive. I give thanks to my heavenly Father for every one of my dear Sisters in Christ.

I am especially grateful to my parents and five younger siblings—Jerri, Patti, Candy, Mae, and Peggy—who either shared their bedroom, or made, purchased, or gave me *hand-me-ups* of lovely current-style clothing. I felt comforted as I osmosed into the lay life in the second half of the stories of my life.

My husband, Chris, prepared hearty salads or opened canned soups, and constantly brought snacks of fruits, nuts or peanut butter on toasted raisin bread. He actually mashed *OFF* on the remote so I could concentrate. I cherish his many hours reading, critiquing and learning secrets of my life.

My family and friends in Texas and Nevada knew many of my unusual stories in the convent and of my modeling experience. They were my great encouragers to write it down. However, since we moved to Panorama Retirement and Convalescent Center in Lacey, Washington in 2011, I've kept those twenty-three years of my life a secret. Most of the 1,200 residents in Panorama knew I was writing. When I finally revealed the title, they kept begging when it would be on the shelves. Thanks for your *patient patience* that prodded me to keep the screen on my laptop vertical longer.

If it weren't for Charlotte Wiseman (facilitator) of the free *Write Your Life Story* class on our campus, I probably would not have started. We did not critique. We read our story aloud, but I had a great goal to write and still more encouragement to write a book. Thank you, Charlotte, and class members.

Humble gratitude goes to Bryan Willis for his PanWriters class. Bryan, an international playwright, has taught Panorama Seniors since 1998. He and his substitute, Margo Benedetto, excel as teachers. I always left the class with swollen encouragement to publish my stories for others. Bryan has helped to edit and to make my manuscript print ready. His positive, up-lifting during computer-to-computer transferring challenges kept me going. His many, "We're almost there. It won't be long now, Mary Jo," blotted my tears in times of frustration. I can't thank you enough, Bryan and Margo.

Pat Dixon, you excellent author, thanks for your kudos for me when you subbed for class, too. Bob Chester, for your professional advice.

I must give thanks for the last three years of my writing with Patricia Swan, whom God sent to Bryan Willis' class when she moved to Panorama as my neighbor. An accomplished author herself, she volunteered to read my stories and to critique them weekly. What an honor and privilege! How much we learn from the aged, when they share the talents left in themselves—specifically, tutoring a skill, such as writing. Training someone to write is probably the most difficult to teach, since the student must be able to share feelings and express them in a unique way. To sit at the feet of a master, to absorb and not feel that the master is bored, exhausted or wants to stop—that is the student's fear, I think. To gain much and return little, yet be able to *express appropriate gratitude*: that is beyond words in writing.

I had expressed those words to Patricia in 2015. I will never forget her response, "Mary Jo, as a teacher yourself, you know that a teacher's motivation and satisfaction comes from a student's eagerness to learn. If you ever want to stop learning, I will get tired in a hurry." That's Patricia.

Patricia Swan and Bryan Willis, I never felt you tired of me and my efforts. My acknowledgment paragraphs should be a separate *book!* Thank you, thank you.

Last and most important, I dedicate to and thank God for the time and gift to write this particular book. I hope it gives Him praise and leaves a legacy in His honor and His glory.

CONVENT

RELIGIOUS LIFE THEN AND NOW

Please read these three important pages very carefully. Thanks.

About 100 years after Father John Martin Moye founded the Sisters of Divine Providence in France, some of the Sisters packed many old, religious customs, rituals, training, and rules into their bags, boarded ships, and traveled to Castroville, Texas. I inherited much of the culture when I began my life as a religious Sister in 1955.

The first old custom I qualified for was my age. Girls as young as twelve entered the convent. I was sixteen, still very young, but I had spent much time in deep, serious prayer and guidance. I knew God wanted me to work as a religious Sister, and I still do. I lived with them for thirteen years.

If I were interested in joining the Congregation of Divine Providence (CDP) today, I would be required to have a degree, or training in a skill or a profession. The Sisters would offer me retreat days with prayers and guidance to help me in a mature discernment before entering. Many girls entered as young as 13 and lived and loved religious life. Many became leaders, superiors, Ph.Ds and so forth.

Back in the 1950s, we Sisters wore traditionally long, cumbersome habits with many yards of black serge and heavily starched headpieces. Today I would have entered and continued wearing civilian clothing, except for a simple crucifix, pin or other item. Perhaps you would recognize I was religious by my life of simplicity, and love and respect for others.

Formerly, for religious ceremonies at each step of formation, rehearsals involved hours of exacting practice as a group and individually. I remember almost bursting into tears as we prepared, saying our vows aloud with a speech professor to raise or lower our pitch and volume on certain words.

After memorization, I felt I just wanted to concentrate on the words, relax, and express them with sincere love, but my heart pounded as I tried to focus on the details of performance. Today I would plan and prepare my service, and I would have a peaceful, loving emphasis on the real meaning of my ceremony.

When I interviewed, as required by the Reverend Mother before each stage of training, I entered her office, knelt on the floor, asked permission for acceptance to the next level, and then waited for her approval to rise and sit. If I had to kneel before her today, I might question the ritual, or at least, I would not be inspired!

In my novitiate, a question hovered over me. Should I plant garden bulbs upside down, or should I ask whether the Sister instructing me knew they were upside down? Alternatively, should I accept it as a test of my obedience and comply? We studied about saints and mystics who encountered those kinds of situations. No one in our formation class inquired what was proper to do. Surely, I did not then, but I certainly would today.

Looking back, I wish I could have used the valuable time studying after meals, instead of dusting shelving or decorative panels in the hallways daily when dusting even every other day would have been too much!

We used to wait for "obedience day" in the summer when we found out what and where we were assigned to teach the next school year. Today I would be in on those decisions to spread God's word and to fill His needs with my God-given talents.

I remember a decade after my entrance when Sister Elizabeth insisted we call her Sister, not Reverend Mother, and her title would be simply Superior General. She also announced she would polish her *own* shoes when needed, not every night. If we bowed to her in the halls, she "would not be bowing back." She continued, "I am a Sister with a vow of poverty, chastity and obedience like the rest of you." Times were changing.

If I were considering the convent now, I would have the *Come and See* opportunities to help me discern God's will, such as retreat weekends, visiting-the-convent weekends, and reflection days. I could attend the *Guest House* program to get a closer look of religious life by living for a time in the convent for a small fee for room and board. I would share duties, develop relationships of religious community life, and take part in common prayer, Mass, and receive spiritual direction. I would continue to teach music and stay in contact with my family and friends.

I would be living in an atmosphere where, fortunately, most of the external traditions have dissipated, but where the spirit of abandonment to Divine Providence is still alive and adaptable to the current times and needs of society and the world.

These are many stories of *my* life as a religious nun, or Sister, including the mysterious, the fun, the hilarious, the questions, the answers, the reasons, the deep prayerfulness, the friendships, the work and the challenges.

Would I do it again? Of course. I would do it in a heartbeat, full of love and gratitude.

MYSTERIOUS MYSTERIES

My knees locked into a kneeling position. It was the summer of 1955. I'd prayed many private hours and during retreats to know whether God wanted me to be a Sister of Divine Providence in San Antonio. For a year I'd felt His calling, but uneasy thoughts haunted my sixteen-year-old mind.

Heavenly Father, You've been closest to me in my challenging times—especially when I needed to talk with someone. When I thank You, You give more. What is it You desire from me? I want to work with a pure motive of honoring You every moment of my life. I see You working through the Sisters in a joyous, loving attitude. Please quiet me, so I may listen to Your word and Your inspiration.

Throughout the year, that was my prayer. Through doubting and questioning, I prayed more intensely. God shepherded me through daily Mass, spiritual reading, visits to the Sisters' chapel at school, and days of recollection.

Each Sunday my family traveled to the mother home of the convent on Our Lady of the Lake campus to visit Mom's sister, Sister Clair. My heart would beat with joy, curiosity, longing, and eagerness to pray, work, and love as they seemed to live. Each two-hour stay enhanced my longing, and saying good-byes pulled my heart-strings. I found it hard to express these feelings to anyone except my school counselor, Sister Miriam Fidelis. Everything pointed to my decision.

In the recesses of my heart, I knew and prayed, *Provident God, I have a strong sense of peace, knowing I am blessed to accept Your invitation to enter the convent. I expect challenges, but with Your grace, I pray to respond a firm 'Your will be done, thus, living my motto: to love God more and make Him loved.'*

My resolute prayer comforted me, but I constantly asked God to rekindle my love and thanks for my special vocation—uncontrolled, recurring questions were likely.

Am I doing the right thing? Will I be able to do it all? Some people remark, 'You can't know what you want to do the rest of your life, and many girls leave the convent because they get homesick.' Will I miss home? I love my five little sisters—Jerri, Patti, Candy, Mae and Peggy. I hardly even know Peggy. She's only 22 months old. She probably won't know I'm her oldest sister. Why do these thoughts pester me? I'm eager for the big day to arrive, but the disturbing brainwaves continue.

At the end of the summer, I sat on my twin bed next to Jerri's with a small fan blowing at my feet and opened my sewing box. The little container reminded me of Imelda who had been an aspirant (high school level in religious life) one year and had helped me gather my list of clothing.

I smiled to myself—she was my assigned *angel* who would assist me when I entered the convent in a few weeks. "Mary Jo, just about every item you will wear needs a name tag, especially, if it goes into the laundry. Don't forget!" I snickered when I recalled that demand at the beginning of the summer. I thought she would be a good leader one day. My needle shook again as I tried to sew labels into my new, tan uniform socks—my mind wandered with questions once again.

What will it be like that first Sunday, unpacking, eating, and meeting other new aspirants? What will that first night bring? Where do we undress, wash up, shower or bathe? Do we wash our clothes together, sort and fold them like a family as we do at home? If my heart didn't pound so hard, I wouldn't be reminded to be nervous. What a silly thought! I've been so eager to join the Sisters for over a year, but as days stacked up, so did my nerves. *Lord, keep me in the palm of Your hand to receive the calm of your plan. I'm not perfect, and I'm thankful You don't expect perfection. I give You who I am.*

Questions snuck in quickly once again. *Do the other girls shiver about these things before they enter? What about cleaning up and chores? This small house seems like a lot to clean with our large family. I hear we're assigned duties. And prayer? I've been looking forward to more quiet periods to pray. Will prayer times be too long or too short? I'll discover those black books the Sisters have in the chapel pews at school. They call them "office books." What's with that word—office?*

Wow! What about study time? Will I be able to stay up late? I always needed more time to study than others. Will I maintain my all A report card? There's probably a lights-out time. Will I have time to practice the piano, or will that be part of my precious study hall time? Lord, you won't ask me to give up my piano study. Please?

What really bothers me is how I'm supposed to skip my junior year in high school. I'll have more to study in less time. Imelda had explained: we attend summer classes, start college earlier and get our college degrees sooner. What am I getting myself into? Lord, please be with me again and help me do my assignments to the best of my ability for Your honor and glory, not for my own recognition.

⁓

Sunday, September 4, 1955, brought more than the usual high humidity, heat and mosquitos. It was the day my family would chauffeur me to the convent. I awoke in nervous, eager anticipation.

I deliberated what Mom and Dad thought as we prepared for Sunday Mass. Perhaps they realized, as I did—this was the last day we would go to church as a family from our home. I'd miss riding my bike two blocks away to Mom's parents, Danny and Ahmama Osborn. Aunt Tantan lived with them and cared for them. She had played the piano with me every time we visited since I was a child. We had celebrated all holidays at their home. I'd miss them as much as I'd miss my parents. My heart cried for them.

I put my hair brush down on the back of the commode to dab a tear in the crowded little bathroom. Mae and Peggy looked up and handed me their own little brushes and pink hair ribbons. I knew they didn't realize that was the last time we'd share that opportunity. Oh, God, I'd miss these little sisters. I could hardly believe my big day had arrived. How would I feel that night when I'd be on my own?

I heard Mom shuffling in the kitchen. Her last-minute nerves made her words race ahead of her tongue. "Jerri, hurry! Line up the party napkins. Arrange the forks next to each other." She raised her volume and speed a notch. "Patti, come here! Hide these old pots and pans in the pantry. Anywhere—while I fix flowers on the buffet. Just hurry. It's almost time to leave. We won't have much time after Mass."

I didn't try to talk Mom out of it. I just left her alone, so she could surprise me with her spread of sweet dainties and hearty eggs, bacon, biscuits, orange juice and jellies. When it was time to leave for church, she tore off her apron and scanned her to-do list to which Dad had written on the bottom: *Leave at 2:30 for convent.*

For an hour, tears of joy welled in my eyes as we prayed and sang in the two front pews at St. Ann's Church with my grandparents and Aunt Tantan. My heart rejoiced. *Heavenly Father, thank You for this glorious day. Please keep my family and me close to Your heart.*

On the front steps, Father Martin imparted his blessing on my family and promised me his prayers. We headed home. Our three-bedroom, two-bath residence, sat atop the long mound of manicured front and side lawns at Huisache and Breeden. The doors greeted my grandparents, Aunt Tantan, cousin Kayo, and three of my school chums for a send-off brunch.

I was distracted amid the excitement of three generations of relatives. I didn't want them to think I was eager to get away from home. I didn't want to seem apprehensive either. Everyone needed to be as joyous as I! Maybe some sensed comparable feelings of apprehensive joy, but wore happy faces for my sake. Mixed emotions probably swarmed each of us.

A hand-crocheted cloth made by our loving, former neighbor, Mrs. Krause, draped from the large dining room table. Smells from Mom's luscious breakfast foods, around a small centerpiece of Tantan's variety garden flowers, invited adults and four of my sisters to gather around one half of the table, allowing us teens to crowd and chat together at the other end.

The room felt electric with teenage girl chatter. Cynthia, Mary Jane and Rachel, my three best friends from school, competed to sit closest to me. My sister Jerri and our cousin, Kayo, grabbed chairs next to each other. We hadn't seen much of each other in three months, and we all talked at once.

"Mary Jo, you're so pumped up with joy!"

"Oh, Cynthia, I am. I'll remember you, always. Do you recall the time your family took me to Mexico?"

"And remember those end-of-school train trips to New Braunfels? We swam, canoed, and biked—plus all of that luscious picnic food!"

The conversation was like mounds of spaghetti—copious, hot, jumbled, overlapping, intertwining, yet delicious and exciting. Whoops of giggles followed each girl's comment:

Aren't you scared?" Giggle, giggle.

"What if you get homesick?" More giggles.

"Hey, aren't you going to miss your little sisters?"

"Do we have to call you *Sister* when you get a new name?" All heads turned to me.

Jerri couldn't accept that change. "Ohhh no! She's my sister, but I'm not calling her any *nun name*—no way!"

My little sisters burst into laughter, but the adults looked wide-eyed at each other.

They knew Jerri had a point.

"It'll be so unreal—seeing you in black and white like the Sisters."

"Remember those two years of school in the church basement?" Mary Jane asked.

"Do we *remember*?" Cynthia asked.

"In the church basement? I didn't go to St. Mary's. What's that about?" Rachel laughed.

"Oh, yeah—all eight grades. Those poor nuns!"

"Party pooper! We had a ball. They divided the room with walls for eight grades."

"Yes, and we ate and played in the big open space in the center."

"Right," Mary Jane burst out, "Mary Jo, you and I went to St. Mary's all eight years together, then to Providence these last two years, and..."

"And we're all heading to Our Lady of the Lake University. Maybe we'll be in classes together."

"Hey, remember Don Burnet?"

"The class brain? Who could forget Don? He went to the seminary after the eighth grade," Cynthia reminded.

"But you've got to hear this," I interrupted. "When he entered the seminary, his mom gave me his accordion. I gave it back last week—to enter a *convent*! I won't use it there."

"Hey, enough about school." Cousin Kayo lowered her voice. We leaned in to listen. She grinned and shook her pointy index-finger right at me. "Mary Jo, you'd better remember the party Momma gave you in our back yard a few weeks ago. The fun of the evening was when I snuck cigarettes from Momma's purse that was sitting on the ground—*right next to her feet.*"

"Ohhhhh!" the group chimed together.

Jerri jumped in, "Shhh! I remember that! Kayo said you couldn't go to the convent without smoking at least one *cigarette!*"

"That big circle of parents visiting in the dark had no clue we were hanging out by the back fence a few yards away—puffin' up!"

"We *can't* forget that night, *August tenth*. Remember when you're in the convent, okay?"

"That's a night to remember!"

Pleased at the high energy we girls were expending, Mom set another refueling of bacon and biscuits at our end of the table.

"Yum, Yum." We inhaled those with heaps of jelly. Jerri almost choked trying to curtail her laughter.

Rachel exploded, "Guess what, Mary Jo? When we're finished here, we're forming a parade a real—*entour-a-a-ge*—all the way to the convent."

I tilted my head, "Awww! You all are so sweet."

We continued a while longer until our heads spun. I cherished my dearest friends reminiscing with me.

When the meal was finished, Tantan left the table and beckoned me over to Mom's gold colored, small couch by the living room window. She beamed, and with a slight nod, presented me with a small, three-by-five-inch gift. Wrapped in her customary white tissue paper, and her pink, scissor-curled ribbon, it was special.

I pressed away a tear as I fingered my first copy of The New Testament with gold-gilded pages. I knew she'd saved up to purchase it for me. "Tantan, I'll think and pray for you every time I open this precious book. It's perfect."

I hugged her firmly and whispered.

"I'll always remember you helped me learn to play the piano when I was little, and I'll cherish the many years we spent together. I'm especially grateful for your giving me a ride to church before school the last two years. You've been so good to me. I love you; thank you, Tantan." We bit our lips and smiled.

Dad interrupted and snapped his hands, "Okay, it's two twenty-five. Now you girls go outside. Open the car door for Mary Jo so I can take snapshots of ya'll sending her off."

"I'll ride with Kayo," Jerri offered.

"I'm goin' with Mommie and Mary Jo."

"Me, too!" My other four sisters packed into the back seat of our 1950 Chrysler.

After tight hugs, kisses and many happy tears from my grandparents and Aunt Tantan, we backed out of the driveway and headed for the convent aspirancy. Dad's Barbera Sporting Goods station wagon—with ads and fish painted on all sides—hauled my trunk and suitcases with yards of rope gripping the open back door.

My friends followed in their cars forming the promised entourage. My formal exodus was just beginning.

Exodus

My heart pounded louder than the chatter in the back seat as Mom turned off Culebra onto 24th Street.

I breathed deep. For a couple of miles, the heated wind of the west sun slapped my face. I searched straight ahead. There they were—the tall familiar Gothic spires praising God, pointing directly toward heaven and addressing everyone within a mile on the west side of San Antonio since 1922. Those spires crowned the campus of Our Lady of the Lake Convent, High School and University owned by the Sisters of Divine Providence.

I sat—still oblivious to the conversation in the car—until Mom parked at the bottom of the twenty concrete steps leading up to the ornate arch. Tiny tiles formed patterns on the convent porch. Two elegantly carved, shiny wooden doors with inlayed mosaic, multicolored glass, separated us from the convent inside.

Eleven-year old-Candy announced, "We're here right on time. The tower bells are singing the *Ave Maria*. It's three o'clock on the dot."

"It's my turn to ring the door-bell," five-year-old Mae yelled as she carefully placed her tiny foot on the first step, followed by the next foot on the same step until she reached the top and dashed to the door. Sister Joan Michelle, Mistress of Aspirants, must have heard the familiar six Barbera girls' giggles and noises. She instantly answered the bell and received us with open arms and a big smile, "What a glorious day! Welcome, Mary Jo."

I knew I had come home.

While she hugged my family and schoolmates, I stared at her yards of religious garb they called a *habit*—a heavy, black dress, stiff-starched white headpiece with the long black veil which flowed down her back. Whatever she wore under it must have been soaking wet! Would I be able to tolerate this heat and humidity dressed like that? I was melting in my light cotton dress.

After more pictures for Dad, I tissued my eyes and gave last hugs and good-byes to my three loving friends. This was it. The crowd was diminishing. I hoped I hid my nervous gulp.

Assistant Mistress, Sister Theresa Clare, who had been my piano teacher in seventh and eighth grades, led us from the entrance through a hallway to the back of the convent. "Mr. Barbera, you may bring the car to this back entrance." She turned to another, opened door. "This is the basement for Mary Jo's trunk."

Dad left to bring the car around to the back of the convent.

My sisters glared down the small, steep steps to the trunk room. "It looks dark down there."

Sister laughed, flipped a light switch and continued. "Mary Jo, when your dad returns, get your swimming gear. I'll meet you here in forty-five minutes after you've said good bye to your family. You will walk with the aspirants and me to the gym. After swimming, we'll help the kitchen Sisters wheel the foods to the large grotto in the pecan grove for a getting-acquainted picnic."

My sisters rejoiced. "Wow! Swimming? Picnic?"

Little Mae puckered her lips. "I wanna go to the convent, too, and stay with Mary Jo."

"Not me!!" insisted Jerri.

"Sounds like the convent is fun," said Patti.

Mae looked out the back door. "Here's Daddy with Mary Jo's trunk!"

"Okay, everyone stand by the station wagon and pretend to take the trunk out," he issued.

After pictures he directed, "Mary Jo, Jerri, I'll hold the trunk at the top of the steps, you go first and keep it from sliding too fast. Then it's time for us to go home."

My heart jerked. Bells rang exodus time.

Little hands batted good-byes in all directions from passenger windows as I waved back to my little sisters until the car turned the corner.

I clunked back down the wooden steps to my trunk and grabbed my swimming suit and towel. Imelda, my angel assigned to help me adjust, called down to the basement, "Hurry up, Mary Jo, all aspirants are leaving for the gym."

While marching to the pool, my heart grinned listening to our teenage chatter. It reminded me of the brunch at home with my family and school chums. But that smile grew a little wider: would the pool be filled with Sisters who hadn't had a suntan in umpteen years?

"You're from Louisiana? Cool." Kay asked.

"Are you kidding? It's not cool; it's worse than San Antonio—more heat and more humidity." Suzanne joked.

Of the approximately forty girls, half of the group walked backward jovially answering questions for us new aspirants. Everyone balanced swim gear wrapped in towels or nested in metal wash basins.

We were a happy, joyous, God-loving group, exploding with enthusiasm, enjoying the new friendship of other girls who wanted to become Sisters. It was exhilarating!

We buzzed like a fast-moving swarm of bees. "Hey look!" Elizabeth shouted, "The boarders from South America arrived back for school. They hear our commotion." She pointed up to their building.

"They're waving from their windows." Donna gestured back.

We flapped our arms and raised our voices, "Hi!! Welcome back! Welcome back!!!

"Wow! Look at the college girls waving from their building. Over there."

Sister Theresa Clare quickly pointed out, "Girls, we're passing the important laundry building."

"Is *that* why we needed all our clothes marked?" I asked.

The returning aspirants yelped together, "Ohhh yes! You won't get it back if it's not marked."

"Clothes are washed and put on special shelving labeled for aspirants, postulants, novices and various groups," Sister explained.

Imelda pointed and yelled over the conversations that started up again, "That's the campus library on the left. You'll spend lots of time there."

"And across from it is the science building." Elizabeth pointed.

"And here's the gym for *swimming!*" Imelda opened the large glass door.

The huge swimming pool sparkled clean. Old timers made sure we green-horns were familiar with the large dressing room, showers and lockers.

Imelda, Elizabeth and Donna introduced me to other seniors, including Phyllis, Beverly, Donna, Maxine, and Suzanne. We didn't stay long, just enough time to shoot water with our palms, swim a few laps to cool off and be introduced to the layout of the pool area. Only aspirants swam—no paper white Sisters! Everyone dressed quickly with no concern for wet coiffures and makeup—the hot sun would dry our dripping hairdos.

After the swim, we retraced our footsteps to the growl of hungry tummies. Imelda, Elizabeth, and Beverly speed-walked ahead to roll out food carts for the Sister cooks. Everything was lined up at the edge of the pecan grove. We swarmed around salivating.

I felt comfortable on those grounds. Even the first floors of the entire campus and the convent chapel that accommodated hundreds of Sisters were familiar. I reminisced about my family when we spent many Sunday afternoons visiting with my aunt, Sister Clair, in and out of the buildings. My heart went out to those from long distances and those who were new to the campus. I presumed they'd be especially lonely on visiting Sundays.

Sister Joan Michelle broke my short distraction, "Silence, girls! Time for grace before meals."

Instant silence! Wow. We turned off like a radio switch.

Sister continued, "In the name of the Father, of the Son..."

Our picnic was a delight—simple, but plentiful: sandwiches, homemade German potato salad, crushed pineapple mixed in lime Jell-O squares, and gallons of milk for seconds and thirds.

The most blue-ribbon remarks centered among aromas wafting from huge trays of Sister Emil's mouth-watering snickerdoodles.

Our nervous chatter persisted and hid most homesickness, except for one girl. Elaine was a new, thin, tall, brownish-blond, senior.

Imelda whispered, "Mary Jo, Elaine is ready to burst into tears. She's eating very little and keeps her fingers to her lips hiding a fever blister. She didn't want to talk with me."

I got the hint. Normally shy, I had no challenge making friends with old or new aspirants. I stepped away to sit on one of the empty chairs next to Elaine. I asked her name and where she was from, but her teary, red eyes under her plastic rimmed glasses took a quick glance at me while she held her fingers to hide her lips. She shook her head when I offered her an oversized cookie. I felt sad for her, but helpless. Eventually, I sat quiet for a while, hoping she'd say something, but she wanted to be alone.

Other girls traveled from Louisiana, Oklahoma or other parts of Texas. For the out-of-towners, family visiting would be more limited than mine. They admitted, "You're lucky. You'll see your family every month on visiting Sunday."

A few girls overheard the sharing of open feelings and edged over to our little group.

"I'm from Louisiana. I won't see my folks 'til I go home for Thanksgiving," Norma said with puckered lips in her thick southern accent.

Freshman, Charlotte added, "My parents have a farm and can't get off."

"I've never been here before." Phyllis had traveled the farthest, from Oklahoma.

"Oh, I never thought about things like that," I sympathized. "Someday you'll meet my five little sisters." Smiles perked up.

Standing next to the picnic serving table, Sister Joan Michelle tapped a metal bowl with a long stainless-steel fork. "Aspirants, I have some important announcements before returning to the convent. Each new girl is assigned an old aspirant called your *angel*. She'll help answer your questions about where to go, what's next, where things are and points like that. You're welcome to come to Sister Theresa Clare or me, but your angels are a big help for all of us."

She read the long list of angels and their assignees. I had already met my angel, Imelda, who helped me shop for necessities.

Sister had another important announcement, "We'll all help load the carts to take things to the kitchen. After meals you'll each be doing an *office*. Office is another name for chores. I'll read the duties now. You'll do these for a few weeks until I assign new ones."

"Scullery work after meals will be Mary Jo, Imelda..." she named six other girls. "Any questions so far?"

"Uhh. Ye-ah!" I said slowly. My bulging eyes fixated on Sister. "What is a *skull*-e-ry?" Bursts of hilarity behind me almost blew me forward.

Teasing laughter subsided, even from Sister. "Mary Jo, the scullery is the kitchen area where the dirty dishes from three dining rooms and the kitchen prep-dishes, pots, and pans are washed, dried, and returned to their proper places. Imelda and Elizabeth, two other seniors, will show you what to do. There won't be much tonight, since we had a picnic for supper and didn't use as much glassware."

I was thinking. *This is going to be a piece-of-cake! I used to do all the dishes, pots, and pans by myself at home when it was my turn. Sister named eight of us to work together. How easy and fun that's going to be. We'll be out of there in no time.*

We walked into a long, narrow room parallel to an industrial-sized kitchen. At the left wall sat a majestic, stainless steel dishwasher with long attached stainless steel tables on each side. There were heaps of two feet high, efficiently stacked grubby dishes, bowls, glasses, and serving utensils. Large dirty pots balanced in five sets of about six or eight pots each.

I detected something that looked like Mom's mix-master attachment she used for making cakes. The ten-gallon steel bowl on the floor sized up to the mixing accessory. Sister Emil must have used it making the snickerdoodles.

Imelda issued instructions, "Here are plenty of towels for the plates, utensils, and serving bowls. We use these damp ones to dry the pots and pans. Mary Jo and I will run the machine. No one touches it but us. Before we leave, we sweep; then we wash. Mop your way to that door, so you don't have to walk over the wet, clean floor.

"We don't talk while we work. It's a time of silence. You'll have lots of questions for a while, so if you need to talk, please whisper. Just work fast, and we should be done in thirty or forty minutes."

She proceeded to announce who would stack dirty items to the flat baskets that would run through the dishwasher. She delegated girls to dry, and others to put away clean dishes and bowls in the kitchen or into cabinets in the three large dining rooms.

The dishwasher was a steam sauna. Every time Imelda pulled up the door on the right, to slide another basket of soiled dishes inside, clouds of hot steam burst out and fogged her glasses. I got the same bath as I lifted the left door to pull out the clean basket for the girls waiting to dry them. Imelda, Elizabeth and I worked well together, seeing where to pitch-in to help each other. We plowed on like workhorses the entire forty-five minutes. So much for the piece-of-cake, fun, out-in-no-time experience of Scullery Class 101!

I prayed, *Lord, I offer my work for Your glory, no matter how hard it is. Be with me and with these new friends as we live and work together.*

After an exciting, somewhat stressful day, we were eager to unpack and get settled. Sister announced, "Line up two by two according to height. We're going to Sacred Heart Main Chapel for night prayer. We walk in silence."

Silence? Again? I reminded myself that was what I wanted. I had to remember to stay quiet. I hoped no one talked to me. I'd feel rude if I didn't respond. If I could answer with a nod, that might help them remember, too. I asked Jesus to help me to be faithful to silence. That would be a good time to pray with Him.

After many, "Which one of us is taller?" questions, my partner was Frances Ann, another senior who had been an aspirant since her freshman year. We easily found our two spots—the very back.

I was overjoyed. *At last I get to go to chapel. Thank You, Lord.*

The chapel seemed gigantic, but only enough lighting shone to walk and to read. The older aspirants lead the chant; new-comers mainly listened. The soft, pure, young tones floated gently as if on angels' wings. The phrases tapered off beautifully and lightly. The Psalms made perfect endings for the day, including Psalm 33:

> I will bless the Lord at all times;
>
> His praise shall be ever in my mouth.
>
> Let my soul glory in the Lord.
>
> Glorify the Lord with me,
>
> Let us together extol His Holy Name.

After prayer, we tried to tiptoe upstairs to the dorm. Our heavy, bulky suitcases accidently banged the left wall or the spindles on the right of the staircase. Additional belongings, like purses gripped firmly under our arms, made it harder to climb gently and quietly.

The forty of us sounded like a herd of Texas Longhorn. I wondered whether those antique steps were going to collapse. I recalled looking up from the first floor, wondering what was up there, when we visited Aunt Sister Clair on Sundays. It felt hotter as we climbed. We'd gone only two flights, and had two more to go.

I stepped aside from the group to observe. Restrooms were on the large landings. Commodes had long chains hanging from the tanks high over the toilets. I remembered flushing the toilet with a chain like those at grandparents Ahmama and Danny's house in years past. Special rooms close to the steps on upper floors housed doors to areas just large enough for a chair and bathtub. We had to be close to our fourth-floor dorm. *Lord, thank You for climbing the mount to Your holy cross.* That prayer made my trudging upstairs seem lighter.

※

Whooa! I thought. *I've never seen a dormitory before.*

White coverings over about forty beds, with heads backed to the walls, lined two sides of the crowded dorm. Each waist-high, antique dresser displayed a plastic cup, metal pitcher, and an upside-down metal basin, many draped with a washcloth. Those forty stations filled most available space in the room.

I presumed the veteran aspirants were using the beds with small crucifixes just below the pillow. I was eager to unpack the similar cross Aunt Sister Clair had given to me.

Instant silence from footsteps and suitcases. What was happening? Old aspirants knelt by their beds and gazed at the large crucifix on the wall at the end of the dorm.

Confused, I fell to my knees. It felt good to unlock my fingers from the suitcase handle and stretch them out. Even kneeling rested my stiff cow hoofs while Imelda led the group aloud in prayer, "Jesus dear, the day is over, now I leave my labor light. And before I take my slumber, I come to say a sweet goodnight..."

Still on knees after the prayer, seasoned aspirants bent down to the floor. What were they doing? I watched Imelda carefully as she kissed the floor. I satisfied my curiosity: it could mean an act of humility. Or maybe it was a way to thank God for our shelter—even if it felt like 150 degrees with no fans in sight. Perhaps it was a moment to bow low and tell God we adore and worship Him. I presumed it meant different things to different people. I could handle that!

I opened a large closet door in the wall at the head of the bed Imelda assigned to me. On the top shelf I lined up folded items: blankets, three towels and wash cloths. A chest-height shelf formed a mantel after layering it with a towel and arranging it with my small, stand-up mirror, comb, brush and toilet articles.

On the rod under the makeshift mantel, I hung my uniform and *party clothes* (skirt and blouse I made for Saturday's heavy-duty house work) and used the floor space for my slippers and two pairs of shoes.

Perspiration raced down my forehead to the tip of my nose. I grabbed the corner of one of the men's handkerchiefs, shook it open and grinned at my name tag sewn on the corner edge. I mopped my face and admitted it felt good not to fuss with smeared makeup anymore.

I reveled in mental jest. The heat reminded me of the story of Helen Bannerman's Little Black Sambo. In Africa, lions walked in a circle around a tree, each holding the tail of the preceding lion in his mouth. They revolved so many times in the heat, they melted into a circle of butter. Not us, Lord, please.

Unfamiliar sounds, not loud, but different, broke the *sacred silence*. About twenty aspirants lined up with their pitchers at the one small sink and faucet at the end of the dorm. I stood tall, gripping the metal-pipe headboard of my bed, staring at length to study the situation. With my eyes wide, my mouth open, I intently studied and watched *inconspicuously!*

I took copious mental notes: *we take our pitcher to fill with water, go back to the dresser, pour some water into our metal basin, wash and rinse our face with basin water, then dry off with a wash-cloth. We pour water into our cup, get a tooth brush ready, and scrub our teeth. Then swish water in our mouth and spit into the water that's soapy from washing our face. Line up again at the sink, empty and rinse the basin and fill it again—ready to repeat at the morning's ritual.*

I scoot to the sink when the line wound down and fetched my share of water. Ahh! At my station, I let my face wallow in splashes of the cool, fresh, wet water. I prayed again: *Lord, wash me with Your living water, especially, on this, my first night in Your holy place.*

Everything was still, quiet. I whisked a glance across the dorm and froze.

Everyone else was in bed waiting for me to settle down. I quickly climbed into bed, but wondered why Imelda turned over and stared over at me a few moments. She flipped her sheet off, popped up, and dashed to the center of the dorm. She pulled the hanging chain, turned off the light, and plopped back in bed. I figured that one out quickly.

Good night, Lord. Thanks for getting me through my first day. Whoa! I just have to get used to those lovely tower bells vigorously ringing four times an hour, twenty-four hours a day.

FULL DAY EYE-OPENERS

CLANG-A-CLANG-CLANG. At five-thirty in the morning, my body jerked, and my eyes popped open. Sister Theresa Clare energetically shook a school bell from the doorway of the adjoining fourth floor dorm. Old aspirants sat on the edge of their beds, facing the crucifix at the end of our room.

Imelda began praying loudly, and old aspirants chimed in, *In the name of the Father...* While she prayed, she took her hands out of her pajama top, kept it over her shoulders and proceeded to dress into her undies. I tried not to look, but simply to *observe* how to don myself. I knew we had little time, but I dressed, washed up, and fluffed my pillow on my tautly pulled spread.

I walked like a racehorse to the second-floor aspirancy study hall for fifteen minutes of meditation and morning prayers.

I was accustomed to getting up early every day for church with Aunt Tantan before school. However, I was exhausted from the excitement of entering the convent the day before, and I felt I was walking in my sleep when we lined up after prayer for Mass.

When we arrived from the side entrance of chapel, professed Sisters had been in prayer one hour. Sister Elaine, college music professor, was leading Matins and Lauds, the liturgical morning prayers of the Church, from the mike in the back of the chapel. I prayed mentally with the Sisters' voices responding to the unfamiliar Psalms. I was eager for the day I'd be chanting with them. Sister Sacristan lit the tall, gold-capped candles on the altar and switched on the sanctuary lights.

Father Quinlivan, resident chaplain, took a long time to distribute Holy Communion. There were so many candidates, postulants, novices, and professed Sisters walking slowly and reverently, it seemed they had made the rounds again.

After Mass, I was curious about our first meal in the big, bright aspirant dining room. The room had three walls of tall narrow windows with wooden slats. Low bookcases and shelving for games divided the room down the center. On the opposite side of the dining area, my eyes latched onto an old upright piano in the recreation area. I hoped to be able to practice on it. There was ample space for a sewing machine and table, and about fifty folding chairs formed a large semi-circle.

Large double doors led to a wide porch outside—the length of the long room. Cement steps led to the parking area where Dad had taken pictures of my little sisters pretending to unload my trunk. My heart smiled inside at yesterday's memory.

The rattle of breakfast plates woke me from my short reminiscence. Sister Joan Michele was assigning tables and seating.

I realized we hadn't spoken a word before night prayer last evening. *Surely we'll talk while we* eat, I thought. I was right: it was just a *thought*.

"In the name of the Father, and of the Son, and of the Holy Spirit..." Sister Joan Michele led grace while we stood at our tables set for five. After the noisy chairs settled, Donna, another senior aspirant, projected her voice from a small podium. "September fifth, the feast of St. Bertinas..."

I entered the convent for silence and prayer. Was I getting a double dose? I was hungrier than I wanted to talk, so I focused on the breakfast on the table.

We had a banana before our bran flakes. I was surprised we had more—bacon and eggs with toast, jelly, and milk. I could handle the rule that said to eat some of whatever is at the meal.

I felt sad for poor Elaine. She wouldn't eat the potato salad at last night's picnic because it had eggs that reminded her of taking care of her dad's messy chickens. She didn't need another challenge to her homesickness and fever blister at breakfast.

Elaine and I were opposites. At home, I ate lots of everything—except anchovies—and I probably would have eaten those if I were extra hungry. Mom used to tease her friends when I was listening, "Mary Jo eats more than her dad. I make a meal for the family and a meal for her. I give her the quart of milk with a straw. Why dirty a glass?" I enjoyed the tongue-in-cheek.

I was eager to unload my trunk, so I ate quickly. It was useless. Sister Theresa Clare announced, "Girls, remember to do morning chores before you unpack. The chart by the door has your assignments. Try to keep silence."

I stood on my toes searching for my name over the crowd of other girls. Finally—*Elizabeth, Imelda, Mary Jo: South bathrooms.*

Elizabeth opened the door to a walk-in closet under the steps outside the novitiate quarters on the first floor. We each loaded a bucket with supplies, including a tin can. We also carried one broom, mop, and a mop-bucket to share.

While Elaine used her Babo and rags to wash the tub, I worked on the sink. We observed Elizabeth when she bent over, used bare hands with the tin can to scoop water from the toilet and to empty it into her bucket.

I froze. Elaine swung her dark blond hair back for a better look. We bit our lips, and side-glanced each other with our own tin cans. I assumed Elaine's homesickness either kicked in with abundance of disgust, or was her least concern now—no time to waste. The broom swished, and we *mopped ourselves out of the door*, as we did in the scullery the previous evening.

We hauled our stuff to the second-floor landing to another room with about four commode closets and other room with about three tub-stalls. Elizabeth let us have our *opportunity* at the commode routine.

I prayed, *Lord, as I wash these dirty toilets, please clean and wash me of my unkind thoughts, gossip, and pride. Help me grow closer to You through this work. I offer it to Your glory.* Third and fourth floor landings had about the same set up. Still in silence, we finished, laughed, and pointed to our sweaty blouses. Our large men's handkerchiefs were soaked with perspiration in our apron pockets. Good until tomorrow at the same time!

We trudged down the four flights to the supply closet, draped the wet rags on our upside-down buckets, and hung the mop and broom next to the ones on a long board with C-shaped hooks.

When Sister Joan Michele arrived to check the supply closet, I inquired about time for lunch.

"Mary Jo, we don't *eat* meals, we *take* meals," she corrected.

That expression seemed strange to my 16-year-old mind. Do we take our meals to eat?

Sister continued. "We take our noon meal called dinner. Lunch is our afternoon snack. Evening meal is supper.

Our elderly Sisters from France and Germany must have packed those words on their boats to Texas, I thought. I was starving for the noon dinner, but I needed the remaining couple of hours to gather loads from my trunk in the basement, make trips to our fourth-floor dorm, and return down to my desk in the aspirancy on the second floor.

⌒

At noon my stomach yelled, "Time *to take dinner,* Mary Jo." I dashed, slowly, to the dining room.

Jenna, a large tall freshman, broke the silence with a loud whisper, "Oh boy, French fries." Everyone transferred foods from the carts to the tables. What a spread! Each rectangle table had a platter of five country-fried chicken drumsticks and a platter of exactly 15 fat, homemade French fries. Bowls of mixed peas and carrots, and small, long oval bowls of homemade pickles displayed a well-balanced meal. Carts with scents of cinnamon apple-strudel waited next to the dining room door.

We followed the food-passing procedure. Sister sat at the head of our table. Two aspirants sat on her left and two on her right. The girl on the left presented her the platter with chicken. Sister slowly forked a chicken leg to her plate. Platters and bowls moved counterclockwise.

But:

> Jenna, who was second to last to serve herself, grabbed the platter from me as I stretched across the table to hand it to her. With one push of the large spoon, she scraped the remaining ten French fries onto her plate. She plunked the empty platter onto the table in front of little Suzanne on her right. Jenna, in her Louisiana drawl, whispered loud enough for all of us at our table to hear, "Sorry, ya'll. My big weakness is French fries."

I wanted to shout through the room's silence, *Ours, too, girl!*

24

My eyeballs darted—empty platter, Suzanne, empty platter, Suzanne...who drooped her shoulders, as well as the corners of her lips. I could have inhaled the entire platter of fries, too; but at home, we had to share. Nothing broke the silence after that, except Donna's reading and our chomping of the fried chicken.

While gathered for spiritual reading in the study hall, Sister instructed, "Girls, in community life, we look at the amount of food in serving dishes and estimate how much an individual serving would be for the number of people at the table. How would you feel..." She continued a short discourse on sharing, and then read from a book about Father John Martin Moye, the founder of the Sisters of Divine Providence.

⁓

How would supper fare that first day?

I'd never seen big, half-circle-shaped white bowls with matching fancy lids and ladles. They waited on carts to go somewhere on the table. My palms gripped a bowl toward the bottom. I shivered, *It's just like me to spill this stuff or bump into someone in this hustle and bustle.* I delivered my container of hot, tiny-cut carrots, celery, and potatoes wallowing in beef bouillon. I slowly lowered the tureen next to a ladle directly in front of the head place-setting on one of the tables with five soup bowls. Another European custom reigned at our meals.

Instead of sitting down after grace, we stood while the person at the head of the table ladled two scoops of soup into each soup bowl.

I was confused and thought, *Goodness, we ate soup in winter at home to keep us warm. It's ninety degrees, and there's no air conditioning on the entire campus. We're sweating from working hard, and we get hot soup for dinner? I'm famished. I wonder why Donna isn't reading tonight.*

Sister Joan Michele smiled and glanced around the room. *Domine, miserere nobis.* (Lord, have mercy on us.)

Veteran aspirants responded, *Deo gracias.* Quiet conversation buzzed around the room.

Hunger pangs considered, *What a strange way to say, 'You may talk now.' I can get used to that! But I'm finished with my soup. Is that it for supper? Lord, I'm sorry for complaining. Thank You for the nourishing soup.*

Imelda, Elizabeth, and other old aspirants hopped up to unload carts of serving bowls Sister Emil was pushing into our dining room.

My considering blinked into a positive mode, *Oh, good. Thanks, Lord. Here comes some real food—big servings of creamy macaroni and cheese, spicy sausage, pickled bright red beets, and baked honey-beans. Orange-pink, juicy peaches from Fredericksburg—what a perfect dessert!* It quenched my thirst after the sugary Hawaiian punch we drank with the hearty meal.

Those at my table joshed, "Mary Jo, did you enjoy working in the *skull-er-y* last evening?"

"Oh, it was great working with other aspirants. We'll have even more fun tonight with these big, delicate soup tureens, ladles and bowls. Last night was a picnic, and cleaning up was a *picnic* compared with tonight," I jested back.

Sister Theresa Clare's after-supper grace summed it up. "Lord, as You nourish our bodies, nourish our souls with Your Word and Your inspiration."

First Letter Home

September 11, 1955

Hi, Mom, Dad, Jerri, Patti, Candy, Mae, and Peggy, and Ahmama, Danny and Tantan, too!

First, thanks for the great send-off last Sunday—the fun, delight, and delicious brunch. I'm finally here, thanks to your help all summer shopping for clothes and for a trunk full of necessities. I'm doing fine, and I love the convent. I'm eager to hear how you girls are doing in school and to tell you more about what we do here.

Imelda explained what I have to do in order to complete my junior and senior levels in one year. I'm taking extra classes plus piano lessons from Sister Elaine over at the college. The piano literature is advanced, but I relish it. I hope all of you love it, too.

I will be short one class needed to graduate in May. Do you remember the huge Moye Military Academy building in Castroville the Sisters own? I learned they used it to teach, board, and prepare high school boys for the military. Old aspirants took summer classes there from the Sisters. That's why they are prepared to graduate in three years. I'll take *American History* next summer with several other aspirant-seniors. We will get diplomas in mid-June, but I still do not understand how it will benefit the congregation or me.

With extra classes and not enough study time, I'm doing my best for the honor of God. I won't be sending home all A's as I made during my two years at Providence High. Sister Theresa Clare is very intelligent and gives an overabundance of homework with library work in literature, English, and journalism classes. We learn a lot, but it is very challenging, sometimes frustrating.

Jerri and Patti, you asked me to give you my schedule. Here's for you:

5:30 Sacred silence: rise. Wash-up; make bed with spreads pulled taut. Nothing under beds.

6:00 Meditation in aspirancy.

6:20 Main Chapel to assigned pews in front of Sisters there since 5:30.

7:00 Mass and Holy Communion.

7:45 Breakfast.

8:15 Chores in silence: in aspirancy, or in high school/college scullery: dishes, pots, pans for all students, faculty, and Sisters on campus.

9:00 Bible study, journalism. *Spanish II for me in high school building with day students/boarders. Study hall for other aspirants.

12:00 Lunch in silence.

12:30 Chores in silence: in aspirancy or college scullery.

1:00 *Typing class. Other aspirants have study hall.

2:00 English. Snack.

3:00 Study hall in aspirancy, library research, piano lesson on Wed., visit to chapel, bath/wash hair upstairs (*wash the tub*), hand wash undies.

4:30 Spiritual reading/religious-life training in aspirancy.

5:30 Supper. Sometimes we talk.

6:00 Chores in silence. I practice piano in aspirancy dining room.

7:00 Recreation: volley or basketball, skating, get-together with postulants or novices, etc.

8:00 Rosary and Compline (chanted night prayer) in Main Chapel.

8:30 Dorm. Ready for bed.

9:00 Lights out. No study in dorm allowed.

*I'm the only aspirant taking Spanish II and typing. I go to Our Lady of the Lake High School in the adjoining building for class with students and boarders.

On Saturdays we do additional assigned chores, pick up our clothes from the campus laundry, and do the regular chores extra well, like mopping and polishing. Once a month on Saturday, we will pack the cars with typewriters and go to a printer out of town to set up the MOYETTE, our aspirancy newsletter, for publication.

Now you can have fun checking up on what I'm up to during the day. I can't wait to see all of you in a few weeks.

I love you.
Mary Jo

CHALLENGING FIRST WEEKS

My fingers were lazy. The physical work of cleaning kept them strong, but my fingers and my brain cells lost a week of musical patterns and exercises. *Lord, I want to do Your work, and You know I love praying with others in the convent—but will I still be able to give You glory in my piano playing?*

We had busy days of lining up our classes, learning where to be and when, scrubbing well in kitchens and bathrooms, and learning how to clean and store mops and rags. My legs developed strong muscles running up and down for things I needed in the 4th floor dorm. All of this settling in helped keep our minds off home.

In the midst of this bustle, I missed the joy of making music. I knew there was no standing still in piano. If I neglected a day of practice, I would spend the next session getting back to the previous level. Only then, could I advance and get better.

As I considered that idea, Imelda darted into the kitchen, "Mary Jo, Sister Theresa Clare wants to talk with you. She's in the multipurpose room."

I finished drying the stainless-steel worktable, and wondered what I had done wrong. Whatever it was, it was not intentional.

With hesitant steps, I entered the dining room. "Ye-es, Sister?"

I marveled inside at Sister Theresa Clare's many talents—she was cutting beige fabric for our uniform skirts and jackets. She removed a straight pin from her lips. "Mary Jo," she said, "I haven't heard you play since I had taught you piano in seventh and eighth grades. You must miss your piano practice since you're here." She had struck the right chord!

"Oh, Sister, I do miss it. In fact, I was just praying about it this morning."

She continued sewing. "Sister Teresita says you did unusual piano work with her at Providence during your freshman and sophomore years. She highly recommends that you audition for piano lessons with Sister Elaine over in the college. Have you met Sister Elaine or know about her?"

My eyes opened wide. "I haven't spoken with her, but I met her after the piano ensemble. Some of us from Providence High performed in Thiry Music Hall. Is she the one who was Texas Composer of the Year twice, and USA Composer of the Year once?"

"Yes," she nodded with a grin. "Sister has a large closet with shelves full of her original compositions. You will hear her perform at the organ, improvising as she plays between hymns during Mass. I often see her sitting in one of the Adirondack chairs with her manuscript paper, composing pieces in the pecan grove."

"Composing music with no piano? Wow, she must be good."

"She's extremely gifted." Sister nodded toward the piano in the opposite corner of the room. "You may begin practicing while others do chores in the evenings. I will make an appointment with Sister Elaine for next month. Prepare a good variety of selections you've learned."

"Oh, Sister, I'm heading for the basement to my trunk. I'll get my music books right away. Thanks again." I tore out. Sister Teresita recommended *me*. I hardly remembered getting compliments from the Sisters. I figured my fingers must be out of shape. *Please, Lord, help me catch up. Thanks for the gift of my music. I want to honor You with every note I play. Always!*

Next month moved like a week. I was not used to being nervous before playing for audiences, but my insides shimmered as we walked across the small parking lot and down steps to the Chapel Auditorium for my audition.

I recalled when we visited with Aunt Sister Clair, my family sat on benches at the back of that auditorium in the wide hall. Often, I would sit close to the opaque French doors that opened to the theater. I would open them about two inches and listen to a postulant practicing the piano. I would imagine myself performing the beautiful pieces. I stared over the five-hundred, up-folded seats made of dark, thin, slightly curved wood in the large, Gothic-style hall. The Sisters had preserved the hall well, since about 1895.

Sister Theresa Clare turned on only lighting on the stage and above the front seats. We chatted about piano lessons until Sister Teresita, who had taught me my complete repertoire, arrived. I beamed that she had come from Providence High to support me. Sister Teresita reminded us, "Sister Elaine has a tight teaching schedule of piano and composition writing. We appreciate her coming. You will like her, Mary Jo. Ahh! Here she comes now." We rose to greet her.

Sister Elaine, tall, with perfect posture, was vibrant, energetic, and had a big smile. She got right down to business. "Well, Mary Jo, what are you going to play first?"

My heart stood still—*he* stood still. We stared at each other. We waited. I felt overcome with the warm, welcoming presence of Concert Grand, whose cloak stood high and majestic, under rays of the spotlight on stage. His ivories shone and begged my fingers to play. I craved to respond and savor his loving tones. I emerged to my feet.

After handing Sister Elaine my book-marked music, I hurried to the stage where Concert Grand's lap was awaiting. I announced my favorite and most comfortable, but very advanced piece, *Libestraume,* by Liszt. I sat a few seconds, took a deep breath, and focused. My left hand led with the opening note.

My fingers embraced the keys, and beautiful melodies sang from the piano during the first pages. I hoped Sister wasn't focusing intently when both hands played fast, chromatic thirds in parallel motion, descending three octaves. I exhaled. It was not flawless, but I was satisfied.

In those days, we didn't get compliments from the Sisters or from family. Was it a thing about being humble or proud? Maybe it was another old-country culture. Negative comments seemed to be the norm. I thought, *No comment probably means I passed my Liszt.*

I assumed Sister Elaine would be impressed with a Bach, so I volunteered his *Invention in C Major.* At sixteen, I didn't appreciate Bach and Beethoven. I liked the melodious, fiery, or Latin pieces with big sounds. My cup of tea did not overflow with technical pieces that proved the intelligence of the composer. I did not yet appreciate perfect, classical form of imitation in various keys in two, three, or four-part voices. I was pleased with my playing so far. The Sisters still did not offer comments.

Sister Elaine chose Mozart's *Fantasia in D Minor,* and I was glad. I relaxed with the various moods and dashing phrases. They were at my fingertips. All the

Sisters must have enjoyed that piece. Even Mozart would have confessed he liked it!

"All right, Mary Jo, you're done."

What a break! I didn't even have to plow through my dreaded Beethoven sonata. The three Sisters bent forward on the edge of their chairs. Their stiff, white linen headpieces almost touched as they whispered in a small circle. I remained with my hands in my lap, perched tall on the piano bench, staring down at the keyboard, holding my breath. What were they saying? All I heard was she...she...she. It was over. I resumed breathing.

Visiting Twice The First Time

First time:

Moby Dick would have been a challenge with or without my family's first visit. I dropped my book onto the seat of the rocking chair and positioned myself on the porch overlooking the small parking area, a perfect place for a good hour's study.

I read one paragraph, read it again. I looked up. No, it wasn't Dad's light blue Plymouth coming up the little road on the campus. I read the first paragraph again. I hate *Moby Dick*. I couldn't be more *bored. Why do we have to read stuff like that anyway?*

My eyes focused as I thought, *Oh, here comes a little white Ford station wagon. Maybe it's Tantan's with Ahmama and Danny. No, it stopped. Besides, Tantan knows exactly where to come. My whole family knows this campus after visiting Aunt Sister Clair since the 1930s.*

I counted eight gloomy pages to read. Time was ticking. I told myself to concentrate. It wasn't like me; I knew how to study well. I got up to check the clock in the aspirancy. Whoa! Only twenty minutes left. My stomach was shaking. I ran to the bathroom. Maybe they would arrive a little early.

I settled again in the rocking chair with *Moby Dick* glaring at me.

Our blue Plymouth and Aunt Tantan's little station wagon with my grandparents, Ahmama and Danny, were inching forward. I popped up and beckoned wildly with arms stretched over my head. I could see every size of limb fluttering back to me from car windows. I was torn. I dashed to the first floor to be there when they arrived.

The cars pulled to a stop and my parents and five little girls spilled out. They were still arranging their wrinkled, full skirts that were floating over several layers of starched, ironed petticoats. The girls had been mashed together during the long-heated drive without air conditioning. I charged with open arms to greet them.

Bear hugs for everyone didn't seem long enough. I was surprised that fifteen minutes had gone by so quickly.

I got many looks at my proudly worn aspirant uniform. Jerri's forehead wrinkled, "Why is your skirt so long below your knees?"

Patti interrupted, "Yeah, it's really out of style."

Disappointed, I glanced down at my outfit. "Well, I'm growing so fast; we didn't want it to get too short. Next year I will have the longer black candidates' uniform."

Adults gave polite, loving compliments. It was simple: A-line style, beige, lightweight wool skirt. My short sleeved, tucked-in, cotton blouse donned a simple brown, looped-over *tie* that hung about four inches under a Peter Pan rounded collar. Not much of my long thin legs showed between the hem of my skirt and the top of my folded-over beige socks and brown, laced shoes.

Mom sweetly changed the subject. "Let's walk over to the pecan grove and sit in the Adirondack chairs. That way the little ones can play." She remembered visiting there with her sister, Sister Clair, when she would be at OLL for summer study and eight-day retreat between nine months of teaching on the missions.

Little Mae yelled, "Yeah, the pecan grove! We brought bottles of bubbles with wands. Mary Jo, you have to see how many I can get to fly at one time. Candy can get lots to float, and Peggy and me try to break 'em before they get away."

My smallest sister, who was taking advantage of distracted grownups, had waddled around the parking area. I grabbed her, "Aha, gotcha, Peggy. You're getting so big!"

She laughed, "I'm twooo." I kissed her two little fingers gesturing up to me.

High-pitched chatter mixed with excited scurry while we gathered items to lug about half a block to the pecan grove.

Ahmama entrusted Danny with a white box, and kids grabbed their bags with bubbles. I was asking Jerri and Patti about school, and noticed Tantan tucked a flat, paper bag under her arm. Dad carried a small chest with grape Cool-Aid dancing in Ball canning jars.

Mom offered her arm out for Ahmama's support and latched onto a bag of water-cooler-size paper cups, obviously from Dad's Barbera Sporting Goods.

We slowly strolled in and out of the shade of mature pecans until we approached a grouping of Adirondacks. Everyone was vying for their turn to share the month's activities, school experiences and Tantan and Ahmama's church volunteering. Passing the Lourdes Grotto just before the pecan grove, I emphasized, "This is where we had our welcoming, outdoor picnic after swimming when you dropped me off on September fourth. I'll never forget that day."

I knew Tantan would ask, "How are your piano lessons with Sister Elaine? You must be thrilled to take from her. I can't wait to hear you play." She smiled as she presented me the thin paper bag. "I brought you a volume of *Chopin Waltzes*." She pursed her lips, pausing for my reaction.

"Oh, Tantan," I squealed while thumbing the complicated pages, "I can't wait to show Sister Elaine. I want to learn them all and keep them at my fingertips. Sometime we can go to Thiry Hall to visit so I can play for you." I knew I would do that many times, especially after piano exams. As I write over 50 years later, I glance at that yellow book smiling from my piano with "$1.25" centered under *Chopin Waltzes*, and my 1955 penciled signature on the upper right cover. I often play two of the waltzes from memory.

Danny arranged his chair to touch Ahmama's so he could lay his hand on top of hers on her knee. They sat with soft smiles, Ahmama with a tilted head, enjoying the flutter of one branch of their family tree. Eventually, Danny handed her the shirt-size, white, sturdy box he had carried close to himself. Ahmama perked up as she opened the box, "Oh, yes! Tantan and I made cookies!"

We always enjoyed their delicious, famous cookies. They didn't have to call twice for the children to let bubbles disappear into the pecans' flickering leaves and for all of us to zero-in on the box.

The large bells in Main Chapel tower chimed to remind us our two hours would be over in fifteen minutes. We bustled to get back to the cars in time. The Sisters knew to be already in place, whether in chapel, dining room, or spiritual reading at the assigned time. The Sign-of-the-Cross began when the bells *began* to chime the time of the event.

Clinging hugs and a few tears tinged with joy and homesickness wrapped up my first visiting Sunday. I pulled out my chair in the aspirancy with Chopin, many luscious cookies to share and blessed memories to cherish. It was nice to sit a few seconds and thank God for the delightful day with my family. I was happy to be back inside the convent.

BONG. BONG..."In the name of the Father, and of the Son, and of the Holy Spirit. ..." BONG. BONG. BONG...the chimes struck five. Sister Joan Michele had begun spiritual reading.

Second time:

"Mary Jo, wake up. Jesus is calling. It's almost two o'clock in the morning." I jumped into my aspirant-uniform and slunk into my Naturalizers, the soft, thick-rubber-soled shoes Mom bought me for bedroom slippers—perfect for quiet walking. I heard the same awakening signal for Imelda, sleeping in the next bed. She rushed, too. Grabbing her flashlight reminded me to bring mine.

Imelda led the way. We covered our flashlights, except for a small spacing between index and middle fingers, careful not to shine them on anyone in the dorm. We tiptoed as we sped down two flights, which led us to St. Joseph Hall, the four-floor infirmary for the ill and/or retired Sisters. At the end of the hallway, Imelda slowly opened an ornately sculptured portal with leaded glass windows.

Whoa! Imelda must have opened the Gate of Heaven. Over her shoulder, I scanned rays of sheer beauty. As we moved forward, I witnessed flickering flames of twenty slim candles of three different heights, spaced artistically on three levels of a ten-foot wide marble altar. A white linen cloth with hand-tatted edging draped to the floor on both sides of the bottom level of the altar.

Three marble platforms provided steps to this magnificent altar. I felt over-whelmed by a glimpse of what eternity must be like as described at the end of the New Testament in Revelation, Chapter Four, where it is thought the Apostle John, or his disciple, wrote of his vision of heavenly worship.

A 24-inch tabernacle, covered with a thin white veil, stood impressively in the center of the second level of the altar. The third level held the glittering gold monstrance. The round glass container in its center exposed the three-inch diameter bread-looking wafer—which had been consecrated into the Body of Christ—the epicenter and purpose of the holy place.

A huge, golden dome hovered over the altar, supported by a semi-circle of six, fifteen foot-Gothic marble pillars. A tall golden angel, with head bent toward the monstrance below, stood atop each of the front two pillars. Their hands folded, and their slim, long wings almost touched the back of their heels.

I realized that the majority of the interior of our small Adoration Chapel was solid marble, except for the redwood altar railing and about four or five pews on each side of the small middle aisle that could accommodate about fifty Sisters. *God, this is beautiful, yet I know Your Heaven is more awesome.*

Two Sisters were kneeling on small individual kneelers at the end of the middle aisle just below the altar railing. They rose and stepped aside as we approached. We four lowered on both knees and bowed down very slowly until our foreheads almost touched the floor. The two Sisters prayed their silent *good-bye* as Imelda and I whispered our *hello* to Him. Imelda and I were ready to spend the next hour in this hallowed place.

During the time of adoration, we could pray silently or together from the little booklets under the hand rest of our kneelers. Imelda led some of the invocations, then we prayed the rosary, which is mainly *Hail Marys* (the Bible prayer when an angel announced Mary was to be the mother of Jesus) and the *Our Father.* We had time just to look at Him and to have Him look at us.

I prayed, *Jesus, how can I thank You enough for bringing me to Your home in this convent? Help me always be faithful to You. Help me persevere in my vocation. I want to do everything, even the smallest things, for Your honor and glory. Help me to love You more and to make You loved. My eyelids are getting heavy, Jesus. Please help me stay awake.*

Imelda arose and climbed on a small ladder behind the altar to replace a candle that was getting very short. From each candle, she removed the gold cuff at the top that keeps wax from dripping down the side. Then she clipped the wicks of all of them with some nursing scissors. "Clipping the wick lets the candles last longer," she said later. Time sped slowly.

At two forty-five, Imelda made another deep genuflection, tiptoed the small middle aisle, and left to awaken and invite two other aspirants, "Jesus is calling."

This would be my experience about once a month during years of study or when assigned to OLL campus. Those were my special visiting times that I would always remember and treasure.

SUMMER RECOLLECTIONS
1956

My first year in the convent fast-forwarded so quickly, I could not believe I was still sixteen when I wrote my name on my Psychology 101 final exam at Our Lady of the Lake University (OLL) in San Antonio, Texas. I had left Providence High after my sophomore year, entered OLL aspirancy, and made my junior and senior high school years in ten and a half months by the end of June of 1956.

I picked up my pace walking through the halls back to the convent at the other end of the campus, feeling good about my completed exam. A smile stretched across my face, as I thought of all the happenings in that short year.

Senior aspirant, Donna, and I had gone to five Texas cities with Sister Joan Michele to give presentations and recruit girls for the convent. We enjoyed those two weeks answering questions about religious life and staying with Sisters on the missions, teaching at their assignments for that year.

Hugs and inquiries welcomed us, "What's the news from the convent home front?" They always had special meals prepared at our stopovers. Donna and I delighted doing homework on the road—it broke the frantic schedule of research and study in the aspirancy!

For six weeks in the summer, we aspirants lived at Moye Building in Castroville, 30 miles west of San Antonio, owned and run by the Sisters. The nuns used it for retreats during the early years of my religious life, and later rented it to parish groups for retreats. We would walk about a mile on the property to the outdoor pool to cool off from the hot, humid Texas weather. We were studying to earn last credits for our high school diplomas from our Sisters there.

While at Moye, I told Sister Joan Michele I felt called to a life of more prayer and quiet, perhaps to the cloistered life, where the nuns have many more hours of prayer and live in complete silence. She assured, "Mary Jo, you'll have much more time for silence and meditation as you advance in religious life." I looked forward to those years.

Passing through the familiar high school buildings after my exam, I paused to step into my former Spanish II classroom. Sister Cassiana tutored me in there several times a week after supper, since all but three of us in the class of about 20 knew Spanish fluently. I had no time for Spanish homework outside of class.

I knew if I could study, I could pass. Taking classes in the high school building helped me make two years of study in one. I only had time to cram-study in Sister Theresa Clare's three classes. She accepted no excuses, so I had no choice. I was re-cycling—deleting Spanish words to add new ones. I did not feel I would learn to speak Spanish. I was right.

That thought invited me to collapse into a chair-desk to recall my final exam days in Spanish last May. Sister Joan Michele had pulled me aside at breakfast. "Mary Jo, the aspirants have completed final exams. We're going to spend two days cleaning on all floors of the convent." I froze—my Spanish exam was in two days. When would I study?

Sister continued, "Get your Spanish book. Go outside and sit at that round concrete table by Main Chapel. Study today and tomorrow. Come inside only for prayer, meals, and bathroom. The aspirants are happy you'll have the time. You work hard at everything you do."

During that study outside, I had covered every inch on my stack of scratch paper with verb conjugations of every verb in my Comino Real II book and translations from Spanish or into Spanish. At the exam, I was the first to lay my paper onto Sister Cassiana's desk. She whispered, "Mary Jo, you have plenty of time left. Why don't you try a little longer?"

I whispered, "Oh, that's okay, Sister. Thanks for your extra help this year. I really appreciate it." I raced back to the aspirancy to help with housecleaning.

About an hour later, Sister Joan Michele handed me my Spanish exam, which Sister Cassiana had sent to the aspirancy. I will always remember it. She announced loudly, "Girls, good news! Listen up! Mary Jo made one-hundred on her final Spanish exam." We all danced and cheered. It was a good ending, but I knew I had spilled all of my Spanish knowledge onto that scratch paper and exam, and would not be able to converse in Spanish. I was still right.

My thoughts came back to reality as I bounced up and out into the high school hallway heading to the convent; but I couldn't avoid elderly Sister Typer's typing room! How did I pass that class?

Sister Joan Michele had asked permission for me to type her hand-written spiritual notebook onto small, narrow lined pages. Except for timed tests, my entire learning was the seek-and-you-shall-find method, poking and jabbing on an old manual typewriter with only my index fingers.

After nine weeks, Sister Typer put her wrinkled little fingers on my shoulder, "Mary Jo, I guess you've never played the piano." I jolted—too shocked to say I'd taken lessons half my life. I didn't dare reveal that I learned Liszt's *Liebestraume,* that I played it in my sophomore recital or that I reviewed it every day so I would remember it. It's a good thing she didn't know I would major in music. I didn't even know at that time what it meant to *major* in something!

I decided to let her think otherwise. Perhaps it would evoke a little mercy.

Recalling my brown, aspirant, lace-up shoes that were wear-worn and wrinkled from walking these halls, I looked down and laughed at my shiny black shoes peeking up at me from under my long, black, pleated, serge skirt and petticoat. My mind wondered. I continued through the halls of my past.

Still sitting alone, l looked around to see if anyone was hearing my giggles. I recalled when Imelda and I purchased those black shoes together at Wolff and Marx downtown. We each tried several pairs for comfort and paraded around the department making sure they were the correct size.

The sales clerk sized up his elegant, repeat customers with unpaid parcels in shoeboxes. We knew he wondered what kind of game Imelda and I were playing. Embarrassed, we bit our lips and pondered what else he might be thinking.

We ignored the women with opened checkbooks, zipping dagger-eyes across the room our way. We continued our pursuit for black, chunky one-and-half inch heeled, granny-looking, expensive Naturalizers. We knew we would be wearing them every single day for work, play, prayer, and walking the university campus. We'd be polishing and having them repaired for several years.

Imelda carefully wrapped the tissue paper around her selections and broke the silence. "I'll take these two pairs, please."

"And these two boxes for me, thank you," I blurted.

His jaw dropped. His eyebrows rose. His shoe-horn slipped to the floor when he studied the two teenage girls. He sputtered, "Uh. Okay. Uh, but where on earth are you going to *wear* these things?"

I froze, but Imelda instantly emphasized, "We're going hiking!"

I thought I would lose my lunch swallowing my laughter. Every eyeball rolled at us as we sashayed across the carpet with our Wolff and Mark bags and the elevator door closed.

Once again, I had to remind myself, *Mary Jo, you are on the way to the convent building after your psychology exam. Get back to the now.*

I approached the area under Main Chapel and met my reflection in the glass of the French doors leading to the convent building. In the involvement of my second step in religious life as a candidate—the excitement of longer prayer times, activities, new rules, registering for daily, a summer three-hour college class and studying—I had not observed myself in my new candidate uniform.

My four-inch-wide, Peter Pan, starched, white collar sat on my black, pleated cotton, long sleeve blouse. A white T-shirt provided protection under it—we could wash the blouse weekly, not daily. The blouse tucked into a wide-belted, pleated skirt that touched the tip of my infamous black shoes. The black cotton stockings and long, black, half-slip attracted the heat of the humid summers in San Antonio. I knew I would get used to the uniform, despite no air conditioning in any of the 100-year-old elaborate Gothic buildings.

Prayer, dependency on God to give me the grace I needed to serve Him in religious life, and my desire to *use* that grace, pulled me through my first year of religious life and many years of other challenges.

⌒

Before entering the convent, I cheered inside: how great it would be to have someone helping to wash dishes when it was my turn, or to have someone help clean *my space* with me. I was younger and more naïve by one whole year, so

I hadn't considered that almost a thousand times more people would get the place dirtier a little faster.

The day after my first college exam, I walked into the postulate (the study, gathering room for candidates and postulants) after breakfast. Sister Ann Joseph, mistress of candidates and postulants, had written on the blackboard:

All report to Sister Maude today.

West ballroom of the university at 8:00.

Wear party skirts.

I cornered my newly assigned candidate-angel, Mary Catherine, "Wow! A party in the university ballroom! What are *party skirts?*"

"I'll get you one. It's a simple, gathered-with-elastic, black skirt made from old candidates' uniforms. We wear them only for heavy-duty spring and fall housecleaning in the convent building or when we clean in the high school and university—as we're going to do the next two weeks."

I deflated a bit. "Oh, uh, I see."

After dressing up in our party clothes and black aprons, about twenty-five of us paraded through the halls of the convent, the high school and university.

We eyed Sister Maude just inside the French doors opening to one of the two ballrooms. She stood in the center of a large variety of cleaning supplies: folded, old bath and kitchen towels, backs and fronts of T-shirts, mops, buckets, five-gallon containers of smelly floor-wax, and long extension cords. A huge machine sat on top of circles of soft padding. I spied a large plastic beach bucket of old toothbrushes and a box of various tools. We knew we had *arrived.*

"Good morning, girls." She seemed to beam at the more-than-usual-total of arms and legs that had appeared that year. "Today some of you will do floors, and some will do steps. Tomorrow you'll switch. Those who haven't waxed floors, pair with someone who did them last spring. Same with the steps." It was obvious who of us were new: seasoned candidates quickly moved toward the orderly arrangement; the rest of us didn't even know how to *look* helpful.

"Remember to work in silence, as much as possible," Sister Maude reminded gently.

Mary Catherine nodded to me with raised eyebrows, picked up two 24-inch square rags, and balanced them on top of a five-gallon can of wax. We shoved the pile near to the corner across the room from the door. She pried the can open with the screwdriver she grabbed from her black apron-pocket.

"Mary Jo, spread out the rags. We'll plop globs of wax onto them." We got down on our knees. I imitated her, scooping both hands full of wax and carefully placing it into the middle of the rag. My fingers oozed thick chicken fat that wiggled like dense Jell-O. After we each deposited a couple of quarts, she said, "Now we'll wrap the top and bottom onto the top of the wax, then the sides."

I asked, "It looks like a gigantic burrito. What now?"

"Keep gripping it tightly where the sides and ends meet. Push hard, away from you. Watch. Mash it into the floor."

"Oh, I see! It's leaking through the rag itself, onto the floor."

"Don't let it come out the openings, and try to smooth it onto the floor," Mary Catherine advised. We scooted backward on our hands and knees, working our way down the left side of the room. We walked to the front of the room, again working backward, overlapping the section we'd just finished, sweating like Texas longhorn-rustlers. We had to stop to *refill our burritos* many times in this large room.

"This wax smells like chocolate, doesn't it?" I asked two hours later.

Mary Catherine energetically rolled her waxy rag into a stack. "Yeah, that's Sister Balbina coming with her luscious cookies. Time for our thirty-minute break. Let's go."

The whiff became *whiffier*. My stomach growled. We stepped just outside the ballroom door into the area at the foot of the stairs.

Pleasantly plump Sister Balbina—one of the university's great bakers with hands on hips—smiled from ear-to-ear. She proudly displayed warm mounds of thick, chocolate chip, pecan cookies on the top of an old fashion, well built, shiny polished, wooden cart. Several hefty containers of cold milk and water, with sweat drooling down the sides, parked next to stacks of large paper cups.

She didn't have to beg us to take many cookies and fill our cups "to the top," with milk. We collapsed onto the nearby staircase and inhaled the refreshments. I closed my eyes, used the steps for a pillow, and sunk into a deep sleep—with one eye open—for the remaining eighteen minutes.

Another new candidate, Thelma, unraveled what looked like a ten-mile cord extending from an industrial floor-buffer and began polishing the area Mary Catherine and I had just waxed. Intrigued with the high gloss reflection the machine produced, I asked, "May I try that, too?"

"Yeah, but it's heavy and wants to do its own thing. Be careful. You're kind of skinny, and it's strong."

I clenched the 24-inch wide handle. "Yi-i-ippes, how do I turn it off?" I yelled over its deep growl. I almost tripped as it "did its own thing." It erratically pulled me forward, right, left. The girls clapped as Thelma pulled the plug, and I ended my fitful tarantella dance. I took a deep, grateful bow—grateful to get back down on my hands and knees to finish waxing that ballroom on the first day.

∽

Could the next day be as challenging? Before I donned my *party clothes* for the second day's encounter, I examined my blouse in the light shining from our dorm window.

I had never seen dried out—not perspiration—but downright sweat. The white salt—the salt my body lost under my armpits, across my back and between my small boobs—formed wavy lines on my black blouse. It reminded me of kelp lining the sand as water drifts back to the sea.

I dropped the stinky shirt into my laundry basket, and reached for an old, worn out, clean party blouse. Ahh, I can handle this garden-fresh blouse. Today won't be so bad.

That morning, our pace was a little slower as we walked the hallways to house-clean again. We understood each other's measured, delicate footsteps. Yet, with more of the same exercise, we knew our sore muscles would be *in tune* in a few days.

Faithful Sister Maude stood eager and waiting. "Greetings, candidates, you did beautiful work yesterday." She knew how to pump us up with brownie points. It did help. Although we felt better just hearing it, our muscles had no ears. She, too, was doing her job—in a loving, pleasant way. Someone had to clean the place.

It was our turn to sparkle the steps. Mary Catherine beckoned me to gather a plastic container of baking soda, and two buckets containing hand towels,

45

several used toothbrushes, and water. We hung the buckets on our arms and climbed up two flights.

She sat on the top step of the landing of six-inch, white tiles and began to demonstrate how to clean. "If you know how to brush your teeth, you know how to brush the grout—no secret." I returned her raised eyebrows and impish smile with a teasing hate-squint.

"Mary Jo, you go on up to the fourth floor and work down to this second-floor landing. I'll work here on the second, down to the first floor. See you later."

On the fourth floor, I studied the situation: if I clean the step just above the one I'm sitting on, this'll be a snap. I dipped a wet toothbrush into the container of soda and started scrubbing the grout until whitened. I wrung the towel only slightly to rinse. The routine seemed simple enough, but monotonous. "This is for You, Lord." That prayer made it seem easier.

My wrist zigzagged so rapidly, I hardly recognized it. I laughed so hard inside that beads of water dripping from my forehead provided salt to the soda for added cleanser!

Soon the velocity made my arm cry with cramps. My fingers didn't want to open. I did not have strength to squeeze water from the towel. I switched to my left hand.

A familiar aroma broke the silence: Sister Balbina and her cookie-cart! I met Mary Catherine on my way down stairs, and tiptoed onto the centers of her already whitened six-inch tiles—I wouldn't soil the grout.

I was so sore, I gingerly gripped the rails to inch my aching back into standing position. Mary Catherine clutched her side as we both laughed at our odd postures and descended cautiously to the first floor.

"Yeah! Sister Balbina! You, and Sister Emil in our convent kitchen, sure know how to make a good cookie better," I laughed.

Mary Catherine added, "You make them fat and serve them with huge cups of ice cold milk. These snickerdoodles are second to none." Sister's big smile revealed her set of perfectly fit dentures. I devoured my snack, closed my eyes, and laid my sweaty back on the cool tiles of the second-floor landing—eighteen more minutes of break. I thought about the day so far and the next several hours of the same physically draining work. "For You, Lord, for You," I prayed.

During those two weeks, we continued to clean grout on many staircases and bathroom floors. We waxed, polished, and cleaned many private rooms and dorms for boarders and Sisters in the high school and university buildings. Our muscles *were* in tune by the time we cleaned in the Sisters' demonstration school, St. Martin's Hall, across 24th Street. We worked in silence, and we worked in sweat.

I wanted to show Him my dedication with this menial work that someone had to do. I'd do it to give Him glory. I would clean His house that needed to be ready for the students and boarders who would learn to love Him more and make Him loved.

The Sisters and lay professors would walk miles on these floors and steps, many until they were in their eighties. *They* would be the very ones who would directly "make Him loved."

Not only did silence help us work more efficiently, it helped us stay in the presence of God, praying mentally as we toiled. That is what made my work *easy*. It reminded me of my life's motto I wrote on my application for the convent: *I want to love God more and make Him loved.*

THE LYING NUN

Although the smothering humidity of San Antonio reminded us that there had been a summer, it sped by quickly; I was stunned reading Sister Ann Joseph's note on the blackboard:

Make an appointment today or tomorrow with
Sister Marietta to get your curriculum list
for college registration next Wednesday.

I asked Mary Catherine, "Registration? How do I know what courses to take?"

"Sister Marietta is the Dean of Studies for the Sisters. She lines up your classes for your major."

"Major?" I asked. "What's a *major*? I hope I won't be as pressured as I was last year doing two years in one."

She laughed, "Your major is the field of study. She'll tell you what yours is. I have my schedule already. I'll take you to her office upstairs. Let's go."

Sister Marietta's workplace was immaculate. The familiar smell of newly waxed floor and polish reminded me of the last two weeks' house cleaning. Shelving on three walls held organized books of various educations and curriculum references.

Tall metal files stood intelligently on each side of the door we had just entered. Two stately ferns acted as bookends on each side of her large glossy desk. Below the three bay windows behind her, I viewed St. Martin Hall, the Sisters' demonstration school across 24th Street.

I relaxed when little Sister Marietta smiled, "I remember when your parents brought you and your little sisters to visit with your aunt, Sister Clair. You all were eager to sing *Immaculate Mary* whenever we asked. We're happy to have you in the convent now with us."

She pulled a manila folder from a file. "Mary Jo, Sister Lucy Marie, head of the music department, sent your curriculum for your first year of study. You will take basic classes for all music majors: harmony, ear training, violin, choir with Sister Hortensia, and piano with Sister Elaine. Sister Joan Michele will teach Scripture, and Sister Henry, voice. You will take a placement exam next week to determine your English teacher, either Sister Generosa or Sister Callista."

My eyes bulged. "That seems like a lot to study."

"It is a very heavy schedule," she admitted, "but we think you can do it. You are a hard worker and a good student. Go to Thiry Hall and meet Sister Lucy Marie. She'll give you some particulars on hours dedicated each day to each applied instrument." Timid and terrified, I thanked her, and left.

My pulse quickened, but I inched over to Thiry Hall in a daze. Many questions and concerns flashed through my mind. How did she know I was a "good student"? I didn't do as well in the aspirancy as I had at Providence High—when I could study until late at night.

I still did not know what it meant to *major* in music. I guessed Sister Lucy Marie would tell me. However, English with Sister Generosa? I knew I'd place high in English. Last year's postulants and Aunt Sister Clair always spoke of her with high regard, but with remnants of lingering pain: "She certainly knows how to teach English. I had her in high school and in college."

"She demands the highest quality," another said. "We received a research paper at least every two weeks. We lived in the library."

"You will know your English grammar, Shakespeare, all the classic literature, and writing when you finish her class. Sister Generosa is generous with homework. English majors appreciated her demanding, exacting instructions." The complimentarians were overwhelming and discouraging!

I pulled open the heavy back door of Thiry Hall, which glistened from wax and polish. I noticed the wide sturdy steps built to withstand the 500 pounds of grand pianos. Movers would haul them to any of the three floors or the basement for events like recitals, workshops, and practicing two-piano numbers for concerts. As I neared Room 202, the Bach *B-Flat Invention* greeted me from the half-opened studio door.

I tapped my fingertip, "Sister Lucy Marie?"

"Yes? Mary Jo!" She removed her thick, music-reading glasses. "Welcome to the music department. I intend to practice daily until I die. It's part of my life. If you love music, you'll probably do the same." It seemed strange the Sisters knew me. During those 16 years of visiting, I hadn't memorized all 900 of the Sister's names.

She reviewed my classes, explaining that *each* university credit for applied music (voice, piano, organ, violin, etc.) required one hour of *daily* practice. "You'll have a card to document your practice. If you miss on the week-days, make up the hours on the weekend." As she spoke, she showed me hallways of rooms only large enough for an upright piano and bench. "You may choose your practice room."

She lowered her voice, "You'll have many classes with Sister Hortensia. She's been teaching 50 years, and is very demanding in harmony, choir, ear training and violin. You'll study many more advanced classes with her in counterpoint, harmony and ear training, music composition and violin. But be patient with her, study well, and you'll learn much."

I folded and unfolded my paper-schedule, which ended up a small wad in my palm. I breathed a prayer. *Dear God, I do want to learn, but am I able to handle all of these heavy music classes and with such demanding teachers?*

I visited classrooms surrounded by green boards painted with permanent white staves of five lines and four spaces throughout the entire building, and large organs I would use with lessons from Sister Henry.

Overjoy and *overwhelm* vacillated my brain cells.

"Oh, Sister, it sounds delightful to hear music coming from several rooms already before school starts. I'm excited to get my pieces from Sister Elaine and start practicing." In the eagerness to play again, I bounced on my feet going back to the convent.

However, I had forgotten to ask what it meant to *major in music*.

Now I *knew*, was *convinced*, was *determined*: there was no way I was going to be in Sister Generosa's English class. My plate was full, keeping up with this schedule of music classes alone. I devised only one solution, and it was simple.

A few days later, I entered Room 204 in the university with my #2 pencils with good erasers for the placement exam. Sister Generosa greeted me and whispered, "Mary Jo, I hear you are as good as your aunt Sister Clair in English. Do well. I'm looking forward to your being in my classes."

"Thank you, Sister."

After she passed the exam booklets around and gave the simple you-may-begin sign, Sister Generosa rested on a cloud with *The Iliad and the Odyssey* for the next hour. Girls bent forward over the pages. I flipped page after page, easily filling in the small Easter eggs with my #2. Then I panicked—I had only two more pages to go. My heart pounded so hard, my arm jerked.

My thoughts blared. I hoped she could not overhear them: *STOP! What are you doing, Mary Jo? You're used to trying to fill in the correct answer, STOP!*

I gulped. My eyes protruded. I had to start leaving some answers blank. I had to go back to change some correct answers to incorrect. How many should I do?

My eraser worked fast. Just did it. Got moving.

Weird! I guessed it was how it felt to *cheat* on an exam. *Oh, God, am I cheating?!* My head had assumed the same position of the girls slaving to fill in the right bubbles. I glanced to be sure I was safe. I could not tie myself to the library and to the music hall, only to rip *myself* apart with the pull.

I had to take up for myself, even if it meant the humiliation of scoring low to attend Sister *Callista's* classes. I would have plenty homework with her on a college level. I would not learn anything in music *or* English if I stretched myself from the library, to Thiry Hall and to the postulate, with little time for study.

The next week, I was helping in the registration office when Sister Generosa entered for her roster of students. "Mary Jo, I'm disappointed you will not be in my college English classes."

I glared. How would I explain without hurting her feelings? "I'm sorry, Sister," I lied with a hint of smile. I took a deep breath and attended to the next student. However, I didn't want to wind up a lying nun.

Summer college exams were over; the buildings smelled of fresh wax, and we candidates looked forward to our first classes. All morning I was curious about the notice Sister Ann Joseph, our new mistress, had written on the blackboard. *All meet in the postulate at five o'clock today.*

Later, we scooted to the postulate. Tower bells chimed five, and Sister began, "In the name of the Father..."

The clatter of vintage, high-back chairs scraping the wooden floors and slapping against the vinyl-topped, army surplus desks with big drawers warranted our admonition. We flopped into our seats. We stared at Sister and listened to the contrasting sound of dead silence as she scanned each of our five rows of desks. Finally, with pursed lips, she broke the hush, "Will you please rise and sit again?" We complied.

"Thank you." She knew how to make a point without saying it. She paused and continued.

"Girls, every day we'll meet here in the postulate at five o'clock for spiritual reading. During that time, you will do your mending."

At that, I noticed the old candidates already in the process of opening sewing kits, stuffing a wooden egg into their long black cotton stockings, and darning worn heels. She had to be kidding! Mend stockings? I didn't know it was possible. I could not mend stockings.

Sister carried on, "In case some of you don't realize it, there are two groups of candidates in the room. The new group will remain candidates for a year. All of you will be in silent retreat for eight days beginning on December first. Those who have been here longer will become postulants and receive capes and new collars on the last retreat day, December eighth." We totaled about nine to-be postulants and eighteen of us new candidates. (Some girls left, but others entered the following year.)

"This week you will begin walking over to your college classes. You will be among others—lay students. They are informed not to socialize with you."

I raised my hand. "You mean I'm not allowed to say 'hi' to my friends? I know they'll be attending classes next year after graduating from Providence High."

"Of course, you may greet them. However, you will have many college and religious studies, prayers and activities here in the convent. You will treasure every minute to study. They will understand that." Experienced candidates agreed with firm nods.

"Also," Sister said, "keep in mind: you will be separated from the aspirants and novices and visit only during special recreations and occasions." She looked down at her list of *dos and don'ts*. "This room, the postulate, is normally for study and spiritual reading. You want to respect that silence for everyone else. Before you leave, except for group activities when I know where you are, you should sign out on the board—your name and destination."

I was getting nervous, wondering whether I should have been taking notes. I hoped I would not mess up.

"We kneel to say the rosary with the Sisters in Main Chapel. On Fridays during those fifteen minutes, we pray and reflect on the Sorrowful Mysteries of the Rosary. We recite the short Hail Mary prayer on each of the five sets of ten beads. Those mysteries are the Agony in the Garden, the Scourging at the Pillar, the Crowning of Thorns, the Carrying of the Cross, and the Crucifixion. We hold our arms bent with our hands to our shoulders and hold the rosary beads in our fingers, like this." She demonstrated.

"Wow, doesn't that get tiresome and hurt?" Eve asked. I was glad she spoke up. I didn't have to do it.

"Well, it doesn't hurt as much as Christ did on the cross on Good Friday, when He died for us—don't you think? It's a small way to mortify, offer, and thank Him."

That made sense. I entered the convent to give myself to Him. Now I hoped I'd be able to endure it.

Sister removed her pocket watch from her waistband.

I squirmed. Maybe she's over the worst of the announcements.

Not quite—she had more. "The cabinet next to the entry door in your dorm has toilet articles. You probably brought large supplies of toothpaste, shampoo, bar soap, toothbrushes, deodorant, boxes of Kotex, and things like that. You are to keep only one of each and turn in the rest. I will supply several of each item on the shelf as needed. Take only what you need. You will learn more about this in the novitiate. Any questions?"

I was numb. A newbie raised a few fingers a bit, "But Sister, I brought a whole *case* of Dove soap. It's pure soap, and I like that kind."

I gulped. I pictured the dozen bars of deodorant soap Mom helped me squeeze into the top tray of my trunk. I did not want to bathe in Dove face-soap.

The room seemed anesthetized. I knew I would always hear our silent response.

Eventually Sister scanned the room. "The same applies to all gifts from home." Familiar sound of silence again!

"One last item—when you receive money from home or from anywhere..." she paused.

My thoughts interrupted *that* thought. *Oh no! We don't put our money on the shelf, too! Ahmama, Danny, and Tantan always give us money for our birthdays. They work hard and do not earn a lot. She's not going to tell us she's confiscating our money from home?*

I held my breath.

She continued, "You haven't taken the vow of poverty yet, but you will turn in any gift money. It will be in an envelope in the vault, if needed. After vows, it won't be in *your* envelope, but in the community fund. If you have any questions, you may ask me later. We need to begin spiritual reading now."

Whew! At least for a while, there were no more announcements.

> I prayed: *Lord, You dished a larger portion onto my plate today. I renew my dedication to You. Help me be the candidate You want me to be. Give me the grace to accept all of these new rules in a spirit of love and commitment. I know You will be with me. You always take care of me.*

Buddies, Misnomers
and Shenanigans

Music majors were scarce in the convent—average one a year. My largest college music class was five students—great for learning with personal attention. The Sisters were excellent but demanding. My religious group in the convent was large—18 girls, including *two* music majors: Frances Ann and me.

On our first day of class, Sister Hortensia played a few measures of a four-voice (soprano, alto, tenor, and bass) Bach Chorale. "Write that down in your manuscript books."

I stared at the series of five lines and four spaces on my paper and gripped my sharp pencil tighter. No way I could do that—I'm not even sure whether I could hum it back. I thought, *Is this what it means to major in music? I like to play, but why would I major in music?*

"No, class." Sister assured us, "I just played an example of what you *should* be able to listen to and write down before you get your degree. You'll need to practice much at home; each class is more challenging."

How do I test myself on what I had just played?

I struggled after each of Sister Hortensia's beginning classes of aiming to train my ears to hear the distance (interval) between two notes. What to do?

Answer: Frances Ann was experiencing the same challenge. She'd play a group of notes for me to write in my manuscript tablet; then, we'd exchange roles. We were both desperate and needing a *right hand helper*.

We began to enjoy the challenge and to see our growth. We each scored 100% identifying 100 intervals on our freshman finals. We were survival buddies.

Frances Ann and I were as Siamese twins—relying on each other in several other music classes. Sometimes she had to do research for Sister Generosa's English paper. I would shake in my black chunky shoes if we couldn't exchange dictation.

Another drawback of this dependency? We spent twice as much time, returning an hour of playing for each other. Many of these intensely time-consuming classes were only one-credit classes, which normally required just one hour of daily study.

When Professor Ingram dropped the needle onto a large vinyl 33.3 record for us to name the sonata and movement, the period in history, and the name of the composer, we thought he was kidding. His confident Irish smile said he wasn't. "You'll listen hours on your own to label many others from the large tape-deck." He tapped his pointer on the small plaque on the door behind him: LISTENING ROOM.

Frances Ann and I eyeballed each other to confirm, "See you there!" We didn't know whether the tape or our brains would wear out faster, but we absorbed and stretched our knowledge more than we expected. We could identify composers by their technique and style.

After our sophomore year, Frances Ann could not envision herself as a music teacher. She was more comfortable as a classroom teacher. Nevertheless, I was devastated and shocked. How could I major in music with only my *left hand*?

Sometimes I felt she was selfish to cop-out—that she had let me down after so many hours of dictating for her. However, I realized: she had done just as much for me. She was the one that ended up with the *wasted time*. I felt no one thought about what I was feeling, or how I was going to survive studying by myself.

Sister Hortensia passed out third-grade-level classroom songbooks to the five of us in our Friday keyboarding class in the basement of Thiry Hall. Rain beat on the little 18-inch windows high above the sidewall of the room. Behind Sister's simple desk, a crucifix hung above the green boards painted with music staves—five lines and four spaces.

Sister said, "Now that you know how to analyze the harmonic structure of music, as the *music instructor*, you will often need to accompany on the piano with only the melody written. Open to the song on page sixty. Study it mentally to determine the chords you'd play for each measure."

Whoa! I numbed. *Did she just say I'd be the music instructor some day? So, that's what 'music major' entails! Mary Catherine had said it was 'your field of study.' No one ever asked me. I was never ever going to get in front of a classroom and teach anything, especially music.*

The distraction overwhelmed me. I stepped back from the group and flashbacked to my horrors of why I'd never be a music teacher.

My mind transported to my third grade, the year I could take private piano lessons at school, and I was ecstatic! Aunt Tantan—who never married and lived with my grandparents—was musical and always taught me something at the piano when we went to their home. Often, she would play and sing to rehearse for the San Antonio Opera crowd scenes. I loved to lie on the floor and listen to her. I wanted to play *"that one piece."* It was not any special composition, just any piece.

Tantan showed me an advanced piano book. I never thought that I would *never* be able to play the compositions—I just wanted to do whatever it took to be able to play them sometime in my life. I was willing to work at it: I needed to quench my hunger and thirst for piano playing. Tantan always encouraged me. We'd play *Chop Sticks, Heart and Soul*—anything at all.

As months went on, I improved. We played all kinds of duets—children's songs, Christmas carols, and pretty tunes I didn't recognize. We were thrilled making music together.

One day she pulled out a book of easy classical duets. The deep, overwhelming joy would transform and transport me to another world. I knew the feeling would be as alive in me all my life as it was at that tender age of eight.

Tantan was patient and forgiving of my mistakes. We just kept on playing and having fun! There were never enough hours in the day for me to play, never as much as I'd like.

༄

Going back again, to the summer *before* third grade actually started: Mom took me to Sister Teresita to inquire about piano lessons. Since the Sisters went to their Mother Home on their university campus for further studies and eight-day retreat, Sister would not be teaching piano until September. Jerri and I started lessons with Sister's advanced, high school piano student in the summer.

My dream would become a reality!

Each week Rosalie taught us together at the piano. Looking back, that was a weak foundation. She was a student herself: no teaching skills in the importance of fundamentals at the very first lessons—hand position, theory, note reading, rhythm— especially with young children.

I remember the sessions. Playing together, I kept playing wrong notes, since Rosalie had us play faster than I could keep up. Jerri did not seem to miss as many notes. Finally, Jerri whispered, "Mary Jo, just keep your eye on the finger numbers above the notes."

Wow, that John Thompson book was great. Every single note had the finger numbers, and it was wonderful! I could play well—for a while—as long as we were in C POSITION. I didn't know it would be a downfall and challenge later.

When Sister Teresita came back to school in September, I was elated and eager to learn from a real piano teacher, but found that she was always, *and I mean always*, very upset with my piano lessons. I practiced at home every minute I could, but I always played many errors. I did not have the ease to decipher the more complicated rhythms, which Sister assumed I had learned from Rosalie.

As those first years of piano progressed, I figured that if you took piano lessons, you simply put up with the ruler's hitting your hand repeatedly and having the teacher yell at you. Accusing me of not practicing at home was more devastating and painful than the dreaded ruler. My little tummy fluttered; my eyes watered as if they were *under* water.

My tiny heart slowly swelled with unleashed tears. Instead of letting them burst out during my lessons, I looked straight ahead at the wall, trying to block out what she was screaming. I pretended her words were ticker tape going in the right ear and coming out the left. When she'd bark, "Now do you understand?" what could I say but, "Yes, Sister"—even though I had not a clue about what she had just lectured.

My mind constantly asked: *Where's the fun like I have when I play with Tantan? She never yells at me. Music's supposed to be fun. I want to play pretty music. I want people to listen and let my playing help them be happy—happy like it makes me.*

The joy and pain of learning and sharing my music: were they misnomers? When no one was around, I'd sit on the piano bench or on my bed as tears flowed down both cheeks as a child. I'd reach for my flowered, cotton hankie already soaked with salty water. Was I poking my tiny piano finger into that hole in my little heart that wanted to unleash the flood of emotions of joy and sorrow? Would the tsunami erupt one day during my piano lessons?

I never told my mother, Tantan, or anyone about piano lesson traumas, since the Sisters were always right...right?

For three years, Tantan and I still had fun playing our duets together. During my study with Sister Teresita, I learned many pretty pieces—very beautiful ones that I loved and performed well—despite the challenge at the lessons. I felt pleased to see myself advancing musically, but I knew I did not understand fully what I was playing.

∽

Two eye-opening experiences jolted me in the fifth grade.

Often when Mom dropped us off at St. Mary's School, I said honestly, "Mommie, I feel like I'm going to throw up." She'd look at me, feel my head, and say I'd be fine. She was right. However, after a year or so on one such occasion, she patted me on the head and said, "It's Wednesday, Honey. You'll feel better after your piano lesson." She was *always* right.

The second experience was when Mom took me for a Saturday make-up piano lesson. "I'll be across the street in church until your lesson is over."

I sat and waited a few minutes in the music studio while Eugene finished his lesson. My heart danced when Sister smiled and seemed in a good mood: "Eugene, you had a nice lesson." I eagerly hopped over to the bench, but the same struggle of incorrect rhythms and notes spun Sister into frenzy.

She slammed her pencil down onto the keyboard, "Mary Jo, you will never learn to play piano if you don't practice!" Lips pursed. Forehead dug deep furrows. She flew from her chair, turning her back to me.

She knew where Mom waited. "March right over to church. Tell your mother I want to see her. Immediately!"

Mom entered. Sister brushed her veil back, raised both arms, and raved, "Mary Jo just does not practice." Tears welled up again, but I swallowed a big gulp.

Mom remained calm with a lowered voice, "Sister, maybe Mary Jo doesn't play correctly, but never once in these three years have I had to remind her to practice. She absolutely loves to play. In fact, when her sisters leave the piano before their practice time is up, Mary Jo runs over to perform."

That was the first time I heard Mom disagree with one of the Sisters, and I always remembered how respectfully, honestly, and gently she spoke. Right then I learned that I could grow up and disagree with others, but I should do it courteously.

Mom soon discovered and informed me that Sister Teresita had cancer. "She's probably upset and just not herself. Pray for her and be kind." That helped me cope a bit with Sister's impatience and strengthened my own patience with her. I cherished whatever it took to see myself growing in my music.

For confidence in piano recitals and playing well, I practiced repeatedly and always had a big *audience* of little sisters running around me. I learned to focus despite distractions.

For a few moments, I woke from my daydreaming in that keyboarding class. Was I training to be a music teacher? What was going on? No one spelled it out for me until Sister Hortensia made her remark about teaching singing as a music teacher.

I recalled that I volunteered to tutor algebra almost every morning before school my entire sophomore year. I also taught *Esta Son Las Mananitas* and two other songs to our Spanish class when our instructor attended a convention three days that same year. That was different and fun. However, I always said, "I never want to be that mean old music teacher. Never. Ever!"

Sister Hortensia broke my moment of deep concentration, "Beautiful work, Jeanette."

Wow! Sister Hortensia actually handed out a compliment to one of the students! Jeanette was a very talented, creative musician and composer. She received many well-deserved accolades from Sister Hortensia in music classes.

I was excited for her and her creativity in music. She was the oldest of many peers and had as many responsibilities as I did.

When I knew my homework with Sister Hortensia was quite good, I never received a compliment or encouragement. She'd just shrug her shoulders and raise her eyebrows as if to imply, "Well, so what? That's what you're supposed to do." She could dish out the negatives, shake her head with displeasure, and wrinkle up her face. Maybe she thought we postulants would become *proud* and needed to learn humility. Maybe she felt threatened. I wondered what the girls thought about the Sisters—what they told their parents.

Sometimes I wanted to slam my manuscript book on her desk, "Why can't you admit that my homework today was darn good? Why make class harder than it is?" My mind stamped its feet again: I'm *not* going to be a *mean old music teacher!* It still hurts to have flashbacks of my first formal piano lessons.

I loved music and hung in there once again, despite the challenges from a demanding professor and it paid off.

While working Beethoven's *Pathetique* at my piano lesson, Sister Elaine commented, "You played that measure very nicely." I unintentionally programmed Sister Elaine's comment and reinforced hearing it every time my fingers played those notes after that. The compliment I received didn't make me proud or pompous—it helped me in my decision to continue as a music-major.

I wouldn't have to be that *mean old music teacher.* Why couldn't I encourage with a deserved compliment? If a student had improved on a composition, why not let him know the hard work was worth the effort?

If the improvement was greatly improved or mastered, why couldn't I celebrate with downright joyful praise? Why not let students enjoy playing piano, as I did with Tantan when I was young?

At Sister Elaine's invitation, I brought her a piece I'd written for a composition class with Sister Hortensia. After I played *Fiesta Fun*, she was smiling, "Mary Jo, it has a good Spanish tune and rhythm. It's an excellent beginner composition. Are you sure you haven't heard it before?" I sat taller on the piano bench. She continued, "It's going to stay in my mind. I'd like to hear more. How about a middle section in a minor mode?"

Talk about a compliment! This one was from Texas-Composer-of-the-Year twice and Composer-of-the-Year for the entire USA once. Sister Elaine's encouragement far trumped Sister Hortensia's discouraging comments.

I had discovered I was a music major—a future music teacher determined to encourage students to enjoy the talent God had given them, whether they majored in music or learned it for pure enjoyment. I knew I'd never regret my decision. I'd always thank God for the Sisters who helped me find my niche of making Him loved through the inspiration and beauty of music.

Music misnomer? Resolved.

❧

In any group of teens or young adult girls, there are individuals you expect to pull off some shenanigans, but the tease punches more intensely when they work together—whether in study, prayer, chores, recreation, or in a convent. Case in point: Marie Gubbels, Pat Slater, and Dolores Sullivan.

Together those three had exhausted the wits of professors at Our Lady of the Lake University. They were all our funny bones could handle when one by one they entered OLL Convent at the opposite end of the campus. They hardly opened their mouths that a quick, loud, or whispered wit didn't cause our entire group to break silence in laughter.

Close to the end of a semester, you could *hear* my stress in the dead silence of the large postulate (gathering/study room): *Oh, God, help me. Second half of my final in Sister Berenice's biology is first period tomorrow. I know I did well on the first half when we had 100 specimens to identify by class, phylum, genus... Tomorrow I have to trace a sandwich of bread, ham, tomato, and cheese through the human body, describing the changes in enzymes and whatever in each organ from tongue to toilet. Where IS my tablet?*

I opened and slammed drawers of my huge, wooden-with-vinyl-top, ex-military desk. I mouthed a *sorry* at distracted frowns zipping my way. There was silence once again. Finally, I recovered my steno-pad.

I had to keep calm and begged my heart to slow down so I could cram my notes; those tower bells were going to chime *Ave Maria* in an hour at five. Time slithered by, undetected.

Sister Ann Joseph left her desk, a reflection of ours, and glided from the back to the front of the room. I read the signal and exchanged my books and papers quietly for my sewing basket.

We began to prepare for the next thirty minutes before supper when Sister would read aloud from a spiritual book. She'd stop often to discuss applying the virtues in our lives. To keep our hands busy, we would take advantage of this time to mend our cotton stockings, to make tatted edges, or to hem altar cloths. I didn't realize *busy* hands in the postulate would encourage busy hands *forever*.

We rose and stood next to our beautiful, antique chairs and waited for Pat, Marie, and Dolores. They arrived at the last minute on Tuesdays and Thursdays after their advanced anatomy class in the college building. Their thick, large, slippery books and sewing boxes shuffled around, making a commotion. Sister stayed motionless and tall, waiting for quiet. She turned to the large crucifix on the wall, "In the name of the Father, and of the Son..."

After the prayer, we gently pulled our chairs out together to sit, maintaining the slow, prayerful environment.

"Y-i-i-e-e-e-k-s!" My sudden shrill threw everyone into the same intense mode. Marie's chair at the desk next to mine had four layers of two-page, wrinkled newspapers laid out and opened wide.

Frantic, girly-squeals hovered around Marie's point of distress. After dashing moments of repeated viewing, running away, returning to the scene, our entire group was in frenzy. "It's a dead, d-i-s-s-e-c-t-e-d CAT!" I screamed.

A huge animal lying on its back with broad eyes stared up at me. Its lips were wide open and revealed a mouthful of sharp teeth. With clinched fists at their faces, girls were yelling:

"Yuck. It smells like formaldehyde. Pee-uu-eey‼"

"It looks like it's lying on an electric chair and wired for an attack!"

"Yeah, those long legs sticking straight up—horrible!"

"Look at all those innards just thrown back inside. Y-u-u-ck!"

Sister Ann Joseph was not impressed, but her pursed lips hinted a grin. "Get! That! Thing! Out! Of! This! Room! NOW! Girls! Back to your desks."

"Yes, Sister," was our trained, quiet response to just about everything.

As usual, Pat and Dolores lowered their heads and displayed impish, pouting lips of false repentance. Silence—except for the ruffling sound of old newspapers quickly wrapping the carcass again. The two pallbearers headed toward the burning incinerator not far from the dining room windows.

The strong scent of formaldehyde and barbequed dead cat gave a special ambiance to our evening meal in the usual silence thirty minutes later.

Oh, God, help me keep from laughing aloud, I prayed. My prayer didn't help when I raised my head and observed the six at the next table with their heads bobbing up and down from inner, constrained laughter.

Across the dining room, we were trying to chew, yet clinch our teeth, to fend off laughter and delight in another *professional* episode of Pat and Dolores. Incinerator odors of roasting feline floated through the tall dining room windows. With the challenge to avoid curled noses and vinegar lips, we forked and knifed bits of what was usually scrumptious: barbequed ribs on the bone!

⌒

During the middle of my first semester of college, Sister Elaine announced, "It's time to prepare for your jury exam in December."

"Jury exam? Why?" I asked. "What did I do wrong?"

Those words hit between my eyes as Bach glared back at me from the cover of his *Preludes and Fugues* on the piano-stand. Finally, I'd hear *the secret behind the mysterious doors* of the convent. I sat tall and stared.

Sister Elaine chuckled. "It's called applied-music jury exam for piano or other instruments. You need to select and memorize a composition by Bach, a movement of a Beethoven Sonata, a romantic, and a contemporary composer. The entire music faculty will listen to you play, and decide on your grade for the semester. We'll be working specifically on that repertoire from now until then."

I melted with relief with the verdict—not guilty—but a usual stress shrouded over me. I knew I took longer than others did to learn a composition, much less memorize it well enough to play for someone else. That *someone else* would be other than my family and friends at a recital.

Professors of music would listen, discuss, and grade. I had two and a half months of dedicated work ahead. I had other courses to study: English and theology. The most challenging would be Sister Hortensia's harmony, ear training and keyboarding. What about violin, organ and voice? They were applied music courses, too. I was in a daze. Where would I begin?

After selecting the repertoire, I bee-lined to the practice room to begin the memory work; but I was distracted by the faculty in the scenario—sitting in the tiny room in my mind.

Sister Henry, my organ teacher, verified Sister Elaine's shocking news. I would perform my organ jury exam immediately after the piano. My dream as a child was to learn the organ, especially the one in St. Mary's Church across from school. Now my joy of organ skills and opportunity had come—with exams included. However, I was grateful I was old enough to appreciate Bach's genius ability in his musical form, including intricacies on the keyboard and foot pedals.

The weeks of lessons and hours of daily practice evaporated too soon. And surprise! Jury exams would be a twice-a-year event—for many years to come. I loved music, and was willing to do what it took. I considered it was as working toward any degree: you sweat doing it, and rejoice when it's done.

In December I stood backstage in the dark with only tall, maroon curtains for support. Frances Ann finished her last piece, left the piano, and sighed in relief as she exited. "Lucky you," I whispered back. Sister Lucy Marie, department head, called me into the hot spotlights.

A semi-circle of six or seven familiar bodies sat in chair-desks on the stage around the concert-grand Steinway piano next to the three-manual, full ranged foot-pedal organ.

I beamed the entire few seconds greeting the faculty individually—more to help myself relax than out of respect! Trembling, I bowed slightly, gripped my music books, and presented them to Sister Lucy Marie. Bookmarks with the title of the composition popped out from the top of each volume.

She wore a serious smile. "You may take the piano, Mary Jo. What are you going to play first?" I was able to choose? I eased—just a tad—selected my favorite, *Spanish Dance* by Jose Iturbi, and aced it. I knew Sister Lucy Marie would want to hear *Bach's Invention in B-flat*—my mind and fingers were prepared.

After several other selections, I moved to the organ. First, I chose and belted Bach's famous *D Minor Prelude and Fugue* with all the pomp and circumstance it deserved. I knew I would play it many years after that. My favorite section was when no hands played, just the feet.

This *jury exam* had reminded me of playing for Sister Elaine in Chapel Auditorium a year earlier when I had tried out for lessons to determine whether I would take piano from her and major in music! Again I had heard, *she, she, she,* but this time I listened more intently and picked up one comment: "She *does* have a love and knack for the Spanish composition." Duh...they finally got it! I enjoyed Sister Elaine; she selected a Latin piece each semester for me to study.

I learned from those *jury exams.* Each semester I ended up with a large repertoire I could play from memory. Those exams—with Sister Elaine's tutoring, prepared me for teaching: to give recital selections months in advance, to give students works they enjoy, and to bracket challenging measures for extra practice. Students must play their recital piece well—at least two weeks in advance—for another person, then play it often for a group of several persons before the performance day.

Although I did not appreciate the jury experience when I was seventeen years old, I knew I would become friends with the Sisters in music and always be grateful when applying their hints and techniques as a teacher later in life.

POSTULANCY, INVESTITURE
AND NOVITIATE

In the summer of 1958, most important on my mind was preparing for the special event about to happen: Investiture Day when I would receive the full garb (the habit) and my religious name as a Sister. I would become a novice.

After a year and a half as a candidate, I became a postulant and received my cape, part of the habit. I endured many music courses, realizing the more I learned, the more there was to learn.

Sister Ann Joseph continued as mistress who observed, questioned, directed, and helped us discern whether God was inviting us to proceed to the novitiate.

For a few weeks, we eighteen postulants moved into the novitiate suite with the *soon-outgoing* novices, to ready ourselves for *eight days of silent retreat*.

I treasured those days of quiet and reflection. That was a big part of my reason for entering the convent—more time to spend one-on-one with Him. The priest gave four lectures a day. I spent the rest of the precious time in private prayer, meditation, and spiritual reading, and a day that included confession and private spiritual direction from the retreat master, in addition to the daily community prayer, Mass, rosary and further discernment.

However, I questioned, *Please, Lord, is this what You want me to do, or is it just a fantasy of my own imagination, wanting to do what I want? I hear and read about the odd things novices must decide to do as a test. Will I be able to handle a year of testing? Is my excitement overwhelming the realities? Am I strong enough mentally and spiritually? Will this be a dreaded year, eager for it to be finished? Some Sisters say it is a wonderful year; others say it wasn't over soon enough. Help me to remember: the tests are tests!*

Will Sister ask us to do things like plant flower-bulbs upside down? Or, on the other hand, clean things that don't need to be cleaned? Seems that's a waste of time and energy. However, if it is a test, then do we just go ahead and do it? It's scary. I had many questions and prayed for the grace to persevere.

The annual retreat always ended on June 21, Investiture Day, after a most interesting and inspiring ceremony in the congregation.

Still in retreat-silence, we postulants in 1958 dressed alike in long, white, gathered-at-the-waist, long-sleeved, bridal dresses, and waist-length, white tulle veils handmade by Sister Ann Joseph. The dresses symbolized the postulant's invitation to become a *bride of Christ.*

I was elated that my parents, sisters, grandparents, some aunts, uncles and cousins would be at the big celebration. However, I hoped the elaborate ceremony and white dresses wouldn't distract from the recesses of my heart: to do His Will.

My expression of inner joy with my usual big smile squelched instantly just as the group picture in bridal dresses was about to be snapped before the ceremony. Sister St. John, mistress of novices, arched her eyebrows and peered from the bottom of her glasses. She articulated in her slow lisp and slight German accent, "Now, postulants, this is not the time to be advertising for toothpaste."

We froze and posed more somber faces, experiencing one of our first *lessons* we would learn in our upcoming novitiate year.

After the photo-shoot, we lined up by twos according to size. Rose Marie and I brought up the rear as usual. Still in retreat silence, we walked to the vestibule, and waited to proceed down the aisle.

My joyful eyes teared as I gazed. The huge, gothic Conventual Chapel emanated its highest regal appearance. Old black and white photos did no justice to the elegance. The sacristan's week of dedicated work paid off. All candles and lights sparkled in the flawlessly clean, white marble floors, pillars, three altars, and long altar railing. An abundance of tall, crimson gladiolas and hunter-green ferns—grown by the Sisters—pointed their long fingers to the heavens as they burst and fanned out from tall, thin gold vases.

Hundreds of double pews for the congregation, including the choir loft across the back and sides of the chapel, shined for His love and glory. Sister Elaine pulled out all stops on the huge pipe organ accompanying the Sisters'

Choir directed by Sister Hortensia.

As our group floated down the aisle, I could not control myself. My little sister, Mae, grinned with pride, next to the middle aisle at the front of the chapel. A quick smile back was a gesture I knew my loving God excused.

The choir intoned the opening of the Mass written by Sister Elaine with the Kyrie Eleison (Lord, have mercy). They sang her meditative hymn appropriately written for the occasion: *What Shall I Render to the Lord for All He Has Rendered to Me* at the offertory.

Before his sermon, San Antonio Archbishop Robert E. Lucey sat on a red-draped chair in front of the altar facing the congregation and summoned our group to come forward to the inside of the marble railing to receive religious garbs, neatly folded into small bundles. Having practiced several days, we were at ease with the procedures of the important ceremony.

Individually, we knelt in front of the Archbishop, and extended our opened arms to accept the two-foot-square bundle, neatly kept together with three-inch long, round-headed hatpins that were needed when dressing.

After all received our treasure, we processed to the room behind the altar and climbed old wooden steps to a large storage room, arranged somewhat as a dressing room. The Archbishop delivered his twenty-minute sermon to the Sisters and guests during that time.

Still in silence, the big rush began. Each of us had chosen two Sisters to help us dress; they were waiting by eighteen assigned chairs. With help, I marked time stepping out of the bridal outfit and sat on the small wooden chair.

Aunt Sister Clair, began ruthlessly whacking clumps of my thick, wavy, black hair with large scissors as I and others said *good-bye* to our loving locks. Meanwhile, my friend Sister Mildred unpinned the bundle and readied the headpiece for speedy dressing.

When Peg was dressed, we knew everyone else was ready, but double-checked to be sure. There were no mirrors, but we smiled seeing our friends for the first time in full religious habits, except for the *white* veils that signified we would soon be novices.

We inched our way down the rustic steps in our long garbs and, chunky, lace-up, shoes like the ones our grandmothers wore.

We filed back into the altar area, forming a semi-circle around the Archbishop. We, as well as everyone in the chapel, waited in anticipation to learn our assigned religious names. In contrast to the jubilant sounds of organ and choir, the chapel was numb with silence. Ears cocked. Many Sisters came prepared throughout the chapel with pencil and paper to write down names as the Archbishop announced them.

"In order to show that you are no longer of this world, you will not be called by your baptismal names. Mary Jo Barbera, you will now be called in religion, Sister Mary Janet."

I bowed. My body tingled from head to foot. For all to hear, I responded a sincere, "Thanks be to God." I loved my new, simple name and kept repeating it inside my heart. I always felt sorry for those called Sister Cunegunda Marie, Sister Polycarp, or Sister Mary of the Sacred Heart. We novices returned to our pews in fresh habits and with new names. The glorious Mass continued to its last Amen, and the eight-day silent retreat was over until next year.

The celebration with families and friends continued the blessed day in the pecan grove. Mom spread out my favorites of her fried chicken, potato salad, lime gelatin with cottage cheese and crushed pineapple. Tummies made room when Ahmama and Tantan opened the large round tin of their hearty fruit-rock cookies.

My sisters and cousins wiped foreheads with sweaty little hands gripping cookies and asked me, "Aren't you hot with all that stuff on?"

I questioned myself. Would I be soaking in yards of black surge and stiff-from-starch collar and headpieces? "I guess I'll just have to keep telling myself that *all this stuff* will help keep *out* all the heat." Aunt Sister Clair sat fanning her legs with her yards of serge. I hoped perspiration sinking into my shoes didn't send a squishing noise when I walked.

I was glad Aunt Sister Clair was nearby so I could ask whether my hair was peeking out from under my coif, the white cap covering my ears and hair. I had recalled being embarrassed when Sister Alice Marie pulled a lock of hair forward while removing her eyeglasses in the sixth grade. I shouldn't have been concerned; my family knew I had jet black hair.

The afternoon dissipated amid the excitement of new dress, new name, festive foods, and visiting family and some relatives seen less frequently.

Tower bells closed the celebration with hugs, kisses, and teary, joy-filled eyes. The family paraded back toward the convent and car. This time the children repeated and teased loudly, "Bye, *Sister Mary Janet,* see you next month, *Sister Mary Janet.*" As the car pulled away, I gasped at my reflection in the rear window, "Oh! Wow! Full habit. So, *that's* what I look like. No wonder I'm sweltering."

We novices hurried to join the professed Sisters for the first time in the front pews of big chapel to pray the rosary and to chant the Office of the Church—Vespers and Compline. I loved the feel of the half inch, rose shaped beads strung together to hang about 36 inches from the waistband of my new habit. With no air-conditioning, *beads of perspiration* racing down my chest competed with the *rosary beads* for attention.

The hour of prayer completed, Sisters gathered into the refectories for dinner. In the novices' dining room, a separate table with a fresh, white cloth displayed something special. As a personal gift for me and the novices, Aunt Tantan expressed her love and attention into a unique 28-inch diameter, four inches high, heart-shaped cake with high white peaks of marshmallow icing, topped with tiny silver balls. Many of her handmade, delicate little sugar flowers and leaves tucked amid the peaks of icing. Thick gathers of four-inch white tulle inched out from under the refined masterpiece.

Because of the celebratory day, Sisters in the novices' and professed Sisters' dining rooms had permission to talk during supper. The Sisters knew Aunt Tantan well. (She, Mom, and Aunt Sister Clair were blood sisters.) The conversations across the refectory included her famous cakes and cookies.

I was thrilled the Sisters loved and respected Tantan. She had been very close and instrumental throughout my eighteen years; she deserved every kind word that evening. I wondered whether I'd miss her and all of the fun we had playing piano duets, baking, riding the bus together, and other favorite times.

We novices appreciated an early retirement that night. In sacred silence, we studied how to pin the headpiece, so we would be able to assemble it the next morning. We discovered how to hang up and/or lay out parts of the garments on the chair next to the bed for quick dressing. No extra time for attiring, just more to *add* to the wash up, the bed making, and the walk over to the main chapel within 30 minutes.

The next morning, fifteen minutes after the wake-up bell toll, one of the Sisters who had helped us dress during the ceremony appeared to assist her new novice. Keeping sacred silence, I hugged Sister Clair when she surprised me. I knew she *must* have arisen before the bell. She had dressed, walked from the other end of the campus, and arrived to our dorm 15 minutes after the wake-up bell.

We emerged on time in chapel for Mass and half hour of meditation. Sister Elaine intoned the chanting of Matins and Lauds, and the Sisters bowed in unison to "Praise be to Thee, O Lord..."

Thus ended my first 24 hours as a novice Sister of Divine Providence. I was elated, except for the challenge of figuring how to flip the pages in the Office Book for the first time. I knew each Sister had been in my big, black, lace up-shoes themselves. In fact, that morning, I would be quite *more involved and sooner* into the procedure than I expected.

OIL IN A DAY'S WORK

"Yeah, Okay." I was eager to run an errand for Sister St. John.

She abruptly peered through the gloom of a dark cloud. "Did I hear you say *Yeah, Okay,* Sister Mary Janet?"

I stared back.

"We don't say *Yeah* and *Okay,*" she corrected.

"Huh?" I frowned.

She lagged her words as if in frustration, "We say *Yes, Sister* and *All right.* And *Huh* is not in our vocabulary."

I knew that. Mom always harped on us to use proper etiquette. I never talked like that to the Sisters at school, just at home. I was thinking I was at home. Maybe Sister St. John was training me to be polite all the time so it came naturally. The Sisters were always respectful and polite to each other and to the public.

I prayed, *Lord, help me in my enthusiasm to be a Sister. I do appreciate the corrections. What else will I be doing wrong?*

From the gate we learned Sister St. John was not wasting one day of our novitiate year. While other novices were doing chores, she informed Sister Celine Marie (Frances Ann) and me to go with her to the main chapel to practice leading the chant during the Office of the Hours for the congregation—starting that evening. When we arrived in chapel, we transplanted our spiritual books into the double pew at the center front, left of the middle aisle. We received a limited crash course on how to find the proper pages for the particular day.

In answer to my silent perplexity, she whispered speedily, "Now Sisters, don't hesitate, but immediately intone each psalm, on pitch, and loud enough to be heard throughout the chapel. You will have your backs to the congregation the entire time. Stand, step into the middle aisle, bow toward the altar when you come to the antiphons printed like this. Otherwise, stay in the pew, but stand up to chant.

"Pronounce distinctly. If the congregation gets flat, raise the pitch when it is your turn, and the Sisters will match. Remember that Sister Elaine starts the Office and has special, long lines to chant. She is on the mike at the back of the chapel. You have no mikes. Sister Mary Janet, you will be leader number one—Sister Celine Marie you're number two." She continued with detailed instructions.

My heart pounded as I tried to absorb all the information to be prepared for our first experience at evening Vespers and Compline. I was petrified. We hardly knew the procedures to follow the proper pages. How would I know whether nuns in the back could hear?

Sister Celine and I practiced a few pages aloud. I worried for her. Obviously, she was more nervous than I was. Her voice kept cracking, and we knew that Sisters in the back pews would not hear her. After about a week, she and I were a bit more comfortable, but I felt I was yelling harshly in that huge chapel. Chanting became easy and pleasant with a smaller group, when most Sisters left for their missions.

Back in the novitiate, we all gathered with Sister St. John. In her German-accent lisp she began, "Now Sisters, this is your first full day as novices, so you will be instructed on things you need to start practicing and doing today. Sister Mary Janet, you will read during meals starting tonight at supper. I'll give you instructions later."

Did she assign that to me as a test? I'd always hated to read aloud. I know if I read the material at least three times privately and aloud, I did it well, but I wished she'd selected a better reader. I prayed: *O Lord, I will practice obedience and see You talking through Sister St. John to me. She is a very spiritual and religious person. Her training is a privilege. I'll have to use some of my private prayer times to study my readings. That'll be a task, but I'll accept the challenge for You.*

Sister continued, "We'll be studying the three vows of poverty, chastity, and obedience this entire year. You will want to practice them daily beginning today. In the postulate you turned in the extra toiletries you brought from home. The novitiate supply closet is in the back west room. When you need things, remember they are not yours, but are for your *use*. Ask permission to use them, not permission to *own* them. You will not own anything. In that way, you learn humility by asking, poverty by using and not owning, and obedience by following the Rule."

Wow. That would be a change. At home, Mom kept bathroom shelves supplied, and we just took what we needed. Seemed embarrassing to ask for things like Kotex.

There was more. "When your family gives you something, you bring it to me during your novitiate year and to your superior on the mission. Turn it in for someone else to use. Only if you need it, show it and ask whether you may use it. Also, all money—big or small—goes for the use of the community."

From the back of the room, I could see all the white-veiled novices sitting like statues in their tall-backed, fancy, antique chairs with thin rungs. They clasped their hands on their well-kept, polished desks with lift-up tops. They were probably as numb as I was with the onslaught of new rules and regulations.

I reflected. My aunt, Sister Clair, turned in the money our family gave her all of these years. She turned in the candies and cookies they made for her, too. I thought that would be hard to do. We saved our birthday money to buy what we wanted. What other shockers were we going to hear?

"You'll take good care of your clothing and shoes, wearing one habit for daily use. You get another for Sunday or special occasions. When the daily one wears out, use it for heavy Saturday or seasonal cleaning and picnics. With permission, rip out your deep-pleated skirt and wash the fabric well. Take the ironed fabric to Sister Maxentia, the seamstress.

"She will make you a new skirt by putting the worn edges of the pleats *inside* the pleat so frayed edges will be hidden. Wear that until it can no longer be re-pleated. Your skirt should last several years. Eventually, your Sunday habit becomes your daily one. Notice that the habit has parts that snap in, like the large black sleeves. You only replace what is over worn."

I was still trying to digest what she had said, when Sister removed her lightweight black apron and continued. "You may wear the aprons you brought from home, but when they're threadbare, you will get long black ones like this one." She held it up. It was lightweight, black and pleated with no bib. "This may be worn all of the time and in the classroom, but not in chapel. Send shoes to Juan in the shoe-repair room next to the campus laundry. He does a good job replacing soles and heels." She replaced her apron.

Sheesh! We did learn to take care and recycle. That was part of practicing poverty; I began to realize I would appreciate many of the practices later in my life.

Sister went on with her list. "You will talk and walk quietly in your steps and in your mannerisms. We do not jerk our heads or arms; do that in recreation. We keep silence during the day, talking softly, and only when needed. However, after night prayer until after breakfast, we observe Sacred Silence everywhere—always. Never talk in the dorms, but step into the hall and whisper, if needed. You're used to the silence, but now you want to be more observant of it, especially in your physical movements."

I deliberated: *Oh yeah (oops, I mean, yes), I notice how the Sisters are in the custom of moving slowly and quietly. I have to work on that. There's so much to remember. Hope I can learn it all.*

Sister put her finger to her cheek, "I've noticed that some of you are forgetting to address each other as *Sister* and her new name. You must make more effort to do that."

I smiled inside. *She said I'm to remind someone to say* Sister Mary Janet *if I'm addressed as Mary Jo. I guess that makes sense. Memorizing seventeen new names will take a while. That should be fun to practice.*

"You are not to talk with aspirants, candidates, postulants, not even the professed Sisters or the college students this year, unless you are given permission, such as during special activities. You will not leave the campus or go to other areas on the campus except for rare doctor appointments or other unusual reasons. When you do, you will always go with another Sister and will put on a black veil. You never leave in a white veil."

I noticed a few raised eyebrows and glances of surprise across the room, including my own.

"The only Sisters who will be permitted into the novitiate rooms are the several who will be coming to teach church history, the history of our congregation, the life of our founder—Father John Martin Moye—or Sacred Scripture.

"You will be memorizing most of the Holy Rule and the Constitution of the Sisters of Divine Providence every day. I will instruct you in those two classes daily. Father Quinlivan comes for instruction once a month. This will be a year of intense spiritual classes only." She paused, lifted the corner of her apron, and wiped a smudge from the horizontal glass door of the bookshelf.

I calculated I wouldn't have as much free time for private prayer, meditation, and spiritual reading as I thought I would have that special year.

"As you had a required visit with Reverend Mother two weeks ago before becoming a novice, you will have another interview with her before your first vows at the end of this year."

Yes, I remembered that visit. Individually we entered her office. Reverend Mother sat at her large desk facing us. I learned to go to her desk and immediately kneel down facing her. When she nodded to me, I requested, "Reverend Mother, I ask permission to become a novice as a Sister of Divine Providence." Then she asked questions like was I *doing this freely and with good will,* and asked *why* I wanted to be a novice. I was nervous about the formality of the interview, but also very curious about the questions and my answers.

"Sisters, that's enough for today. You will have more to learn. It's almost time to take noon dinner, so remember to start practicing your walk quietly and slowly, in a reserved manner."

We gathered to leave, but Sister had one more item. "Sister Mary Janet, come. I will give you the book to read while we take our meal. Oh, yes, did you notice, Novices? I said we *take* our meals? We don't *eat* them."

No heads moved, but everyone was exchanging side-glances, ready to burst. That was a classic ending.

⟡

"Now Sisters, when you dust mop, be careful that the mop does not get dirty."

Oh, yeah, I mean yes—that I had to see! Will we observe some kind of miracle? How great not having to shake out those dust mops.

Sister St. John held a five-foot long wooden handle with a 12 by 36-inch mop-head at the end and picked up a large oiled, folded-over cloth. "Fold the cloth until it is the size of the mop head; put it on the floor; put the mop-head on top of the cloth, and slide the cloth with the mop to clean the floors. Be sure to keep the cloth under the mop. Sister Charles Andre (Imelda) will be in charge of oiling the rags after they are washed."

Jumping to conclusions, I asked, "Oh, we just pile the dirty rags, and Sister Charles Andre washes them?"

She looked over those spectacles so I could see her frowns adding more wrinkles between her eyes. Lowering her voice in frustration, she lisped, "No, Sister Mary Janet, you do not just pile the dusty rags to be washed. You shake them out and beat them on the incinerator. Then fold and put them in the box on the floor in this cleaning closet."

"Oh, okay. I mean, yes, Sister." I knew all about the incinerator (where Pat and Dolores discarded the dead, dissected, formaldehyde-smelling cat when they were postulants) not far from the dining room windows. We used to beat the cloths there as postulants.

I don't know why I thought that just because we were draped in yards of black and starched white linen and white veils, we were abstained from dirty work. I learned fast there were no prima donnas in the convent, *especially* in the year of novitiate. Hopes were not shattered. I had intended to work, and I received princely helpings.

As weeks passed, simply dust mopping the floors after breakfast was not so bad. Grabbing the corner and shaking out those half-inch-thick-with-dust, oily rags all over me was the real corker. The mop itself at the end of the five-foot-long handle would have been bad enough to shake had it been dirty; but it stayed clean, thanks to the cloth we pushed under it.

Year round when I approached the six-foot high, square, brick incinerator, I unwrapped the rag carefully to avoid any unnecessary dust clinging to me. I gave one wimpy beat at the corner of the structure, and then dashed a few yards away until the dust flew into the humid-hot or rainy-cold atmosphere. Then I crept back and gave another whack or two.

Clinching a different section of the filthy cloth, I repeated the scenario. Toward the end of the task, I just shook and beat until the cloth was tired and gave up the ghosts of dust. Nevertheless, the rags made my hands oily, and the gray powder covered my sleeves, habit, and face before classes.

It was a yucky way to start the day. Sometimes you could tell who had dust-mopped: she wore a slight smell from amalgamate of old cloth, strong, dirty dust, and a good dose of rancid oil. That sharp odor stayed and felt like a slit in my nostrils. My novice friends were pleasant and good-humored about those foul tasks. They didn't complain either. I supposed they also considered it a part of learning to be humble and obedient. Actually, the floor was the only thing dusty daily. Our habits must have collected the dust all day and dropped it on the floor constantly.

Dusting the bookshelves and the decorative wooden walls in the hallways daily sometimes made me feel Sister was finding *busy-work* for us, as classroom teachers do for children who finish their desk assignment ahead of time. I learned to pull out a few books on just one or two shelves, clean their tops, and dust the shelving behind them. I avoided heavy duty cleaning of shelves on any one day. Obedience to Him made me more energetic to work.

The walls in the hallways had vertical wood-trim below the wainscoting. Dusting them, we had to bend over all the way to the floor, up and down see-saw-like, stepping forward or backward.

I walked up the inside of my long skirt. My cape was pinned back over my long veil, but it came forward over my low, bent-over shoulders wiping the floors. My veil kept winning that contest. Dusty, oily hands painted splotches onto my white veil when I tried to push it back. After a half hour of playing piggy back, my knees hurt to stand straight. However, it paled with His pain on the cross.

These oily cloths seemed to weave around our prayers in our daily schedule. Aerobic dusting on the steps from the fifth to the first floor, spindles and wainscoting that climbed up from the hallways gave me time for free exercise. Bending over was just about the only way to tackle that job, unless I intended to use my habit to pick up the fuzzies. Sometimes I worked to vary the monotonous chore by doing the spindle-step-wall, then the wall-step-spindle. On the first step, "All for Your honor," second step, "All for Your glory," third, "I love You, Jesus," until the final step from the fifth floor to the bottom of the first floor. I always prayed, "Help me be the Sister You want me to be, even when I'm *oil* absorbed in my work."

Novitiate was the year we novices in white veils and new religious names experienced discipline—mentally, physically and spiritually—studying the three vows of poverty, chastity and obedience. We spent numerous hours studying the Constitution and Holy Rule of the Sisters of Divine Providence. We expected more time for private and community prayer. I rewarmed memories of the year that was ending.

A mature pecan tree offered shade as I rested on a cement bench, which sat there since about the 1920s on the novitiate-patio. With my spiritual notebook now closed, I wondered how I had survived the important, demanding twelve months. Yet, my heart wished I had another year of novitiate before stepping into the world as a religious nun.

I pondered: *Maybe if we had not polished things that didn't even need to be cleaned, or had toilet brushes to work quicker, we would have had time for more spiritual reading and private prayer. Yet I always tried to make my work a prayer.*

I'd hoped I would retain the exact wording of many lines and their references in the Bible. I'd spent long hours memorizing the Congregation's Holy Rule and Constitution and prayed to remember them. I struggled for years with the inability to retain Spanish studies and histories of all kinds—world, American, or music—a challenge I still do not understand. I prayed that those precious hours of memorization in my important year of novitiate would remain fruitful. I'm thankful, knowing for some reason, I still remember music theory.

I had anticipated that was the year I was to have a "full set of false teeth in three years." Our family dentist had always told me, "Besides looking like your dad, you have perfect teeth. Just like his."

Sister Ann Joseph had sent me to the Sisters' dentist when my teeth begged attention. He was perplexed, "You're eighteen years old? Haven't you ever been to a dentist? Your mouth is full of cavities."

He had cautioned, "If you eat any more sweets at all—and I mean at all—you will have a full mouth of false teeth in three years." His order made me cringe. He was stricter than Sister St. John. Religious obedience overflowed into the dentist office.

Now I calculated: refraining from sugar the last three years, along with the intense physical house cleaning was why I dropped from 145 to 110 pounds. My 5-foot, 9-inch physique didn't need to lose 35 pounds in one year. I used no sugar on cereal, coffee and tea. I abstained from candies, cakes, pies, ice cream, and even Ahmama and Tantan's carefully crafted homemade cookies—but my teeth were all intact!

My eyes captured the bright sky hovering heat rays. I whiffed imaginary cool air to my legs with my long skirt. That combination of heat and habit recalled another reflection.

With the mission Sisters home for summers, the west sun raced over the incinerator and blasted itself directly through the tall windows in the packed dining rooms. The large chapel had a few fans aimed at a few Sisters, but ignored the majority. Their white, starched head and neck gear bled perspiration most of the year. I thanked God for tolerance with heat, but felt for those born with less.

I considered myself blessed with the hard discipline and spiritual growth. However, I would encounter more expected and unexpected events—some fun, some not so fun—in the next years of my religious life.

Profession Day

Sister St. John wrinkled her forehead, pursed her lips slightly, and obviously waited to study a response from her statement: "Sister Mary Janet, you're the only novice who never left the campus the entire year. Other novices went to doctors or as companion to other novices."

Perplexed, I said, "Yes, Sister."

"How do you feel about that?"

"It didn't bother me at all, Sister. I rather liked staying home and having the time to pray, study, and read." I meant it.

"I see," Sister St. John said, slightly biting her bottom lip and nodding in confirmation. "God go with you, Sister Mary Janet."

We novices had only two more hours of our eight days of silent retreat. Sister St. John had been calling us individually into her office to give her verbal blessing before we left the novitiate.

I wondered. Perhaps having to stay on campus was one way of testing me. Others seemed excited to leave, remarking that they could accompany Sister-So-and-So.

Sister St. John left her office and announced, "All right, Novices, it's time for Chapel."

Profession Day had arrived. We would receive our black veil and make our first vows of poverty, chastity, and obedience for one year.

Just before lining up, I glanced out the window by my desk. My little sisters piled out of the car to attend their big sister's next step in religious life. Tantan parked right behind with another load of family members.

A bomb of questions exploded in my mind: *Oh, God! What am I going to do? My big family's here and we are supposed to have a picnic in the pecan grove. It is going to be crowded with families of the new final-professed Sisters and the eighteen of us new annual-professed after the long ceremony. I can see us trying to find a cool place with my dear, elderly grandparents.*

We can't drive cars on the grass. I cannot run around looking for a place with enough tables and chairs. Even if I do find a place, how do I save it while I run all the way back to tell them? It's blazing hot out there. Ahmama, Danny and Nona cannot even walk that far, if I do find one. Everyone else will be rushing to find a tree with tables and chairs, too.

I tried to calm myself. We had gathered in the crowded vestibule as postulants dressed as brides a year ago. We waited again to process down the middle aisle. Sisters who gave up their seats for visitors assembled around us, also. Despite my efforts to remain serene, my mind was limp, exhausted, and in a turmoil. My last moments of retreat should experience deep, meaningful prayer, expectation, and joy. I thought. I prayed.

I cannot go into this ceremony with this horrible distraction the entire time. My mind should be only on what God is offering me, and my response to Him. How do I get rid of these thoughts? I have to figure out something, some solution, soon—in the next few seconds. Please, Lord, help me know what to do. Okay, Blessed Mother Mary, I place this predicament into your hands. Please take it to your Son and place it in the palms of His hands. I know He will take care of this.

As at the switch of a light—a weightless, thin cloak—a calm of restful peace enveloped my entire mind and body. Within seconds of that encounter, Sister St. John tapped me on the shoulder and whispered slowly in her lispy, German accent, "Sister Mary Janet, I know you have a big family with grandparents here today. I have reserved tables and chairs close by—under the pecan tree at the back of the convent. They can use the restrooms and cold water fountain at the top of the few steps several feet away."

Sister St. John did have a soft, loving heart amidst her pillars of discipline.

Immediately my eyes welled, "Oh, Sister, thank you, thank you." I knew I would cherish this experience and share it with my Mistress of Novices at an appropriate time. God blessed me with a sincere faith and trust I would want to communicate to others.

Sister Huberta stood to speak:

> Sisters, you will dedicate this year to your academic studies.
> Next to your prayer life and the living of your vows of pov-
> erty, chastity, and obedience, your year will be one of intense
> study to earn your academic degrees and do student teaching
> or student nursing. You will still observe the rules of silence.
> Lights are out at nine in the dorm, but with special permis-
> sion, you may stay up until ten. You rotate on your cleaning
> jobs after meals when I post them. Hours of night adoration
> will be two hours instead of one. You will go less often and
> sleep an extra hour the next morning. Sister Marietta is ex-
> pecting you in her office to receive your course of study and
> list of college books.

She was preparing us for our year as Junior Sisters.

I took a deep breath and eagerly raced upstairs to Sister Marietta's office, then over to Thiry Music Hall to meet with Sister Helen Mary, my assigned music mentor. With a short build—business-like with dancing eyes and sweet, pursed smile—she greeted, "Sister Mary Janet, I'm looking forward to helping you teach singing and music appreciation in grades one through six the first semester. Sister Alexandrine will mentor you in grades seven through high school next semester."

I hoped she did not hear my heart in allegro tempo. "But I don't know how to teach or how much to cover at a time."

"You're not supposed to know that now." Sister Helen Mary laughed and turned toward her library shelf.

"How do I know what the children can do in each grade and what they're expected to know at the end of the year? Then there's discipline. I don't know how to handle the boys as the Sisters did when I was at St. Mary's School and, and..."

"Slow down, Sister Mary Janet. You will have music education courses in large classes of five music majors this year. Each grade has a teachers' manual for its songbooks. By graduation, you will know how to teach just about anything, and you might *have* to teach *just about anything* on the mission."

Panic! She had a lot of trust in me. "But I'm taking music education, English, theology, and I'm supposed to practice an hour a day on my applied instruments of piano, violin, voice, and organ."

She answered my concerns. "We work together, and we pray a lot. You will see. Let's go to St. Martin's Hall. It is a teaching-demonstration school owned by our Sisters, and teaching there is a privilege. We mentor education majors—studying from our university—right here on the campus."

We chatted about student teaching as we strolled across 24th Street.

"Oh, Sister, the rooms and bulletin boards are bright and cheerful. But now my heart's beating fast. I don't know whether it's because I'm *excited or nervous* about standing in the front of a classroom."

Sister Helen Mary shook her head and spoke softly, "You're normal. You will not teach until you are ready. Before I teach a class, I will explain my lesson plan to you and show how I am going to present it. You will observe from the back of the class, take notes, and write down questions you need answered later. You'll be a fly on the wall."

I laughed. "I hope you won't swat at me."

On the first day of school, donned in hooded raincoats and galoshes, we sloshed together to St. Martin's Hall (SMH). After removing our raingear, I followed her into the first grade room. The children stood up. "Good mo-o-o-r-ning, Sister."

"Good morning, first grade, this is Sister Mary Janet. She's going to sit in the back and enjoy our classes. Later she will be teaching you, and I will sit and enjoy. You look so grown up in your first new uniforms."

The proud little six-year-olds turned their heads right and left sharing their big smiles. Then crowns of first-day-of-school hair-dos twisted for my approval. After I sanctioned their praise, Sister raised her hand, "When I point to myself, you listen while I sing. When I point to you, it's your turn to echo back what I just sang." Pointing to herself, she sang the first verse of *The Wheels on the Bus Go Round and Round*. Her hand showed when the notes were going up, or down. I took copious notes.

That afternoon, I bounced into her studio and dug out my folder while rattling off questions like why we did not give songbooks to the first graders.

"Sister Mary Janet, they can't read yet."

A few weeks later, Sister Helen Mary helped me make my first lesson plan that included reviewing and teaching of new songs. I learned to let students request old songs and to insist on raising their hands to do so. We clapped rhythms and played games to enhance retaining and listening skills. I wrote my scope and sequence for each day.

She observed every class I taught, and reviewed the same day in her office. "Sister Mary Janet, you often called on a student before asking the question. Do you know why you should ask the question *followed* by the student's name?"

I raised my eyebrows and shrugged my shoulders. "No, I never thought about it."

"Many other students don't bother to pay attention to the question, since they realize you're not calling on them to answer."

At our last tutoring session, I put away my folder and held it close to my chest. "Sister Helen Mary, I have a wealth of skills, methods, ideas, and hints I will review and treasure. You will flash before me as I ask a question before calling on a student." We both slapped our knees with laughter. "I appreciate your patience and openness. Children are fascinated with the printed page of music theory. You made it fun—one note at a time. I'm exhilarated to go on the mission to share the joy of music and singing with God's little ones."

During the second semester, tall, kind Sister Alexandrine and I worked together in grades seven through twelve in studying choir and music appreciation.

"Sister Mary Janet, listen to Smetana's *The Moldau*. It's a musical portrayal of the main river which runs through the countryside of Czechoslovakia. Plan an art and music listening class for the eighth grade."

With excitement, we entered the classroom on Friday. She observed from a back desk as I passed out large white sheets of art paper.

"Class, take out your colored pencils. I'm going to play a recording without telling you anything about it. Just close your eyes and listen. Picture what you see. When you're ready, draw what *you* see. Don't get ideas from your neighbor. You will have forty-five minutes."

They smiled to each other, sat tall, and expressed eagerness. I dropped the needle onto the large, round, black glass record. Sister Alexandrine nodded in agreement. I wove through the aisles of desks to observe the works-in-progress.

They finished in time to share their masterpieces. What a surprise for all of us—students had beautiful underwater scenes with colorful fish, blue waters, floors of sea-waving plants, shadows, and/or light rays.

I thanked the comments, such as "Sister, this was fun." "Can we do it again sometime?"

I felt assured realizing I could use original ideas for music listening, thanks to Sister Alexandrine.

However, I was not as relaxed teaching in Our Lady of the Lake High School. When we worked on a musical, I lost sleep at night, was distracted at prayer, and torn between practicing piano for the musical and spending hours on my college-required instruments. I did not want to complain. Would I lose college credit for opting out of playing accompaniments, or perhaps fail the course? I prayed to know a solution.

Finally, I worked up courage. "Sister, I've worked on playing for the musical, but I know I won't be able to learn them properly in time with all of my other studies and instruments to practice. I feel I'm holding the progress back instead of helping."

"I understand," Sister Alexandrine said. "I'll play the accompaniments. You observe what goes into putting on a musical. When you are on the mission, you will work the time into your teaching schedule. Playing will get easier with practice, too."

I felt comfortable and eager to teach classroom music in all grades, but hoped I would not have to be responsible for upper level *choirs*. I had not sung in the Providence High Chorus, just Sister Hortensia's convent choir, which I knew was completely different from teaching high school students.

I had attended a Choral Conducting Workshop for only one week at Jefferson High School not far from our university. I reflected: *I had a few moments in that workshop to direct five other music majors. What kind of training is that?*

I don't feel able to handle high school choir on my own. My mind trembles at the possibility of that assignment on a mission in the future.

I knew I would implement many of my two mentors' one-on-one tutorials and critiques, and I'd always appreciate the constant interest and energy with me as a Junior Sister. I wished I had had another year of teacher training and studies before going onto the missions.

How excited I was for visiting Sunday—to share my good feelings and experiences with Aunt Tantan, who had given me my first love for music at such a tender age!

POWERFUL THRONE

Did you ever have someone in your life whom you owed many thanks, someone who influenced you and guided you tremendously, but dominated you to your wit's end? Someone over-exercising *power from a throne?*

I experienced my first, exciting Obedience Day the summer of 1960.

We received a thick brown envelope as about 900 of us entered the huge chapel auditorium to close the annual eight-day-retreat of complete silence to grow closer to our Lord. I blindly prayed, packet upside down on my lap waiting for permission to read the contents.

My heart pounded. *Lord, give me the grace to accept my first mission and work-assignment with joy and obedience. Help me be the Sister you want me to be and to pray, work, eat, and get along graciously with the Sisters I will live with during this coming school year.*

Before she gave permission to read our obediences, Reverend Mother Amata read words of our founder, Blessed John Martin Moye:

> I entrust you to Divine Providence whose daughters you are. Put your confidence in it, and it will never abandon you. Abandonment to Providence is the virtue that earns you the name *Sisters of Divine Providence*, because you are founded only on Providence.

Our silence ruptured with the rattle and crackle of thousands of sheets of 8.5 by 11 inch paper. My fluttering fingers searched for my name on my stack of stapled papers. Where was my name?

"Abilene!" I yelled out loud. "I'm going to Abilene! Sister Gaudentia is my Superior. Wow! There are ten of us in our community. I can't wait to tell my family."

I studied the names on the list for Abilene. I bit my lip and thought: *I don't know all of these Sisters. Some of the names are familiar, but I've forgotten their faces. I know Sister Blanda. She seemed strict and firm in her summer voice-workshop when she used Frances Ann and me as her demonstration 'dummies.' She's been teaching many years and has lots of experience. I should be fortunate to work with her.*

I clammed up when I realized I had lived in San Antonio all of my life. I had never been apart from my parents longer than a week—when Jerri and I stayed with our grandparents. Ten months without seeing my family? I hoped I wouldn't get homesick.

My new community gathered to meet in Sister Gaudentia's summer room in the university before lunch. I felt heartily welcomed, relaxed, and excited to begin my new life on the mission after summer school.

By August we had all traveled to the red sands of Abilene in west Texas. I was to teach piano, mainly. Sister Blanda was my mentor and easily in her 80s or older. She took the advanced students and assigned me mostly beginners with a few intermediate ones. From Germany, she was a determined woman who was decidedly easier to live with when she got her way, and everyone knew that.

Sister Blanda was a little bent over, walked as if her feet hurt, and shuffled along in her wide, timeworn, lace-up shoes. Her oval, furrowed face—with protruding lower lip—arrived slightly before the rest of her body. You surmised correctly that she was in a sour mood when her eyebrows were arches, and she looked ready to fall asleep.

At least 20 years earlier, doctors had declared her dead and covered her with a sheet while her mission superior and other Sisters in the room planned her funeral. She lay all day trying to show some signs of life. Hearing they were going to ship her body from Louisiana to the mother home in San Antonio for burial, she managed to wiggle a toe.

She was not going to be buried, especially *alive*—not Sister Blanda! She and the Sisters involved confirmed the story. It was a timeless one, to be sure!

At St. Joseph Academy Boarding and Day School in Abilene, she immediately took me under her wing. Her studio wall shared my studio wall.

In August before school started, she convinced our superior/principal, Sister Gaudentia, to purchase and deliver an old, but "perfect" grand piano she had seen in San Antonio a month earlier. She "needed" it delivered to Abilene.

"Oh, it won't need any repairs, and I'm sure the owner will send someone to fix it for me if it does. He's an honest man," she insisted.

The pedals ended up sitting on the floor after a few months. She shoved a board under them—which did suffice—but looked rather strange. She haunted and persuaded Sister Gaudentia to call the seller to drive the five-hour trip to stand up to his word to repair it. That never happened.

She issued, "Now, Sister Mary Janet, here's a year's worth of music literature for your own enrichment: Bach's *B-Flat Prelude, Beethoven's Pathetique, No. 1*, all three movements! Quite difficult, but you will work until you master them. We can do some of the Chopin Waltzes from the album your aunt Tantan gave you.

"I will give you piano lessons on Sunday afternoons, and you will practice about an hour every day and extra on Saturdays. When you go back to Our Lady of the Lake University for summer classes, you will have these prepared to play for Sister Elaine. If you pass her piano exam, you can earn one hour of college credit."

Alleluia! "Oh, Sister Blanda, I'm excited. Thanks for your time and interest. I'm very fortunate, and I'll start working right away. I love to play piano. I can't wait!" I meant every word.

She ignored the fact that practicing and teaching piano was not my only assignment. Just three months before school started, I learned I would be book-keeper for the year. I had never experienced the pages in the two books. The first had single pages about two and a half feet long and waited for entries. Then the second, measuring about one foot square when closed, received figures from the first. Both books needed time-consuming entries and hours of effort to balance.

You must realize—no one had written one figure in those books the entire previous year! I learned by balancing nine months of the former school year during only *one* month while I attended summer school at OLLU. The treasurer of the congregation, Sister Modesta, patiently worked with me in our *free time*.

I was ready. I sent out monthly bills, which included fees for tuition, piano, kindergarten, science lab charges, etc., for about 400 students in grades K through 12. I entered and balanced the figures into those monstrous books.

Boarding school? I became "Assistant Mistress of Boarders." My tiny bedroom was on the 3rd floor with the residents' dorm, private rooms and baths. On Saturday afternoons, I would monitor study hall to give the Sister Mistress of Boarders, who was also an eighth grade teacher, necessary time to herself.

$$\backsim$$

During the school year in all our elementary classrooms, I enjoyed teaching music appreciation and singing. I accompanied Sister Blanda's choir on organ at Sunday Masses, but could not attend rehearsals—I had to teach piano lessons during choral time.

I practiced the hymns on my own, but often she forgot to give me the new music in advance. She did not seem bothered that it was a constant concern on my mind every week. "Little Sister, you need to improve your sight reading," she would scold when I reminded her.

Too often, I was on the huge organ trying to play music I had never heard, on two manuals and with full foot pedals. If I made a mistake, instead of ignoring it, Sister Blanda stopped directing with both hands to use her right one to shake and wave my way. She would blast out, "Sister Mary Janet, you're playing too many wrong notes." In addition to the girls who were singing and heard my admonition, members of the congregation turned around to look up into the choir loft. Maybe I should have stopped the music, stood up, and taken a l—o—n—g, deep bow and played an *encore of errors*!

I had no one to talk to about my ordeal. I wasn't one to talk negatively about people, and I did not want to start. After months of praying about it, I spoke with our superior, Sister Gaudentia, who understood. I did not mean for her to do anything about it. I just needed a sounding board.

Perked up with relief, I was practicing piano the same day. My studio door flew open. "Little Sister, I hear you're complaining I'm too hard on you. I think you'd rather be balancing those books, making out bills, and doing things other than practicing piano."

My jaw dropped. I jumped in, "Oh, Sister Blanda, I'm sorry; I just was overwhelmed. Please, please. You know I appreciate your teaching me piano. I love piano practicing. I'm privileged that you tutor me. Please forgive me. I wish I did not have to do those books, but the classroom teachers have many papers to check and lessons to plan every day. It is my assignment this year. Someone has to do it."

She raised her eyebrows, "Sister Mary Janet, you also have those large, front-entrance school-steps to clean each morning and the teachers' bathroom."

She did not understand. I could accept the extra duties—all teachers had extra assignments. It was the constant hovering, constant demands from the person in direct charge of me who misunderstood my fulfilling of these duties. In her mind, I was avoiding piano practice, which I would much rather have been doing! So, where was I to go for reprieve from the power of this throne controlling me?

Only one place: bathrooms have powerful *thrones*!

LITTLE ORGAN IN ABILENE

Little did I know what I would be getting into two days before Christmas in about 1963!

On answering the phone, I heard a quiet, slow, obviously elderly voice with a *heavy* Hispanic accent, "Seeestair Jaaanet. I am Angela from Our Lady of Guadalupe over far from where you live. Our veddy small church is one hundred years old on Christmas Day. We don't have a choir. Most people don't climb to the loft veddy easy anymore. Six of us have been singing carols for weeks. Some, like Katrina and Elena warble. Well—me, too, sometimes. And when Clara sings high notes, she hardly makes it, but we're excited and work hard."

I pulled up a chair—sounded like a long conversation ahead.

"My great-granddaughter, Leenda, goes to piano lessons with you. She gave me your phone number last night when I told her we practice carols, even if we don't have anybody to play for us. We'll get to church veddy early on Christmas Eve to sit and rest in the loft before singing. We won't be here many more years, and we want the old fashioned, holy Christmas, like many years ago.

"We helped each other climb up to the loft yesterday to look. The girls went back downstairs. I stayed up there to dust a little and, Seeestair Jaaanet, I found an organ! It's little, but it's good. I tried it out. I played piano maybe sebenty years ago. May we beg you to play the little organ for us? Please?"

"Oh, Angela, I play our Mass at Sacred Heart on Christmas Day," I responded quickly with a sigh of relief.

Angela came back with a more excited, positive, quicker-paced response. "Glo-o-ria Dios! Aieee, Seeestair Jaaanet, that is w-o-n-d-e-r-f-u-l! We sing the *Midnight* Mass! We are ready to sing. You don't practice with us. Just two days before Christmas. You know, we are too busy to practice more now. We bake pies, wrap hundreds tamales, make huge pots of refried beans and rice for a fiesta grande after Mass. Then we shop, put up decorations. You know, veddy busy now."

Listening to Angela's joyful excitement and devotion in working to make the sacred celebration a success, I wondered whether I would be as committed at her age.

Angela continued. "We just finished practicing carols for the last time today. Now they're all at church putting up the beautiful Christmas crèche with live trees and poinsettias in buckets and, at our ages, we just can't move veddy fast as we used to, you know. Besides, we have to keep sitting down to rest. Big Bertha—her legs—so swollen. We don't know how she gets her tired feet into her slip-ons. She carries things across the wooden rough floors huffin' and puffin'. She keeps dropping her cane, and someone picks it up for her. She laughs with us about it all. Everybody has a good time. It's going to be such a blessed day. You on the organ and us girls singing out, I can't wait to tell them the veddy good news."

Getting over my narcissistic twenty-three-old self and feeling quite ashamed, I said, "Oh, Angela, I'd be honored to play the carols for you."

After asking necessary information, I slowly, thoughtfully, hung up that receiver. Was there a floor under my feet? What on earth had I gotten myself into? I had just committed to play for some ladies who might collapse from heart failure. What would I do if one of them keeled over?

Angela asked me to perform cold turkey, no rehearsal, no usual practice for hours. She just didn't catch on that if I played her Midnight Mass, I'd be up all night. I couldn't go home and sleep all day—I had to play our early, nine o'clock morning Mass.

When the big night arrived, I pulled out into the dark unknown with my music mentor—loving, unselfish, elderly—Sister Damienne.

I've seen old churches in my life, but this little relic earned the antiquity-appearance award. The ladies greeted us as if we were two of the three kings (or at least two of the shepherds). They hugged us and exchanged exclamations in Spanish to each other. Each wooden step "ouched" as if in pain as we climbed so delicately and wound around a tight twist all the way to the loft. How did those women manage this flight up here?

Where was the organ?

That? Older looking than the church, it had been thoughtfully positioned in front of the six rickety, matchless, wooden chairs. The organ stood proudly 30 inches tall and 24 inches wide, wearing the nicks and stains of time.

My thoughts froze, *Oh, dear, only three and a half octaves. I'll have enough keys for the right hand, but my left hand's going to run out of keys. Major adjusting on the spot. Where are the pedals? Uhhh? It's a pump organ! I remember pictures of these from music history class.*

Proudly, enthusiastically, Angela announced, "Seeestair Jaaanet, Bertha told me her papa played it at home for her mother and their thirteen children to sing. He gave it to the church. Here, Seeestair Jaaanet. This is Bertha. She speaks veddy little English, but listens and understands."

Bertha's big smile and energetic shaking of her head let me know she understood what Angela was relaying. We got a quick introduction to the other lovely, tired, but-pumped-up-with-adrenalin senior ladies. Their body language expressed their enthusiasm and thankfulness.

I had to move on with what to do with this little vintage organ, before Mass started in 30 minutes!

A quick prayer put me at ease. *Okay, Lord, this one's on You and for You, in honor of Your birthday. Be with me, as You have so often when I place situations in Your Hand.* I sat on that stool and held a C chord. I kept my toes pushing down, then my heels going down, toes, heels, toes, heels. I had to keep air going into the bellows. Time was ticking away. I played a few chord progressions to get the feel. I was focusing.

I plugged through *Silent Night* with jerky rhythm, as I tried to coordinate hands in various rhythms against the constant even wave of my feet. Eventually, I got the feel. I could see the ladies smiling and nodding with approval and joy of an organ.

When Father was in the middle aisle ready to proceed to the altar, I began playing *Away in a Manger*. The choir chimed in. Suddenly, the church went pitch black. Parishioners had flaming candles—the only light for a few minutes.

They would blow them out when the priest reached the crèche to place the Infant Jesus figurine in the manger.

I could not see the organ, much less the music book. I stopped playing. The choir continued singing with no direction. They didn't need direction! They just kept belting out joyously—heartily. The warbling was noticeable, and Clara's not-quite-high-enough notes, were not quite high enough. They were singing with what talent was left in them for God's glory on His Son's beautiful birthday.

"Luminares! Luminares!" Clara was yelling over the balcony.

When the lights came on, I continued with the choir, but not for long. My hands were still playing, but the reach was much farther away. My pumping feet were pushing the organ forward. The remedy? Play a few seconds; pull the organ back, play, pull, play, pull, and repeat the *entire* evening. Mass continued for an hour and a half. Tears of joy from the women spoke louder than words.

I give thanks to the little unassuming pump organ when I was twenty-three. I had been given a challenge; and with God's help and the example set by a parish of dedicated and gracious, elderly people, we made a joyful noise for the Lord.

ABILENE FLASHBACKS

"It is!"

"It ain't!"

"It is so!"

"No, it ain't!"

Two third grade Dyess Air Force family boys were sitting on the lower outdoor steps leading to their classroom. Crumbled, brown paper lunch bags rested in their laps. Their opened juice drinks sat on another step. Fearing a mini-wrestling match was about to explode, I rushed over to them, while prefecting the playground. "Hey, boys, what's the matter?"

They didn't look up. Their eyes were fixated at my feet for a long stare. Pointing at my black, lace up, chunky heeled shoes, the one on the right yelled, "See, I told you—it's a man! Look'et them boots!"

Sister Gaudentia laughed in her familiar, low-pitch. She and I were sharing stories of the past four years together in Abilene, my first mission. We were walking after supper in the summer, in front of the long row of buildings of OLL campus. "That was a good story, Sister Mary Janet. Do you remember during Spiritual Reading when one of the Sisters sneezed, making a funny noise—all of you laughed uncontrollably while I was reading aloud?"

"I do. That was embarrassing. But it was a weird sound," I added. "You frowned and pointed me out emphatically, 'Sister Mary Janet, that's enough!' Everyone stopped immediately. We needed that."

"You were the youngest Sister, and I needed to stop the laughing," she said.

"That was a compliment in my mind—you knew I'd take it well," I said.

"I was blessed to have had Sister Damienne as my mentor these last two years when she took Sister Blanda's place. I got the best of both worlds. Sister

Blanda taught me piano, but seemed to push the children too fast at piano. With respect to leveling, Sister Damienne emphasized giving many materials at each step and having the children clap and write rhythms more often.

"She always gave me the choir music in plenty time to prepare and was frank with me about how my students sang. She told me, 'Unless you have perfect pitch, don't teach singing without a piano.' It was excellent advice—I treasured it. I learned to have the children know the recital pieces at least two weeks in advance of the program. I will stress that as long as I teach."

Sitting down under a large pecan tree close to the tall Main Chapel steps after a long walk, Sister Gaudentia said, "You always got along with the Sisters and had fun teasing and helping the community. I want you to know: the Sisters said that you brought something to the group spirit that picked them up. I appreciated that, too."

That boost was a *shot in the arm* for me!

"Did you have any mission experiences you didn't expect and you are happy you got to do?' she asked me.

I jumped at the opportunity, "Oh, yes! I enjoyed teaching under Sister Blandina in her eighth grade. She showed me how to teach English and spelling in interesting ways.

"When I taught third grade religion, I'd show my face through the door-window so Miss Smith knew I was there. The children would eye me, and wave their hands, while pointing to the door mouthing, 'Sister Mary Janet is here.' Also, you let me sub when you had to be out at a principals' meeting or convention, remember? I got to teach your diagraming in English class—I've always loved diagraming."

Sister smiled, shook her head, and waited for me to continue.

"I didn't want to be a teacher, especially, *the mean music teacher* when I entered the convent, but I know teaching is what God wants me to do."

"Does anything stand out in these last four years in Abilene that was particularly fulfilling for you?"

I sat tall on the edge of the bench. "Yes! Two stand out. The first was on the first day of school. I listened for out-of-tune voices. Henry was singing in the basement.

"I taught fast: 'Henry! Play a teacher game with me. Quick! Stand up! Listen! Sing *my* tone: w-o-o-.' My hand indicated my pitch at my chest level. No go! He tried, but was still too low.

"I lowered my hand *and* voice to *his* level. His eyes popped—He heard tones matching. I upped my voice and hand a tad higher—so did Henry! We alternated Teacher w-o-o-ed, Henry w-o-o-ed. Teacher. Henry.

"He was on tiptoes about five notes higher. He limped out of breath—with a huge smile. Third grade buddies exploded with claps and cheers! Before long, Henry was on his way."

Sister Gaudentia, waved her arms, slapped her knee, and belted her hearty, low laugh. "Don't you sometimes get tired teaching music?"

"Never! And classroom music is my *recess* during school hours."

"It sounds like you have fun teaching. No wonder the kids like music. You said you had another story."

"Yes, fourth grader Katy took lessons four years. She loved piano, was eager to play, but could handle only finger exercises, eventually crossing hands over. Key names and reading the simplest printed page? No way."

Sister Gaudentia frowned, "That must have been frustrating for you and her."

"Somewhat, but I was confused. I told Mrs. Williams that Katy was a sweet little girl, but I did not feel right taking payments for finger exercises. 'Oh, Sister, Katy adores you and plays the piano without reminders. Just keep doing what you're doing. We know you're a good teacher—Michael plays well, loves his lessons, and we enjoy listening to him.'"

"I heard her and Michael play solos and duets in recitals. What did you do?"

"I let my *seeing-eye-dog* help Katy!"

"Another bag of tricks?"

"Well, when I said, 'the set of two black keys are the roof of the doghouse, and the white key in the middle of the two black keys is *D for dog*, Katy said nonchalantly, 'Oh, okay!'"

"She found all the Ds on the piano. I wanted to bark with excitement! I dared to introduce C—no problem. She went home knowing the entire keyboard and became one of my best students."

Sister Gaudentia nodded her head, removed her glasses, and rubbed her eyes. "Only a teacher can fully appreciate the dedication of parents and student—the reward of teaching."

The sun blasted in the west. The tower bells would be tolling, but we had one more incident to recall.

Sister Gaudentia put two hands at her face, "We were in chapel for morning prayers, waiting for Sister Reynold to come upstairs after getting the coffee started in the kitchen. The big wooden doors to the chapel jerked opened. She stood in the entrance waving her arms, using her sing-song, strong-nasal voice, 'Whut time 'er we gettin' up around here e-e-nyway?'"

Other Sisters passing us during evening recreation enjoyed our hearty laughter as we anticipated the story's ending.

I added, "I always automatically woke up in time to get you all up. I'd switch the alarm OFF button and ring the hand bell. The night before, I wound the Little Ben clock, but accidentally put it upside down on my table. At 12:55 I awoke. *I'm late! It's 5.55!* I rang the bell. We'd slept three hours."

Sister Eileen left her pew and headed to the door saying, "Do I undress, go back to bed, get up in a few hours, re-dress in all this habit, and remake my bed?"

Sister Lillian whispered, "I'm going to take off my head piece and lie on my bedspread until time to rise again." We all got over it, and eventually delighted in that unusual event.

Sister Gaudentia shifted and softly asked about another subject. "Sister Mary Janet, you confided in me about wanting to be a cloistered nun, instead of making your final vows as a Sister of Divine Providence. Have you discerned that with God yet?"

"Sister, I've spoken with my spiritual advisor, and I've been praying intently. I know God has given me a special vocation in music. I love teaching and being a part of our active Sisters. Thank you for your help and guidance. I know this is where God wants me. Thanks for asking. Please continue to pray I'm the Sister He wants me to be."

BONG. BONG.BONG...The tower chimes above our heads tolled 8 o'clock. We had many more flashbacks for other times. "I tell you what," Sister Gaudentia said, "today is the twenty-fourth of June. Let's pray for each other in a special way each month on the twenty-fourth."

I jumped at the idea. "Great idea, Sister!" I always knew we'd keep that simple promise!

FALSE AUTHORITY

"Ahmama, I'm going to be teaching in San Antonio this year!" I was excited and could hardly speak to my grandmother when I phoned her on Obedience Day in July 1964—the day we learned the city, mission, and work for the coming school year. "I'll be teaching music at St. Henry's Elementary School on South Flores."

She seemed more excited than I. "Oh, how wonderful! We'll get to see you more often. It'll be good to see my old school again. Did you know that's where I went to kindergarten?"

"No way," I said. "Ahmama, what year was that?"

She was silent a while. "Well, let's see. I was born in 1890, so it would have been in 1895. The Sisters of Divine Providence were good to us little ones."

We chatted for a short time. I had other family members to call, and I wanted to be the one to announce the good news to my other grandparents as well.

"Nona," I said to Dad's mom, "I'll be teaching in San Antonio at St. Henry's this year. Do you know where St. Henry's is?"

"Sure I do," Nona said. "But I haven't been there in a long time. It's a very old school now. I went to kindergarten at St. Henry's."

"You're kidding! Did you know that is where Ahmama went to kindergarten, too? What year were you there?'

"Well, it would have been in 1895."

"Then you and Ahmama were in the same kindergarten class! I just spoke with her. I can't wait to call her back to tell her—and Mom, and Dad, too."

A few months later, Mom and Dad treated their mothers to a visit with me at St. Henry's School. My grandmothers, who seldom saw each other except at weddings, held hands as they struggled to climb from Dad's car. Their eyes surveyed their surroundings.

The campus blanketed the entire square block. Splotches from humidity blackened the Sisters' rock, three-story convent. It stood on the end of the campus resembling a saltine box on its end.

Still holding hands, partly out of joy of seeing each other—but probably for support and balance—they walked slowly at age 74 (an old age in 1964) reliving memoirs of kindergarten 69 years ago. On the way to the elementary one-story building, we stepped into the tall, white, Spanish-architecture church.

"We kindergarten kids sat in the front pews and didn't dare look around. It was good for us. Good discipline," Ahmama recalled.

"This hall to the lunch room seemed so long and wide. Those Sisters had us march like little soldiers."

Nona stood straight with her feet together, "Yes, with our arms folded and in silence."

"We had good hot meals, too! Oh, I can smell that big plate of Mexican food—handmade tamales, enchiladas, rice, beans and a glass of milk."

"For only fifteen-cents!" Ahmama licked her lips.

We groaned at that bygone fact as we headed to the Sisters' dining room for a quick snack of Sister Emil's snickerdoodles and hot tea, then strolled back to the car in the large parking lot next to the convent.

I built my own great memories of teaching at St. Henry's, but I earned a special serendipity for my family and especially for both matriarchs that year.

After Sunday morning Mass, my eyes protruded as we seven Sisters strolled through the crowded parking lot back to the convent. I had turned to page three of the parish bulletin to jump-start planning my first week of preparation for teaching music at St. Henry's School.

I questioned Sister Mary Rose, my new superior, also experiencing her first year at this mission, "Besides the weekly Sunday Mass, there will be three funerals to sing, and a Quinceanera Celebration Mass (Quinceanera is a Mexican traditional rite of passage for girls reaching age 15. It is a long, high Mass with 15 teenage girls and 15 boy-escorts dressed in formals and tuxedos) on Saturday morning. Then there's a wedding to play on Saturday evening. I have to see

Father Carmody right after breakfast. There must be a mistake."

"No, Sister Mary Janet." Sixth grade teacher, Sister Euphrosine, grinned to her shoes on hearing my alarm. "Welcome to St. Henry's. No need to see Father Carmody. Remember, this is a very old and very large parish."

"But what does that have to do with so many high Masses in one week, and all in Latin? That's massive!"

"Well, old people die," she teased. The Sisters chuckled at my naivety. "I'll show you the file where Sister Roslyn kept the Latin *propers* for the day, so you don't have to print them. Over the years, each music teacher typed the proper if there was none prepared for a particular day. I'm sure there's one for tomorrow."

After breakfast, I trailed Sister Euphrosine to my studio. My face lit up viewing years of collections. "This is a real treasure of time, but Wednesday's a high Mass, and school starts next week."

"These kids read Latin like they do English," she said. "They read the bulletin, and a few dependables will show up to sing on Wednesday. You will see. Call little Mary Ann, the seventh grader who plays organ year round. She'll show you where things are and the procedures."

The next day I jerked at a knock on my opened, studio door indicating a strong piano hand. "Hi, Sister, I'm Mary Ann." A stocky, simply dressed, brown haired Hispanic girl took a strong step inside the familiar room. "I brought back this music Sister let me take home last summer."

"Thanks for coming to help, Mary Ann. I'd love to hear what you studied on your own," I hinted.

She nodded her small, oval face with raised eyebrows that made her eyes appear to be *listening* to everything she saw. Without hesitating, she jumped onto the piano bench and beamed. "One of my favorites this summer was Bach's Two-Part Invention in B Flat."

My face froze. She had to be kidding. I had never heard a student with a comment like that. Bach? I hated any piece with letters B-A-C-H on the page until I studied the gifted, music-genius in college. This girl was a gem—and only in 7th grade! She played Bach almost flawlessly. Her tiny hands had a firm, sure grip—teacher's dream.

"Mary Ann, I'm impressed. We'll have a good year together."

We found what we needed for Wednesday's Mass. Before she went home, Mary Ann said, "Sister, I'll call the girls who came to sing funerals and high Masses all summer. They'll be here on Wednesday, but won't show up 'til the last minute. I'll get Theresa and Marie to come tomorrow to help put new covers on the hymn books."

I mashed three fingers to my lips—mesmerized with Mary Ann's leadership and eagerness to help. Was my massive assignment for this year going to shrink a tad, or was this just a first, great impression for a new teacher?

Wednesday morning Mary Ann bounced early into the choir loft. She greeted "Mornin', Sister" as she darted around old pews used for seats. Her small legs raised her little body onto the front edge of the bench so she could reach the full spread of foot pedals at the big, old pipe organ.

Out the corner of my glasses, I watched as she selected stops for the three manuals and arranged the music. She leaned forward—her arched eyebrows revealed her dedication.

I had not realized my nervous anticipation until it began to disappear. This small figure perched on that bench is where I wanted to be at her age—playing the organ. I was happy for her, yet thrilled for myself now. But was I going to sing a solo? Where were my faithful choir members?

BONG, BONG, BONG...

Six giggling, bubbly, *eager-to-meet-the-new-music-teacher* teens rustled up the old wooden staircase and bounded into the choir loft, just as Mary Ann had predicted. The first ones to emerge stopped short in shyness when they eyed me, causing girls behind to slam into the front three.

More giggles—until I smiled to greet them quietly with a finger to my mouth. "Sh-h-h. I'm Sister Mary Janet, girls. Thanks much for coming. I want to meet each of you later. But right now, Father Carmody's downstairs waiting to process with the coffin."

I was handing out the small, vintage, black books *Mass on the Day of Funeral* when Mary Ann intoned the entrance canticle. I glanced over to her, shocked with pleasant astonishment and gratitude. The girls began chanting in Latin, before they located the page. I nodded my confirmation. It was all in a day's work for them, as I began the arsis and thesis of directing the beautiful Gregorian chant. Thank you, Lord!

However, that treasure of Latin propers filed for many years was about to see its own *death*. The Catholic Archdiocese of San Antonio sponsored a contest to compose the official music for the first English high Mass. Catholics would have Mass in the vernacular (language of the particular country).

What a change for the church and another challenge for me! I had to teach entirely new Masses. I was just getting used to the busy routine of many Masses in Latin.

After months of anticipation, NEWS FLASH in churches, newspapers, and television: *"Sister Elaine Gentemann, from San Antonio, Wins the First-English-High-Mass Music Contest!"*

When I unpacked new music in choir, the students read *Sister Elaine* and could not pass the music out fast enough. "Yes," I said, "that's what it sounds like." They were humming their parts before I was ready to begin the class. To generate instant excitement presenting a future choir or piano selection, I would say, "Here's another Sister Elaine." They liked it before hearing it, no matter the title.

As God would have it, each time a challenge appeared, He was closely present with His solution. I appreciated His sending Mary Ann and her entourage of reliable peers. He shrouded me with the warmth of Sister Elaine's first English high Mass to present to this beautiful, antique, and dedicated parish.

End to Latin in the Catholic Church. *Deo Gratias!*

What an experience! Sister Mary Nora and I survived a year sharing a tiny attic room in San Antonio, Texas.

The small attic, divided into two miniscule bedrooms, had one bath atop the three-story home built in about 1889, with no air-conditioning. The heat and humidity of San Antonio was blistering.

Our room kept us hostage for a year at St. Henry's in the mid-1960s, while I was in my 20s. It offered only a stingy walk space between our single beds along opposite walls, two chairs, two large chests of drawers and a shared closet.

The wall facing the small entrance had a tiny attic window a few inches from the floor, half my height. We had to glare at it every time we entered. It worked conspiring with the room to influence its control, also, by choosing to open only at rare and random times.

My roommate, little Sister Mary Nora, was a serious, dedicated seventh grade teacher at least fifty years my senior and from a hard-working Hispanic family of meager means. In the evening's sacred silence, she sat on the wooden chair with her legs crossed checking classroom papers on a clipboard in lieu of a desktop. Papers waiting their turn lay stacked on the single bed next to her. In her black, long half-slip, moisture soaked her white T-shirt straight down the front between her generous bosoms.

The extreme A-frame ceiling hovered over me, demanding that I keep a deep, bent-over-posture above my bed when pulling up sheets and bedding each morning. I learned my lesson early when the ceiling began slamming my head if I raised my back too soon when assuming a straight posture.

Even the slanted overhead surface above the raised tub on fancy legs in the closet-sized bathroom warned the same demand: "Sister Mary Janet, you'd better keep that bent-over posture, if you don't want me to slam your head in here, too."

Weekly that little window dared us to lift its panes. Why? This hole-in-the-wall gazed down onto the church's huge parking lot. On Fridays, long tables with chairs filled the area for BINGO that ran from seven o'clock until midnight, fifty-two weeks a year, except on Good Friday and Christmas Day.

The huge, old parish had mainly retired, hard-of-hearing, dedicated BIN-GO-playing seniors because they knew they were donating their retirement income to their church.

The amplified BINGO numbers blared through the jaws of that little window faithfully, as we tried to sleep.

Despite the noise, we looked forward to those Fridays. We Sisters made our *orders* for steaming tacos, bulging bean burritos, refried beans, tamales, rice, fries, and even sweetened, fresh squeezed lemon-flavored iced tea. Sister Mary Nora and I delivered the list of orders across the parking lot to the gym kitchen when volunteer workers began heating the stoves and ovens.

Two hours later, one of the helpers knocked on our door. "Seesters, I am veddy happy to be the one to bring your delicious dinners tonight." The aroma of warm, yummy Mexican seasonings—escaping the tall folded-over-the-top brown paper bag—trailed from the convent entrance to our dining room.

After supper and night prayers in chapel, Sister Mary Nora and I gathered our bits and pieces to haul to the third-floor attic—up the old wooden, very steep, narrow staircase. I carefully balanced my body hugging my belongings, taking one step gingerly, placing the other foot next to that foot, step by step.

I laughed envisioning myself, *Lord, help me get up there safely with all this junk. I offer this sweat and exhausting climb to Your honor and glory. I submit it as part of my climb from this earth to my heavenly home. But this sweat, Lord, would delight in front of a fan in the oven called our bedroom here at St. Henry's.*

I shuffled my bundle to turn the doorknob—even the door squawked its weird welcome.

There it was—that tiny attic window stared at me and my arms loaded with paraphernalia! It seemed to grin, knowing it got extra attention from us if we dared to close it on sweltering Fridays.

Sister Mary Nora and I got along well, and later in life, we mused about our unusual surroundings. That building still serves its parish—many years since my two grandparents attended kindergarten together in 1895. I've had many false authorities in my lifetime, but the heat in this episode wins the *toaster*.

I stared at the opened trunk I needed to pack in my attic bedroom in summer's 95 degree with 90 percent humidity and no air conditioning. Despite the heat, I sensed a twinge in my heart and began reminiscing about both this past school year and its summer at St. Henry's School.

I would miss shy, little porcelain-faced Sister Emil, our mission kitchen manager, as her fragile voice called, "Here, Kitty-Kitty," from her little pantry while cleaning up after supper. Sisters would chuckle and shake their heads as they hauled dinnerware from the table. They were used to our routine.

"I'm coming," I'd call, scurrying to the kitchen for a small plate.

"There's no way to unscramble eggs or serve a few tablespoons of veggies or meats to seven people," Sister Emil would announce over her old, silver-rimmed glasses.

After stuffing a pile of black stockings in the corner of my big trunk, I gazed at the white wall bucked up against the side of my bed and watched an imaginary movie continue to run through my mind. I'd miss those monthly first Friday trips, when I drove Sister Emil to San Antonio's gigantic Farmers' Market before classes began.

While I studied signs to the market, Sister Emil un-wrapped a breakfast burrito she had made for me. In the cold of wet winter, the aroma of warm tortilla with scrambled egg and sausage made the before-school trip worth every mile. She would reach over to me with the snug, folded-over rectangle poking out of a container of butcher paper so I could bite off a mouthful while I was driving. Every few bites, I'd wash it down with her luscious hot coffee.

I giggled as I observed her having fun, her shoulders bobbing up and down as she tried to laugh under her breath, enjoying every minute. This was our monthly ritual, dodging heavy traffic of canvas-covered pickups and large vans advertising restaurant names as we neared the market in south San Antonio.

The market's vendors welcomed us nuns as if we were the Pope. Picking out our veggies, we selected items like lettuce with bruised outer layers, but fine on the inside, or slightly wounded fruits or injured taters or turnips.

Sister Emil would try to push cash into cold, wrinkled hands, but the hunched over, Hispanic man insisted, "Ohhh no, Seestair. We love the Seestairs. They teach me when I am little. Next, my six little cheeldren. And now, my little grandcheeldren. We l-o-v-e the Seesters. God ees so good to me. I no take your money. No, Seestair."

Sister Emil bowed reverently and promised, speaking slowly for ease in their translating, "All the Sisters thank you very much." Their large smiles exposed their remaining, crooked teeth. We assured them with warm hearts, "We will pray for you when we enjoy the beautiful foods." And we did.

I fingered my new, shiny gold ring—with the symbol of the Eye of Providence—that I had received that same summer, when I made final vows. It was one of the most important days of my life.

Then I noticed the little crucifix below my pillow on my threadbare, white bedspread. I pleaded again, "I know I'll have challenges, Lord, but please be with me all of my life. I want to accept the challenges and do all for Your honor and glory."

BONG-BONG-BONG—chimes from church prodding me to get on with my packing.

Moving a few items around in the top of the trunk's large shallow box, I spied my graduation diploma. I gripped it, swung it over my head, and scraped the knuckles on both hands on that pitched ceiling.

"Yes," I whispered aloud. "I finally got my music education degree this summer after 10 long years." Strange how Sister Marietta (education director for the Sisters), all of the Sisters in the music department, and even *I* forgot that I had not graduated yet.

All I had needed was the *first half* of American history for the previous five years. I had 72 hours of music credits (needing only 36 to graduate) and many other classes not necessary for my degree, such as biology and 26 hours of Theology. That summer I finally earned the few credits for graduation.

I was the solo graduate in music and the last one called to the stage. "The bachelor degree in music education is conferred upon Sister Mary Janet Barbera."

The entire audience cheered. Were they clapping because the ceremony was over? Even the president clapped. I turned toward the audience. Most Sisters standing knew it was my *at last* moment. The standing ovation was for me!

High in that old attic, I sat at my trunk giggling aloud when I awoke from this diversion. I fanned myself with the padded diploma, pushed my chair aside, and closed my trunk.

Across the room, a picture of Mary sewing and of Jesus helping Joseph—at his carpenter bench in their simple home—put me in a prayerful mood. I thanked God for my family of Sisters there at St. Henry's Parish. The attic room was hot, but it never intruded on the fun and spiritual life we experienced. The parish was poor in earthly means, but rich in the spirit of a giving God.

I left for Lawton, OK, taking with me a trunk of many loving memories wrapped in generous blessings.

Bus Flight to Lawton

Alone and feeling self-conscious, I was dressed in my long, black and white habit in 1967, the year the popular TV show *The Flying Nun* was playing its first season. Because of the wacky, naïve, silly antics played by Sally Fields, I felt the public thought some real nuns were somewhat ridiculous, especially the young ones. I chose a place to attract the least attention in the crowded Greyhound Bus station in San Antonio, Texas. My chair happened to be in the center of the large room. The hustle and bustle of travelers alternated with periods of still and quiet.

A wound up, small, five-year-old boy began running back and forth on the long, shiny floors in the wide space between my strip of seats and the row facing me. He'd pick up momentum, then slide the last few yards in his slick-soled Buster Browns. After about eight such rotations, he noticed my black garments. He continued his laps, but as he passed me, he slowed down to study my presence.

I strained not to play, entertain, or converse with him like I normally did with my students or when introduced to little ones. I was familiar with *out-of-the-mouths-of-babes* incidents. I didn't want this babe's attention, not in this place, not while I was alone, and certainly not while everyone was noticing my growing unease. My head was down, but distracted from my book. My headpiece failed to conceal my eyeballs from the crowd as I watched his footsteps.

At his third time of pausing and staring for about fifteen seconds to ogle me from head to foot, I kept my head bent toward the pages in my lap, completely ignoring him.

Oh, no! Why does he glare at me every time he passes? What's he thinking? Is he ever going to run out of steam?

The little sprinter stopped short, parked his feet firm and far apart. He stared at me with hands on his hips. Between huffing and puffing, he took a big breath, and blurted out for the entire station audience to hear, "CAN YOU FLY-Y-Y?"

Travelers snickered. Newspapers jerked closer to their faces. Complete silence.

I lifted my head, stared the boy down and gave him a loud and slow response, "Little fella, if I could fl-y-y-y, I wouldn't be sitting in this bus station."

Newspapers collapsed. Surprised at my own clever response, I smiled across the crowd to relax myself and others. Everyone laughed and applauded. "Way to go, Sister!"

That little boy didn't know how much I detested *The Flying Nun*.

⌒

When I recall my mission in Lawton, my heart hoots happily. A combination of personalities, environment and coincidences added to the bubbling stew of fun, but with challenges.

Sister Margaret Rische, superior and principal of the twelve grades, was a sport overseeing our antics and wise cracks. The fun began in the kitchen, since we took turns cooking for the community of about nine Sisters. The consensus ruled: the person who complained anything about the food had to cook the next time for the Sister who had prepared the complaint meal.

I was reading aloud during silence at breakfast. After the usual first course of fruit and cereal, each Sister took one of Sister Preparer's soft-boiled, still-in-shells eggs as they passed around to us seated at the large square wooden table in the dining room. Sister Marie Anna cracked hers open.

As it spilled out on to the buttered toast, she stared at her plate of transparent and yellow mucus-looking slime. She blurted out, "Oh no!! The eggs are ra-aw-aw!" But she instantly emphasized, "Just the way I like 'em!!"

We burst out laughing. We knew she'd just realized she'd broken the rule of complaining and had to cook for Sister Preparer. Sister Marie Anna Gubbles was the comic in my novitiate group and in Lawton.

In the quiet of subsided hilarity, other Sisters stared at the little white, innocent objects on their own plate, and eyed Sister Margaret with questioning looks. She turned to Sister Preparer, "It's all right, Sister; just gather all the eggs—crack and scramble them quickly." Superiors were good for all kinds of solutions.

I continued reading, but we saw school busses arriving for classes. All hands doubled time washing dishes. Sister Marie Anna (we called her Gubbles, since it seemed to fit her better) passed the plates through the mounds of soap suds at the sink for others to rinse and dry. "Hey, Gubbles, the plates are still dirty!" warned Sister Eugenia Ann.

"Come on. You're supposed to do the *dry-cleaning*." Almost every time she opened her mouth, Gubbles had a witty joke or pun.

My bus flight to Lawton took me to one year full of memories. I didn't realize what was in store for me in Enid.

Just Say No

My short time in Enid, OK, was years ago, but it was traumatic, life changing, and it all started the first day of my arrival.

On Obedience Day (the day we received our mission assignments for the coming school year), Sister Erma, my new superior, asked, "Sister Mary Janet, since you have to stay at OLL another month to take care of Jubilee Day, do you think your family would help you get to Enid? That would save the community the expense of a bus or plane ticket."

I thought that quite strange—the first of other strange events.

Why would I have to depend on my family to get to my mission? The mission community bore that responsibility. However, I humbly asked, knowing Dad had to work. Southern Texas to Oklahoma was a long trip. Mom kindly offered, so she took my two little sisters, Mae and Peggy, to have someone in the car driving back home.

We arrived after two days. The smooth, wide Texas highway bucked right up to the rough roads of Oklahoma. They dropped me off at the convent, and Sister Erma invited them for breakfast at seven in the morning. That was early for us after the long trip, but it would be fun for the Sisters to meet Mom and my sisters for a short time during a meal.

Sister Superior directed us to sit at opposite ends of the large table on opposite sides—for breakfast and lunch—and we ate in silence! I was shocked. I appreciated the meal, but on all missions, on rare occasions when family members shared a meal with the Sisters, we always were able to converse. My family left after lunch.

I was confused in Enid. Sister Damienne had taught 86 piano students twice a week in groups of two or three and was an excellent teacher. I had always taught piano privately, and very well, but never in groups. I had many unanswered questions about it.

Teaching all 86 privately would be a nightmare. Even 30 privately twice a week would be a challenge. School started in only three weeks.

My thoughts were in turmoil, *I've got to talk with my new superior (Sister Erma). I don't know where to start to get ready. She asked me to take guitar lessons so I could teach interested students, too. She said I could walk the mile to town with my guitar for the lesson on Saturday afternoons after teaching all morning and walk back home. But I already have too many students. Maybe I'll just give guitar a try and drop some piano students.*

I was to teach on the first floor of the disastrous looking, condemned school building for the first year, so I began the challenge of making it look somewhat presentable. Powder, sand, dirt: a space to be my chorus room was filthy, but I gathered chairs and put some handmade stick-kid-figures along the top of the blackboard: a 3D paper-folded, but slightly open, *sheet music* was in each little figure's hands.

Opening from the choral room was a closet for a 55-year-old repulsive commode. The name "Nasty" would have been a compliment, and it didn't look any better after I scrubbed it vigorously several times in and out with an entire container of Lysol. That disinfected, chipped, and rusty-stained toilet probably ended up cleaner than the tables in the new building across the campus.

Very tall, narrow windows occupied most of the three 16-foot walls of my very large piano studio next to the choral room. The brown wooden blinds had slats that were long, skinny little banquet tables with untouched fabric cloths of years of dust and dirt. Despite my great distain for disgusting dust, I did not write those blinds onto my "to-do" list with the shortage of time for greater priorities.

The brown wooden floors would gain much attention when school started and pupils dragged construction-clay, dirt and debris into the building every half hour. Yes, I had the honors of cleaning those floors every day before school.

I didn't know when I'd have time to go to the music store for the students' piano literature. Sister Erma wasn't easy to talk to, and I always had a challenge asking to talk with someone when I needed advice or help. Would she let me drop some pupils? I couldn't purchase music books until I knew how many students I'd have and the interest and needs of each one.

How could I start teaching those songs on those shelves of choral music—until I had time to instruct myself? Also, the pastor wanted me to teach a new high Mass "to begin singing on Sundays in two weeks after school starts or sooner, if possible," as he put it.

Answers to those questions never arrived before I received another assignment. Our parish would host the annual Ecumenical Protestant, Catholic, and Jew Fest. I'd be in charge of selecting, teaching and directing the most "festive hymns" because it was "our" special year, as Sister Erma explained.

I don't remember why it was special. My brain cells must have liquefied into a blur just before she mentioned the reason. Sister Phyllis Ann was sweet to offer to clue me in on other details, since she had attended the past year. I wouldn't even have time to *attend*, much less be in *charge* of the entire event!

What's going on? I quizzed myself. *If this school year's going be a joke, I hope I make it to the punch line.*

School started.

Several weeks later I cringed: *I wonder what I look like in my black and white habit toting this guitar with no case, walking to town for my guitar lesson every Saturday. I feel like the singing nun—a little silly. I don't like getting attention like the lady across the street looking in that store's big window, obviously using its reflection to stare at me. I know what you're doing, Lady! Sorry, Lord, that wasn't kind. I do love my religious garb. Maybe she's thinking of talking to me to be consoled, or to share a challenge she's enduring.*

Robert was a good guitar teacher, but I felt guilty for not telling him I was a music teacher. (I wanted to study his teaching method for greenhorns, since I'd be teaching beginners.)

"Sister," he stopped playing and stood his guitar on his knee, "since you are practicing hard and advancing so quickly, you deserve a set of nylon strings." Unintentionally, he was messaging my guilt wounds.

After my lesson, we climbed downstairs, and he actually replaced my steel strings, no charge! I was very grateful and later took him some of Sister Sharon's famous fudge. I could tell he appreciated it.

During my walk home, I switched my guitar from my left to my right hand so

I could rub my four fingertips with my thumb. The steel strings had made cuts into my fingers, but they were beginning to get hard and firm, as he said they should.

Guitar lessons were fun, but I still had the challenge of my heavy-duty schedule. The Sisters arose daily at five o'clock to pray morning Lauds, walk to church for Mass, meditate for one half hour, and walk back home.

Sister Erma said I could "grab a quick breakfast and be excused from morning chores" so I could start teaching by 7:30. I'd stand over the kitchen sink for a piece of toast and juice, rush to be at the piano studio and have materials ready for students and choirs for the day by 7:30 a.m.

After chaotic mornings of non-stop teaching, I had only 30 minutes at noon to run across the campus for lunch, stand in line, sit to eat and "visit pleasantly with the high school students" (per instructions from Sister Erma), and dash again to begin frenzied afternoons.

That lasted only three days—soon I opted out of lunch all together. Instead, I'd rest on my *throne,* yes, that repulsive potty! It would substitute for lunchbreak and be my only *resting place.* Sister instructed me to teach piano during community prayers of rosary, spiritual reading, Vespers and Compline.

At 6 p.m., the hectic teaching day paused. I'd race to the house for supper, chores, bath, bookkeeping, and few minutes of prep (with no piano) for school. I was to pray alone privately during most of the one hour of recreation, practice guitar with a flashlight—next to my sleeping roommate—then collapse into my own bed.

We learned in the novitiate with Sister St. John that our holy rule said we were to obey our superiors, go, and do our assignment. However, if we truly thought and prayed over an appointment that we could not handle, we should present our concern to our superior.

I petitioned, *Oh, Heavenly Father, You know I've always accepted where and what I was assigned. I've had challenges on my missions—we all do—but I had prayed, and together, You worked it out with me. I've loved all my missions. I'm not a complainer—I want to do what you want. I need Your help. What do I do?*

I barely slept with those issues gyrating in my mind, night after night after night.

Proposal for Danger

Despite little time to prepare for the hectic year envisioned ahead, school started.

On that first day, I started passing out copies of music saying, "We're going to learn the new English High Mass written by Sister Elaine."

Suddenly, a panic, almost fight to get a copy, made me stop to observe. "We l-o-v-e Sister Elaine's hymns, Sister," Beth said over the laughter of agreement she educed from the other students.

I was relieved. With no time to teach myself other works for the first days of school, I had brought a generous supply of printed copies from Sister Elaine. "This Mass won a contest put on by the Archdiocese of San Antonio for the best English Mass for the church in that area. Let's start learning it. First, I want to hear how well you can sing it by sight."

The group was excited with the ease and lovely melody of the *Lord, have mercy.* "Sister, it's beautiful," Anthony exclaimed, swinging his copy above his head. "Yes, can we do the *Gloria?*" others chimed in.

Our first day was an unexpected round of success. In two weeks, the Mass was ready to sing. I hardly had time to go through mounds of choral music in the storage closet to select anything more to consume our class time.

I had never had someone drop into my choir practice before, but a newly assigned, trim, about-my-age of mid-twenties, sharp looking priest tiptoed in and quietly took a seat in the back row. He looked intent, seriously studying my teaching. When we finished, he said, "I've been overhearing the practice the last few days and had to stop in and say how impressed I am with the new Mass, Sister. You're doing a splendid job with the group." I thanked him.

The students left and Father hung around to chit-chat and asked, "Sister, I'd like to get together with you and talk about another High Mass."

I was shocked. I thought, *What on earth? Another Mass? We haven't even sung this one in church yet.* But I was so disturbed, now running late for my next piano lesson, I didn't know how to respond, so I just said, "I don't have any free time at all, Father, but I suppose I could use my half hour of lunch time. You can come over tomorrow at noon." My smile dropped from my face.

"Oh, I'd rather you come to the rectory. Noon is a perfect time," Father Dan said eagerly.

Thoughts zoomed through my mind as he walked out the door to the caliche ground around the old abandoned school building. (I was using the first floor as a piano and choir teaching area until one was ready in the new school building.) *That's the last thing I need to teach—another high Mass. I've got to go through that pile of music in that dreaded closet, select, teach myself, and present something different to the group.*

There was no time to think about tomorrow. Noon tomorrow would come too soon. I had to focus.

Tomorrow did come too soon. I shivered when I thought: I *haven't even told Sister Erma I'm going over to the rectory. What am I doing? It didn't even enter my mind that I should have informed her. I don't have time now. It's already noon—just go and get it over with. I'll simply tell Father Dan I don't have time to start a new Mass.*

I grabbed a folder of paper and a pen and, with my long veil blowing in the wind, I took a short cut on low mounds of construction rock and debris over to the rectory on the other side of the campus.

Father Dan cheerfully welcomed me at the door and ignored my reminder about having to get back to teach in what was left of thirty minutes of my lunch time. He sauntered over to the array of wine bottles displayed on built-in racks. They were next to upside down, stemmed-glasses with their bottoms slid through slots over a bar area. A large mirror covered the wall behind the counter.

My eye mapped out the large room of several over-stuffed couches nestled by convenient coffee and side tables. Large artificial potted greens softened many areas. Everything was new, finely decorated and arranged.

A quick search and I pulled out a firmer chair—one at the dining room table where I could take notes in my tablet. As I bent over to sit, I popped up instantly as if the seat were on fire when I heard from behind me, "What kind of wine can I get for you, Sister?"

Thoughts raced in my mind like a recorder on fast forward: *There's no high Mass to talk about. I shouldn't be in this house. Sister Erma would have a fit if she knew I was here. And rightly so! I shouldn't be here. How can I be so stupid and naive? I've heard of people like this. Now I know why in novitiate Sister St. John emphasized we should always go accompanied by another Sister to the priests' rectory. Thank God for my busy schedule. Just let me get out of here. I wonder if the pastor knows his new, young assistant is entertaining me and maybe others, at the "perfect time" of noon.*

I yelled tongue-tied at racing speed, "Oh, Father, I really don't have time to socialize. Like I said, I'm missing my lunch and have to teach non-stop until six o'clock. I need to get back. Besides, Idon'tlikewine," I lied.

I grabbed my pad and pen (the pen slid under the table and stayed there), jumped up to get out, but walked up my long black skirt that got caught under the chair's leg. I frantically untangled myself and didn't care what he thought. I just wanted to get out.

I guessed he was glad I didn't drink any wine and wondered what contortions I'd perform if I had! I sailed to the front door, swung it, left it open and dashed out. I was Little Black Riding Hood sprinting from the big bad wolf in a Roman collar.

My shoes were mutilated in those little mounds of caliche and rock as I retraced my steps to the studio faster than when going the opposite direction. I was meeting myself going back. It was too late for lunch, but I sat on the piano bench for my breath to catch up with my body. *Thank You, God, for this dilapidated, dusty old building—my great escape from a proposal for danger.*

I knew I'd pray for Father Dan (fictitious name), build a fence between him and me, and figured he would, too.

I'M NOT ME

I can't keep up like this. Weeks come, go, re-run. No changes, just more responsibilities. I wonder what it would be like to watch one football game with the Sisters, or just read a little on the weekend, or play piano.

I don't have time to rest a few minutes. My stomach shakes constantly, non-stop. Seems it's the end of the school year, and we're only beginning. I don't even know the names of my students yet. That's not me. *I'm* not me.

All those community financial books wait for me to balance each month (as in Abilene, San Antonio and Lawton) and to send results to Our Lady of the Lake Convent office. But it's a nightmare here. Sister Erma actually writes down the check charges onto another piece of paper for me to use. I must have them to tally the totals, and can't see the checkbook!? She must think she'll never make a mistake of transferring figures from one item to another. I'm frustrated, discouraged. I'm constantly stymied and dizzy.

Have I done something she's trying to have me *pay* for? I don't want to discuss it with the other Sisters. That doesn't seem right.

I must talk with Sister Erma. She knows my schedule. She sees me inhale my breakfast, and knows I only have a 30-minute lunch break. But she *doesn't* know I don't eat during that period—I don't have time to walk to the high school lunch room, stand in line, sit, eat and visit with the students, as she wants. Instead, I just sit on that nasty commode to rest. I don't know why she doesn't understand.

I've prayed every day for eleven weeks for wisdom to avoid complaining, to be inspired for resolutions. Now I pray more intently: I sincerely want to do Your will, Heavenly Father, but I can't believe You're asking the physically impossible.

There's only one solution: I will speak with Sister Erma and ask to drop some students during school hours—and some or all—on Saturday mornings.

Lord, go with me now. Help me be calm, gentle, and kind. Holy Spirit, put the correct words into my mouth.

I knock on her door on retreat Sunday, step to her desk next to her bed, slowly sit on the wooden chair, and begin gently, "Sister Erma, thank you for all you do as principal of our school. That's a big responsibility."

Suddenly with excitement, "Sister Mary Janet, I'm glad you're here," she interjects. "I have something I need to ask you. Sister Damienne had eighty-six piano students last year, and you don't have that many this year. Don't you think you could take on a few more students?"

I'm stunned. *More* students? Shocked. Lips quiver. I gasp for air, feeling faint, nauseous. I nod my head slow-mo, left to right. I whisper v-e-r-y-s-l-o-w-l-y, eye-to-eye with her: "Oh—no, Sister Erma, I can't."

That was the beginning—of the end.

Although I was shocked and stunned, I thanked God for two reasons: I had the courage to *request* to be relieved of students after praying sincerely. I had replied a genuine "no" to taking on additional students. I felt no guilt. I was truthful.

Our conversation ended. Sister Erma never knew why I had gone to her room.

Still, each day I felt more feathery and lightheaded, plugging along to teach students and choir, and balance books with no idea what was happening to my body, mind, spirit, and psyche. Where was my usual joyfulness, happiness, cheerfulness, friendly and grateful attitude? My sincere, big, happy smile?

Was I becoming a different person? I used to enjoy teaching, greeting the students, helping in community. I cherished community life—the times for prayer, work and recreation—just visiting together, pitching in when extra help was needed. I loved working with others doing His work.

Lying on my back one night, I grabbed a wad of my bed's top sheet and wiped large, salty tears drifting toward my ears. Tears merged into haunting thoughts: *I'm isolated in our mission community, trying to get only myself and my work pulled together.*

I'm spinning my wheels in a cage, getting nowhere very fast. I'm not me. Talking with Sister Erma doesn't work. Seems she thinks I am not bringing in as much money as last year when Sister Damienne taught groups of piano students at one time, or something like that. I try to see the situation as His will for me, since she is my superior and principal. I have no one to talk to. There just aren't enough hours in each day. It's impossible. I used to get over challenges, but I've never had anything like this in my life. Lord, what do I do?

I was excited Sister Ann Joseph, regional superior, formerly my mistress of candidates and postulants, came to Enid, Oklahoma for visitation. The yearly observation for one week for our mission community arrived with October's fall leaves. I prayed I could open up to her about my challenge in my private interview.

She asked just the right question, "Sister Mary Janet, how are you doing here in Enid?" Here was my opportunity to speak up.

I froze. I choked. I couldn't do it. Speaking negative of my superior Sister Erma would not be appropriate, even though we learned to pray before asking to be relieved of assigned duties. If the superior didn't agree with our request, we were to see the job as *God's will* for us.

I *had* prayed very intently, but I blurted out, "Oh, just fine, Sister."

"I see a very tight schedule here for you. Don't you feel over burdened with it?"

"Oh, no, Sister!"

I had passed up my chance. What had I just said? I had lied. How would Sister Erma treat me the rest of the year, if she knew I spoke ill of her to our district superior?

I was torn between and betwixt. I knew I should have spoken up, and I knew Sister Ann Joseph sincerely wanted my honest answer. She was there to observe and to hear the pros and cons of what was happening. She could be a sounding board, or could put into effect what needed to make situations better.

About two weeks went by. Somehow, so did I.

⁓

Fridays were Mass days for the entire school. All Sisters went with their classes at 11 o'clock to the church, but Sister Erma said I could be "excused"—I could teach three students during that time!

My thoughts were confused: Is it more important to teach to make more money, or to attend Friday Mass and receive Him in Holy Communion? Why can't I have that time with the Lord, my Spouse, to sit quietly, to have an hour to grow more spiritually, and to rest my mind? With my hectic schedule, I need time to unwind, too. I'll be frustrated until the end of the school year.

One Friday during a lesson with Sylvia, every 10 minutes, I had to run to that "throne" with loose bowels, feeling nauseous and extremely weak. I held to desks or walls for balance on the way back to her session.

Eleven-year-old Sylvia noticed my weak physique. Her small, but wide, dark Indian face punctuated two large, white eyeballs glaring at me.

Oh, God, please don't let me throw up in front of this little girl. I can't continue this piano lesson; and I can't send her to the classroom, since her teacher is in church with the class. How do I notify one of the Sisters—they're all in church?

I sat down in the chair-desk close to the piano. My head rested on the back of my palm on the desk. I was humiliated and embarrassed in front of my scared little student. *Please, God, help me know what to do, before I pass out.*

I pointed to my paper pad. Sylvia's vibrating little fingers handed it to me. Jittering, I scribbled out a note.

"Sylvia, I need you to be very dependable. Run this to Sister Erma in church at Mass. Do you know her?" I asked.

"No, Sister," she whispered, shaking her head.

"She's probably in the last pew. If you don't see her, that's okay. Give it to *any* Sister. Her name is on the front of this envelope, and says *or any Sister*." I had simply asked Sister Erma to come to my music room as soon as possible.

In less than five minutes, Sister Erma entered my studio and ignored me, shaking on the chair. She energetically began pulling down all of those tall blinds. The blinds' dust formed little clouds in front of each window. The thick smell was sickening. I was woozy.

I was the one who broke the silence, slowly and with effort, "I'm sorry, Sister, I don't feel good. What do I do?"

She snapped, "We're going to the Catholic hospital across the street."

Sister must have known what was wrong with me. Why would she come in and start closing up my studio before I volunteered that I wasn't feeling good?

Why would she admit me to a hospital immediately? I didn't ask questions. I had no idea why I was sick. I was young and naive.

The hospital was small, had no vacancy, and since they said I "wasn't contagious," I occupied a room at the end of the *maternity* ward. An elderly, grandfather-like, experienced physician I'll call Dr. Edwards, observed me each day for a week.

I was discouraged. How was I going to make up those piano lessons? I didn't need that. I was so concerned, confused and weak, the smells of food made my stomach turn. Three trays of meals returned untouched to wherever each day.

After about a week, Doctor Edwards tiptoed in and sat by my bedside. "Little Sister, I have to tell you," he said seriously, "your blood sugar is zero."

He stared, not moving.

Was he waiting for my comment? What was I to say? I didn't want to seem dumb. He was on *pause*, so I asked, "What does that mean? Is it good or bad? I don't know anything about blood sugar."

I remember exactly these moments—my questions, his answers—verbatim.

"Well, three is larger than two. And two is larger than one."

Big help! What was he trying to say or imply?

Then he commented, "I've never had a patient alive with a blood sugar of zero."

Thoughts triggered, *Sheesh! That's comforting! What am I supposed to do now—roll over and die?*

⌒

When my community came for their evening visit, Sister Imelda rushed ahead of the others to my room. Breathless, she had to "warn" me that the Sisters wanted me "to see a psychiatrist."

At top speed, she almost stumbled over her demand, "Don't do it, Janet. Don't do it." She went on talking.

I was distracted, papering the ceiling with my thoughts.

Talk about comforting! Sister Imelda's very intelligent. So why is she talking like that? Now I'm more confused. What's wrong with seeing a psychiatrist? If a psychiatrist can help me—fine. I'll do anything to get well.

Someone, please help me. Just let me drop some students, so I have a decent amount of time to do whatever I'm supposed to do. I can—I just need some hours.

I'm weak, seasick. Why did I get so sick so fast? I'm angry with myself. I should have been honest with Sister Ann Joseph.

With that, the other Sisters entered the room.

Sister Erma reported that Sister Ann Joseph, who had just returned to Oklahoma City a week earlier after her formal visitation with us, was coming to drive Sister Erma and me to Our Lady of the Lake Convent to St. Joseph Hall, the building on the campus for sick Sisters and run by our CDP nurses.

Guilty thoughts persisted. *It's too late to tell Sister Ann Joseph of my overwork. No need to tell her now. I'll just tell her I'm sorry for making trouble for everyone. Trouble's the last thing I ever wanted to be. It's humiliating.*

In two days, we left for the Mother Home in San Antonio. I didn't get to pack my trunk with personal music materials, expecting to return to Enid. I was a genuine, physical, authentic zombie the entire trip: no talking, force-feeding myself bits of food at stops along the way, as Sister Ann Joseph insisted. What was going to happen next? My mind didn't have the strength to think about it.

Santa Rosa Daze

"Your loss is our gain." With a sweet, calming smile, Sister Florence Marie greeted Sister Ann Joseph, Sister Erma and me at the convent building on OLL campus.

My slow, tired, exhausted mind was asking whether Sister Florence Marie knew what she was getting. I didn't know myself, literally. The three Sisters stepped aside and talked a while about "arrangements," which didn't make any difference to me. I just wanted myself to be *me* again, whatever it took.

I was now part of the convent community with a bedroom in St. Joseph Hall, a three-story infirmary for the sick Sisters, and, hopefully, I'd sleep, sleep and sleep. But day by day, I got worse.

Head nurse (I'll call Sister Mella) came to my room, "Reverend Mother Amata asked me to make an appointment with Dr. James Bailey for you. He's a retired top army psychiatrist. But he can't see you until next week."

I muttered, "Sister, I can't last a week. I haven't eaten in several weeks. I'm weak and need some help now. Please?"

She left the room with a singsong voice, "You'll see Dr. Bailey next week." I saw her only a few minutes each of the next several days.

My sluggish mind thought, *Lord, help me not die before the week is over. But thanks that I'll finally get some help.*

Lack of appetite brought more weakness. At the end of the second day, hired help came to clean my room and shook her head in disapproval as she reached to take another untouched food tray to the dumb-waiter down the hall. Smell of food was still making me nauseous.

I cringed when I learned Mom found out I was in St. Joseph Hall—so sick

I couldn't eat. Being a trained registered nurse, she worried much when we were ill. She called to beg me to ask for some honey for strength, but asking Sister Mella got no response. Eventually, Mom had to deliver a jar herself to the nurse's station. I wondered, *Why didn't Mom come to my room? I haven't seen her since she drove me to Enid. Is she not allowed? I'm glad she didn't—my condition would make her torture worse.*

Although very weak, I managed to remove a spoon from the next tray of food to keep for the honey. Later, when I mustered enough determination to try to force-feed myself, my arm shook uncontrollably reaching to the side-table for the spoon. It dropped to the floor. I was scared. What was wrong with me? Not enough strength to hold a spoon in my hand. It would've been impossible to lift the jar and remove the lid anyway.

I half draped off my bed with miniscule strength to rearrange my drained body. I exerted and rolled onto my back. Instantly my *corpse* began to stiffen, to freeze. The third-floor's quiet and stillness suffered a piercing wake-up when I yelled out irrepressibly. I terrified myself. Soon Sister Mella arrived. Behind her, loving Sisters—aroused from their naps—were asking how they could help.

I felt I was a dissected, rigid cat-in-pajamas lying on its back, unable to move, but crying profusely like a live, newborn baby. I was embarrassed and was sobbing, "I have to go to the bathroom."

Sister Mella reassured me from the foot of my bed in a monotone, "That's fine. We'll wait."

Somehow I mouthed, "I can't get up."

My fingers fanned out straight; I couldn't fold them. My body felt it was petrified, literally. Fragile, elderly Sister Felicia, a licensed vocational nurse, entered the room and came directly to me, soothing with her sweet, soft, supportive voice, "That's *all* right, Sister, that's *all* right. I will help you." Nurse Sister Mella watched and made room for the path to the bathroom.

Sister Felicia wiped my face with her thin, cool fingers, and led me to my bathroom a few yards away. She opened the swinging privacy door to the commode and turned to leave. Weeping, I muddled, "I can't pull down my pajamas. My hands. Stiff. Don't know what's happening. I'm sorry." I was mortified.

"That's *all* right, Sister, that's *all* right. I will help you." I knew I'd always remember those words. She kept reassuring me. She proceeded to help me again. I realized that was one of my few, real aides and encouragement in weeks, not from the registered nurse, but from an *insignificant* little licensed-vocational-nurse. She was one of my religious Sisters in Christ, and I treasured her love and care.

Gentle Sister Florence Marie arrived and smiled. "Sister Mary Janet, the hospital is waiting for you. Sister Charlene is here to drive and admit you to Santa Rosa Hospital. You know we will be praying for you. God go with you."

Ah! The comfort of two more of my loving Sisters gave me hope and love.

A few days later, I learned that head nurse Sister Mella had cared for her own mother in my similar situation. It helped me understand her hesitancy to be able to connect with my needs and me.

The other Sisters assumed someone had tended to me in the infirmary. I knew our Holy Rule stated that the care of the sick Sisters was very important. Their needs preceded the vow of poverty in certain instances, such as the jar of honey.

Was relief in sight? How long? How soon? What was involved?

Doctor James Bailey shuffled into my room early the first morning on the third floor of Santa Rosa Hospital. It was the same hospital run by CCVIs (Incarnate Word Sisters), where Mom had been a nurse. Dr. Bailey was a tall, thin, shoulders-slightly-bent-forward, grandfather-type with thinning gray hair, wrinkled skinned and big concerning blue eyes.

"Doctor Bailey," I said, "I'm sorry to mess up your schedule. I'll do whatever it takes to get well and back to my piano students in Enid."

He reached into his trouser pocket, pulled out a clump of keys and chose a long one.

He asked the nurse to raise my pajamas to expose the area above my knee. While I looked at the ceiling, he took the key and lightly rubbed it across my leg. He said, "Tell me when you don't feel the key." I did.

He asked many questions and handed me six or eight papers to fill out by the next day. I was eager to get well.

I had almost a full day to answer, but it's my nature to start on a project with the first opportunity. I did.

The ridiculous set in. I couldn't understand the short, one sentenced, first question—same with the second—so I tackled the first one again. They were *yes* or *no* answers. Was it a joke? What was wrong with me? I knew how to read!

I kept trying, but as I read to the end of the line, I had forgotten the beginning words. I read much slower and told myself: concentrate, focus, think carefully. Starting over for the fifth time made me feel frustrated, stupid, nervous and depressed with my inability to answer short, simple questions.

Exhausted, I climbed into bed, rested a few minutes, and eyed my Office Book on the side table, thinking, *I'll read the Psalms. They're always beautiful and restful. I haven't read them in a long time.* To my surprise, I became more depressed and could not focus on or remember what I was reading in the usually familiar Psalms.

I looked up and stared at a religious cross on the wall. At that moment, a gentle, sweet voice came from my door, "Sister Mary Janet, this is Sister Frances Jerome, may I come in?"

I sat up, "Oh, Sister, please come in. I'm glad you're here. Maybe you can help me." She was one of our OLL University social-work professors and a patient across the hall, healing from knee surgery.

After I explained my predicament, she generously volunteered to read the questions for me, but to no avail. I neither retained the words nor answered a single question, reading slowly or quickly.

In her kind way, gentle way, she folded the papers, put them back into the big envelope, advising, "Relax, Sister Mary Janet. God will be with you. Doctor Bailey's a very fine doctor. He's helped many military and several of our Sisters. You're very fortunate that Reverend Mother let you have him."

I was falling apart at the seams. I felt I needed to be introduced to myself.

That afternoon, Sisters from our university and from our San Antonio schools made surprise visits to me—not singly, but in groups. As one crowd opened the door to leave, the next cluster walked in.

Oh dear, I was thinking over the sweet voices of the Sisters in my room, *I love all of my religious Sisters. I want to see all of them. I wonder who's out there waiting. I'm exhausted. I don't want to hurt their feelings. I know how valuable time is on school nights—preparing lessons and grading papers. They have the hours of prayer and some have come from long distances. What do I do? What will I say? Lord, help me know.*

Unbelievably, an instant answer to prayer: the CCVI Sister-nurse (Incarnate Word Sisters who owned and ran the hospital I was in) entered my room and addressed my visitors, "Sisters, do you mind stepping into the hall a moment. I must speak with Sister Mary Janet." They left; sweet Sister-nurse remained.

I was relieved. "Oh, Sister, thank you. I want to see the Sisters. They're all my friends. But I'm so drained. What do I do?"

"That's why I came. You're blessed to have so many friends, but you do need your rest. We'll put a note on your door to check with the nurse's station before entering."

That was a preamble to a long stay at Santa Rosa Hospital.

⁓

The following morning? Humiliating!

I taught Sandy in choir at St. Henry's in 8th grade. She was the candy striper who gripped the handles on my wheel chair on the way to the tenth floor for testing. I kept my head down, with my fingers holding up my forehead and covering my face. I prayed she didn't recognize me or remember my name. Except for the day I was admitted to Santa Rosa Hospital, it had been seven years since I'd been seen in public without my full religious garb. In my pajamas and robe, all I had on my head that day was a little white coif (cap) that normally covered my hair, but now exposed jet-black hair above my forehead and on the sides of my face.

We traveled down several hallways, rode an elevator seven floors, and again whisked through more hallways. I said nothing; she offered no comments. She was trained well to give patients privacy.

The sign on the door glared at me: *Sister Marion, CCVI, Psychologist.*

Thoughts fired: *Oh, that's great! Now Sandy knows I'm going to a head doctor. I hope she doesn't spread the word. Maybe there's a rule to keep secrets about patients. I wonder how often I'll be in contact with her in this hospital.*

Sandy walked a few feet to Sister Marion's large, orderly desk—stacked with papers and a box of tissues—handed her a thick, tan envelope and left. Sister quickly sliced the envelope open, squinted as she read its contents, and immediately started a series of tests.

She showed me a series of pictures in a three-ring binder. "What do you see happening in this picture, Sister Mary Janet?"

"A boy playing a violin."

"What about this one?" I answered questions for several more pictures.

Sister asked, "And this one?"

I was silent. I stared at the picture. Something inside made me study it at length.

Uncontrollably, I began to cry, sob. It was a simple black and white picture of a young girl sitting on a low step stool, next to a wall, her head buried in her lap. I continued looking at that little girl. A blanket of depression and sadness shrouded over me.

"What's happening, Sister Mary Janet?" She tore a handful of tissues from their box and reached the fluttering wad across the desk to me.

I managed to whisper, "The little girl is sad—very sad. She's confused. Crying. Sobbing. She's trying to sit as low as she feels. She can't squat any lower on that stool. She can't talk with anyone. She doesn't know what she'd say, if she *could* talk. Just feels lost, no interest. Not her usual bubbly, happy self. Changed. Doesn't know why."

Sister's kind, patient testing lasted about an hour. I felt drained and wilted. Another candy striper wheeled me back the same path in reverse. I never saw Sandy again.

Later, Dr. Bailey shuffled seriously into my room with his large coffee mug. His wide-opened eyes formed creases above his eyebrows. He gripped a large fat, tan envelope and studied me a few seconds; then he snapped the envelope on his upper leg slowly, bringing my attention to it. Holding it forward for me to observe, he implied it had information about the testing and pictures with Sister Marion the previous day.

"Sister, I want to help you, but my patients are on the tenth and eleventh floors. I have a room for you on the eleventh. It'll be more efficient for me to see you."

I knew those floors: tenth was lock-up, for seriously depressed and suicidal patients; eleventh for depressed with pass-privileges within the hospital when they were ready.

Accepting that information, I choked as I held back tears, "But what about my piano students in Enid? I need to return soon. I'll never have enough time to make up all the lessons I'm missing."

"Someone has been sent to take your place. You're not to think or worry about it. Let's just get you well, Okay?"

My stomach was surf with waves, but melted into calm. I wondered which Sister was teaching my large class of students. How would she be able to cope?

Later, I learned that retired Mother Mercedes, a former musician, went to Enid and lasted for about a week. She remarked emphatically that the piano schedule I had was "impossible." Sister Barbara Ann finished the school year with a major adjustment to the schedule.

I was grateful to both piano substitutes, but I never inquired about more details. I wondered what the eleventh floor was like. I was in a daze.

Alone in Room 1109

Why would a nun be a patient on the psychiatric floor? I'm too embarrassed to leave my Room 1109. Besides, I'd be uncomfortable in yards of black serge, hose, lace up shoes and starched head piece. I'm too groggy to take long times to get dressed for the day-room down the hall just to eat, and come back to undress for resting. However, I'm curious and bored. *What do they do down there besides eat anyway?*

I hear food trays coming and patients shuffling down the hall talking about what's for lunch. I reach toward the doorknob. I want to sneak a peek to see what patients are wearing, but the door swings open. With my plastic covered meal in her hands, Nurse Margie asks, "Oh, Sister, are you going to the day-room to eat?"

"Oh, no," I blurt, "I'm just looking to see what's outside my door." She goes into my room. I stay in the doorway and observe two women in nice housecoats and slippers, another in a black skirt and a Halloween pumpkin-print shirt. A well-built young man in jeans and slip-ons seems eager to dine.

Poking my head around the edge of the door frame, I see past about five rooms down the hall. I notice part of the glassed, nurse's station on the right of the walkway. Dining tables wait on the left. Cardboard images of pumpkins and cartoon witches dangle from orange and black streamers.

What am I doing here so long? Am I getting better? I never feel like eating, but I force feed so I don't end up as I did in Enid. I take lunch fast, so I can climb back into bed. They wake me up early and give me sleeping pills. I don't seem to catch up on sleep. I used to be eager for time to read, sketch symbolic religious figures, and hand print a *Bible* quote. I have all this great time now, but doing anything at all appears too taxing. *What's wrong with me?*

The Sisters and my family haven't been coming. I love them all, but I don't want to get dressed or put on a strong face to hide my depression. Mom would be anxious, and that would hurt me. Maybe they remember the sign put on my door downstairs the third day after I came to the hospital asking visitors to check at the nurse's station. I'm alone much, but I get more rest and have less stress. I feel this is going to be a long haul of healing.

I begin to realize that nurses are loving, understanding and encourage me to go to the dayroom. I appreciate that they aren't pushing me to do it. I'll go—eventually.

A few days later, Dr. Bailey walks in. "Sister, we got a piano in the dayroom today. I had to pull a lot of strings to get one, but you're invited to play it."

"Oh, Dr. Bailey, when is a good time to go? Are you sure the piano won't bother the nurses or the patients?"

"You go whenever you feel like it." After routine questions, he leaves my room.

How exciting! I can use my extra time to practice. I'll go down there right now. Wait! What am I thinking?! I can't just appear: I'll get everyone's attention in my religious garb for starters. I can't just sit down at the piano. Dr. Bailey was kind to pull some strings for me. I'd be rude not to play.

My heart is starting to race. I don't need more decisions and challenges. Now my eyes are tearing. *Someone, please come and take me down there—go with me. Why can't I control all this crying? I haven't cried since I was a little kid. Now anything ticks me off. Who have I become? Why can't Dr. Bailey fix it?*

Trying to figure everything out exhausts me, so I lie on the bedspread in my housecoat. *God, I haven't deliberately left You out of things. I'm not myself. Your Scriptures say You've known me before I was formed in my mother's womb. You know I still love You. You've always taken care of me. I know You will take care of me in Your own way and time.*

I'm encouraged a bit—enough that I sit up in bed. I'm convinced to go down the hall to see that piano.

I wish I could just throw on a pretty housecoat or pair of pants and top to walk down there like others, but I can't go without a head piece! I dress from head to foot, even take time to pull on my black stockings. I slip into my soft-soled Naturalizers Mom purchased for me when I entered the convent. I'm glad I dyed them black; no one will know they are my slippers. I'm dressed. I have to go.

I peek carefully from my door—left to right. No one is in the hallway, but I hear patients' conversations in the dayroom. I wonder what that room looks like. Wobbling, I use the hand railing on the left side of the hall. My head is top heavy, but I figure it's normal for being isolated and in bed so long. *Sheesh, I have not walked more than three feet at a time—from my bed to the bathroom. What do I expect?*

Ah! A nice little spinet piano! Inside I laugh. Obviously, someone has wheeled it off the elevator just a few feet, left it there, and gone back to work.

I sit, pull my long black skirt away from my slippers on the pedal, and keep my hands in my lap. I'm ready—staged directly in front of the elevator doors! I inhale deeply, and through thin lips, exhale slowly.

Two patients put down their coffee cups and stare. Behind them, I notice a few nurses hovering over whatever they do at the counter, but peering over their eyeglasses. I giggle inside, *Okay, nurses, I know you're looking at me.*

The top view of Dr. Bailey's bent-over, bald head at the counter catches my attention. He glances up, raises his eyebrows, and grins a *good-to-see-you-out.* I return a fragile smile of thanks.

I'm already exhausted and winded from the long hallway walk. My hands feel limp and intimidated. Everyone expects me—the music teacher—to play all over the keyboard, performing like a concert pianist. My head is dizzy, but I don't care; I want to play. I rest my hands on the keys and look up at the music stand.

What am I thinking? I have no piano book. I can't play anymore. I haven't played in months—I've forgotten everything.

They wait for me to perform. My thoughts race ahead of my thinking. I feel so empty. I finger the opening measures of Chopin's *Minute Waltz in G-flat.* It sounds flimsy and anemic. I jump to the middle, slower section; and I skip to the dashing G flat scale ending measures, which I used to attack easily—now a lousy mess.

Tears well again. I'm humiliated, disappointed and depressed. I never expect to see my stack of favorite music books I left in Enid. I stop and motion to those in the nurse's station that I have no music and can't play without it—and probably *with* it.

Trembling with weakness and clinging to the railings, I retrace my hobble to Room 1109, flop into bed and cry in my pillow.

∽

I remember the questioning from Dr. Bailey in the hospital. Sometimes I puzzled why he spent just a few minutes in my room asking, "How are you feeling?" stand, study me a while, and leave. After days of that, he actually pulled up a chair. "Sister, how do you feel about being a nun?"

A bit surprised, but truthfully, I said, "I love being a nun."

"Did you ever feel it might have been the wrong decision?" he asked.

"No, not at all! I appreciate the convent, the Sisters—praying together, working together and teaching piano."

Dr. Bailey bit the side of his lower lip, "Sister," he hesitated. "I'm not a Catholic, and don't understand about nuns, why they become nuns, their lifestyle—but there are questions doctors like me ask their patients to get a better understanding of how they feel, how they tick, what their deep feelings might be. We do this to help them better help themselves."

I recognized his predicament. "Yes, I know. I've been very open with you and answered every question so far with honesty. I don't mind your asking me whatever you need to know. I probably won't get well until you *do* know, so why put it off? I want out of here as soon as possible to get on with my life of teaching piano."

His face relaxed. I knew both of us were sincere and ready to work.

"See you tomorrow," he said. He pursed his lips with a hint of a smile, nodded and left.

Tomorrow did not come soon enough. I was eager to get going with getting well.

A knock on my door, and Dr. Bailey entered while hanging the "IN SESSION" sign on my doorknob. He sat, crossed one leg over, forming a *desk*, pulled his legal size tablet from under his arm, and leaned back to yank a pen from his medical jacket. As usual he pursed his lips, raised his eyebrows, looked at me without saying a word, and smiled as if to say, *Well, here we go.*

"I'm ready," I assured him before he said anything else.

"Sister Mary Janet," he began, "how old were you when you went to the..." he wavered, "nunnery? Is that what it's called?"

"We call it the convent, or religious life," I said. He didn't know I dreaded the word *nunnery*, so I was glad he had asked. I wouldn't have to hear it again and embarrass him if I'd have to inform him later. "I entered the convent when I was sixteen, after my sophomore year in high school."

His eyes opened wider this time. I don't think he wanted me to body-read his surprise. "Do you think maybe you should have waited until you were older to make that decision?"

"No, I couldn't wait to go, and never wished I'd waited. I've always been excited, cherished my decision and thanked God for choosing me," I said.

"Did you go out or date before you entered?" I knew where that was leading.

"I mainly double dated with my sister or with friends. I went for a while with a boy I knew through childhood. Our parents were friends since their own high school days. He was the oldest of seven, was in a seminary a few years, but had epilepsy and had to leave.

"We dated often, and he took me to the Central Catholic prom when he was a senior, and I was a freshman. Our dads took us in our car—Cactus Pete couldn't drive because of his epilepsy. I didn't have my driver's license yet. He was nice, fun and liked to tease and joke a lot. We were good friends."

"Was there anyone else you dated that you liked?" He continued jotting a few words on his pad occasionally.

"I dated another fella—David. He really liked me, and I went with him whenever he asked. We mainly double dated. He didn't like it when I told him I was going to the convent. He kept begging me not to go."

"How do you mean?" Dr. Bailey asked.

"Oh, he was upset, even angry. He said it wasn't fair, and that if I entered a convent, he'd go to a seminary! I told him that was fine—he could go to the seminary, but he shouldn't go just because *I* was going to the convent. That wasn't a good reason."

Dr. Bailey shifted in his chair and stood up a while to stretch his legs. He shrugged his shoulders up, down, and around. We could hear patients laughing in the hall, probably going to the dining room for lunch. I thought he was going to leave for the day, but he sat down again.

"Sister, how did you *know* you were to be a nun?"

I didn't know where to start and thought it out a while in my mind. "It's hard to explain," I began. "It's like little prod at first: you can't stop thinking about it—can't get it to go away. As weeks and months go by, you get a strong desire to do God's work, to spend time in prayer with Him and to enjoy those times more and more."

Without hesitation, I smiled, "You see the Sisters at work and want to be a part of it with them. It's being in love with God. He is the only One that really makes you feel fulfilled. Eventually, the pull gets stronger. In high school, I pictured myself when I read Francis Thompson's *Hound of Heaven*."

A question on Doctor Bailey's face invited my clarification, "God pursued Thompson so strongly, he compared the spiritual quest to that of a hound. The longer I'm in the convent, the more I cherish each day as a religious."

Dr. Bailey seemed relaxed with my openness, my firm conviction, and the simple, honest joy I had for my way of life. He also seemed to have more he wanted to know. He was quiet. He studied his yellow pad, probably wishing he could understand my Catholic faith to be able to help me.

He couldn't understand why it meant so much to me and to others in religious life. I knew I couldn't explain that to him. I didn't understand his side of the process, either. All I could do is give open, honest answers and let him help figure out what to do to guide me in my journey to wellness.

Eventually he hesitated, as if not knowing whether he was crossing the line to ask, "Don't you miss dating men, enjoying a good time, having a husband and children, things like that?"

"I feel completely fulfilled having Christ as my Spouse; I can't imagine anyone giving me that deep confidence of a trustful relationship. I can't ever thank Him enough for all He does and is for me. I'm overwhelmed with the joy I experience in religious life. I've always enjoyed children—I guess because I was the oldest of six and had many little cousins to babysit. However, I have thousands of children I teach and will teach and care for as a nun. There's no way to explain it to anyone, even to my Catholic friends."

I didn't expect him to grasp that answer. I also felt he would want to know more about my feelings and relationship with God and my religious Sisters.

"Let's talk about your mother," he suggested—or insisted. That jerked me a little.

I wondered: *Why do we need to talk about my mother? That seems a waste of time. I don't have any problems with my mother. But I want to get well, and he is the doctor.*

"Don't you think your mother wanted and pushed you to be a nun?" That was a shocker!

"Dr. Bailey," I smiled and shook my head; "my mother never pushed me. She never suggested it. Far from it—I had a hard time telling her and Dad I wanted to go to the convent. It took me months to ask them, even though I knew they wouldn't object. I felt they'd be happy."

The whites around his blue eyes expanded; his eyeballs bulged.

I continued, "I finally wrote a letter, as I often did, to Aunt Sister Clair. When I finished writing the opening sentence telling *her* that I wanted to go, I called Mom to my desk and let her read that single sentence that was on the page. She patted me on the back and said, 'We've known it all along.'"

He looked puzzled. "If you knew they'd agree to it, why was it hard to ask?"

"I couldn't figure it out myself at that time. Maybe I thought they'd think I was a *holy, holy*. But I got over that. I'm a Sister, and despite the challenges, I treasure my vocation. In fact, knowing all I know about religious life, I'd do it all again."

We'd talk about that *fulfillment as a Bride of Christ* often. It was the most perplexing issue for Dr. Bailey to comprehend, and that was okay. We often wonder why some spouses choose each other in marriage; but they live long, happy, fulfilled lives together despite many, sometimes difficult, challenges.

CHRISTMAS OVERDOSE

Time passed slowly on the psychiatric Eleventh Floor of Santa Rosa Hospital. In the dining/day-room, Halloween witches, ghosts and pumpkins appeared and disappeared. Pilgrims with turkeys came and went, but Christmas trees hovering over manger scenes in cotton snow brought warmth to our spirits. Some of us were veterans who welcomed new patients.

During that time, Dr. Bailey and I had many serious talks from family, convent life, teaching, to sex. I always responded with honesty and trusted Dr. Bailey's questioning. I earned hospital privileges, as long as I signed out at the nurse's station on our floor. It was comforting to walk to the CCVI's (Incarnate Word Sisters) chapel in the building to hear them chant the office and visit my religious Spouse in the Blessed Sacrament.

"Sister Mary Janet," Dr. Bailey asked, "how do you feel about going home for Christmas?"

"Home?" I asked. "Do you mean my convent home, or my family home?"

"Which would you like?"

"I'd love to go with the Sisters. I miss them very much. How long can I stay?"

"As long as you're doing fine," he said. "We'll have weekly sessions in my office on Hildebrand Avenue."

The next day I was delighted when Sister Ramona, my former seventh grade teacher, knocked on my door. "Sister Mary Janet, the Sisters at St. Martin Hall are excited. Reverend Mother has assigned you to stay with us, to rest and get well."

"Oh, I'd love to be part of your community, and I want to help out as much as I can."

"Now remember you're coming to rest and gain strength. You don't have to teach. We'll see what you feel like doing. I'll come for you tomorrow. Sister Blanda is especially eager to have you come. She told us, 'Sister Mary Janet is the only Sister I've ever been able to work with.'"

I panicked. My mind flashed back to when Sister Blanda was my mentor—very demanding in her old age. But she constantly harped I was avoiding practicing piano because I'd rather do my assignments of bookkeeping, writing and paying bills and helping with the student-boarders. There was no way I could live with her in my present condition. I had to be honest, or I'd be worse off than I was.

Through disappointed tears I uttered, "Sister Ramona, I'd love to go to St. Martin Hall with you and the other Sisters, but I lived with Sister Blanda in Abilene. I cherished her teaching me piano—enough to earn college credit each of those two years—but it was an overwhelming challenge."

"Oh, Sister!" Sister Ramona stopped me. "I'm sorry. I forgot. I know Reverend Mother didn't think about that either. She'll certainly understand." She shook her head and smiled. "I know it wouldn't work out either. The Sisters will be disappointed." She hugged me and left. I don't know what she told the community about my not going to live with them. I knew God would take care of that.

Upsetting plans Reverend Mother and the busy Sisters were arranging disturbed me. I was a washed out rag. Nurse Margie brought supper to my room, and Dr. Bailey made an extra visit that evening, too. I was on the verge of tears. Valium knocked me out.

I was still woozy the next day when Sister Marga, from St. Mary's School downtown, came to visit. She was very sweet, rather quiet and reserved by nature; but with a big smile, she announced, "Sister, we are eager and happy to welcome you to St. Mary's. Reverend Mother called me last evening. You'll have the guest room. Sister Frances Joseph says she could use some help teaching *The Little Drummer Boy*, but only if and when you feel like it. Sister Marie Anna Gubbles is eager, too. She says you were together in Lawton when the cook served raw, soft boiled eggs during breakfast silence."

I chuckled. "She kept us laughing." I had collected energy with the friendly visit and good news.

The next day I was a member of my new community at St. Mary's downtown, where I had attended elementary school as a child.

Small, aging Sister Frances Joseph took me under her wing, was understanding and a delight. I helped a bit with the music, but didn't have the energy I needed to help as much as I'd like. Daily naps were humiliating after being a hard worker, but I learned there was no choice. I had to curb my eagerness to be bouncy and bubbly. I was doing good to muster strength to nudge my body and mind to be at least sociable.

The Sisters were kind to take turns to drive me weekly to my appointments with Dr. Bailey on Hildebrand. That was another shaming experience. I had been the driver every summer taking the Sisters, especially the aged, to doctors, running errands, even driving Reverend Mother and other directors all over Texas and Louisiana for their mission visitations.

A few weeks passed. BRRU-U-U M. BRRU-U-U M-M. It was Friday night again. Guys on motorcycles raced up and down the parking areas for hours. I flew from bed and spread the window blinds. On the graded levels of concrete floors, a huge Honda cycle whizzed by, level with my eyeballs. Then the Harley Davidson raced past. BRRU-U-U-MM... My body and psyche made me a wreck on the weekend and beginning of each week. Then it started all over.

I continually heard the BRRRU-U-UMM, BRRRU-U-U-MM during prayer and quiet—all day long. What should I do? Tell Sister Marga? Dr. Bailey? I prayed, *God, please help me. I love the Sisters here. They have adapted their days just to help me.*

My St. Mary's community understood I could not recuperate there. They prepared a special supper of fried chicken, baked potatoes, carrots, peas and cranberries. We had handmade Christmas cookies, fruitcakes, fudge, brownies and peanut brittle in large tins all over the dining room: students' parents constantly showed generosity to the Sisters. Sister Marga packed a tin of goodies for me to share with my newly assigned, next community—Our Lady of the Lake Convent. Before Christmas, warm hugs sent me off to live a new phase of osmosing events which altered my life still again.

"Why do you think you're in the hospital again?" Dr. Bailey asked.

"Overdose of pills!" I exploded.

"Dr. Bailey, what's wrong with me? Except for Enid, Oklahoma, I've always adapted wherever I've lived and worked through many challenges. I'm back in the hospital again and it scares me. I was in my third room at St. Joseph Hall, trying to adjust to mariachi playing from night clubs outside the rooms on the other side of the hallway. The hum of the window air conditioner in my next accommodation was nerve wracking. Tell me. What. Is. Wrong. With. Me?" I begged.

He paused, then spoke gently, "Talk about what happened this morning, as best as you can recall."

I took a deep breath.

"Last night I took too many of those big red sleeping pills you gave me. I overslept and went out to the hanging phone close to my room to call my superior to explain why I wasn't at prayer and breakfast. I picked up the receiver and suddenly it went *up* the wall."

Dr. Bailey raised his eyebrows. "The phone went up the wall?"

"That was the last I remember. I must have passed out at that time. When I woke up, I was in bed. Sister Florence Marie, my superior, was calling my name."

A pause refreshed my memory. "Sister Mella, our Sister nurse who had challenges caring for me before I was sent to Santa Rosa Hospital the first time, came in and set a breakfast tray on my side table. She picked up my jar of pills and scolded. 'You just got this prescription two days ago, and the container is already half empty. Sit up and eat your breakfast.' I was groggy and unsteady, so Sister Florence Marie helped me from my bed to a chair by the little table."

Dr. Bailey's pen scribbled faster. He flipped his yellow tablet page over the top.

"I remember asking, 'Which tray do I eat from?' No one said anything. I asked again, 'Which one is mine? There are two trays. I'm sleepy, and my head hurts.' I rubbed my head and felt a huge bump on the back. Sister Mella said, 'You got that when you fell in the hall.'"

I sat pan-faced staring at Dr. Bailey. Breaths were shallow, but I managed a yawning inhale.

He leaned forward, tapped his pen on his yellow legal pad and nodded for me to continue.

"Later I realized that the phone *looked* like it was going up, because *I* was going *down*. I don't remember hitting the floor. Someone must have put me into bed and I woke up when Sister called my name."

"Do you remember taking the pills?" Dr. Bailey asked.

"You had told me I could take one at night; and if it didn't help, I could take another one, but no more. That's what the label said, too."

He seemed perplexed. "But did you take half the bottle that was missing?"

"Dr. Bailey," I blared, "if I did, I don't remember. And you *know* I certainly didn't do it on purpose!"

"All right—that's why you were told to take only two," he said quietly. "A person can get up and unconsciously take more. While you're in the hospital, nurses will dispense your medications."

I looked at my lap and thought. *They don't trust me to take my own medications. I've always been responsible. Lord, I have to do whatever it takes to get well. I should be relieved, but I accept this humiliation. Please help me work with Dr. Bailey. He's right. I'm not responsible right now.*

"And those two trays?" he asked.

"I aimed at the one on the right and it worked," I mused.

"While I ate, Sisters from the second floor entered. 'We came to see how you are. We heard a loud fall on that concrete floor above us.' They were curious about the knot on my head. Mom used to tell us it wasn't good to sleep after a bad fall. However, my eyelids were heavy; I was overcome with sleep."

I scoot down in my chair. Dr. Baily's head bowed, but he peered over his glasses.

I broke the silence. "After about an hour, Sister Mella woke me up and scolded, 'Get up! You're going to the hospital. Dr. Bailey will be there to meet you.'"

I shook my head. "It took a long time to get dressed. My clothes seemed extra heavy to put on today, but while struggling with my shoes, I realized I wasn't seeing double anymore. I'm still dizzy—and here I am—back in the hospital."

∽

For over two years, I climbed the mountains and valleys between OLL Convent, Dr. Bailey's office and Santa Rosa Hospital. I was gaining strength emotionally and physically. My life mixed with interesting experiences and new jobs—all with many changes in religious life and the Catholic Church.

I remember my stays at the convent when I wasn't in the hospital. We received a new superior, Sister Agnes Ann, who had a heart as big as her large physique.

Sister Florentine, my office manager with the patience of Job, would say, "Sister Mary Janet, you come when you feel like working. You're in this community to get rest and recuperate." In the sixties before OLL had computers, I learned filing, figuring time-card hours and payments for lay workers, and other office work.

A large safe hid stately in a locked area in our office. When the Sisters came home for retreat and summer school university classes, we protected the community's zippered bank-pouches in that safe. Retrieving those items as needed provided me another chance to see the nuns and chat for a few minutes.

Sister Florentine helped retired Sisters, some who had taught sixty years, sign up for Social Security. She and I met them monthly as they gathered for lunch. We took the checks for them to sign or to make their X. I smiled at their fragile little hands. Those delicate appendages spoke years of chalkboard finger work, gentle shoulder-pats, kneading dough in the kitchen, typewriter tapping, limewater mop-wringing, or piano playing.

After signing, the nuns would look up, "It's so good to see you, Sister Mary Janet." "I know Sister Florentine can use your help." "Come visit me in my room sometime." I did go for many visits and played Canasta in the solarium of the retired Sisters' building.

My own room was only large enough for a single bed, chest of drawers, chair, small closet and mirror on the wall.

The room jutted out from the convent building with two tall windows wearing antique, brown, slatted-shutters. They opened the possible claustrophobic feel from the twelve-foot-high walls around the small floor space.

The window openings at the front of the convent looked across 24th Street to St. Martin Hall, the demonstration school for education majors. I could see the entire block of the campus-building complex from the window at the head of my bed.

The tiny room was probably a former storage area, since it was off the squeaky-clean sewing room with huge tables and a complete wall of closed shelving for black serge and white linen. Two Sisters and one layperson quietly fashioned the congregation of about 900 Sisters in yards of perfectly-made habits in that chamber with its own tall windows.

Memories reintroduced themselves when I rested there—each afternoon and every night—in undisturbed and tranquil sleep. I thanked God for another blessing and many that were to come.

LONG ROADS TO RECOVERY

Later, when I was able to drive, I was in the red Chrysler going for my office visit with Dr. Bailey on Hildebrand, waiting for busy traffic to enter the freeway. My mind wondered: *if I were killed in an accident, no one would miss me. I have no family to care for, and anyone can do the work I'm doing. Sure, my parents and sisters would miss me, but they don't depend on me. Sorry, God, I shouldn't think things like that. My work is for You, no matter what it is.* But why did I even think such things? I wouldn't dare tell Dr. Bailey.

So, I thought! Wise, experienced, old Doc read me like a book, and opened it to the right page. I felt relieved and defeated. Relieved, because I had always been open; and defeated, because of how low it made me feel—low enough to end up at Santa Rosa again.

I spent many different hospital stays—with weeks between—after bouts of depression.

I didn't know whether to say, "It's so good to see you again," or "I'm sorry you're back." In a sense, we began to bond.

Thoughts would haunt me during my years of recovery; and the more I'd try to erase them, the more despondent I'd feel. At times, I'd sit at my desk in the convent office and gaze out the window facing me. My mind would go in circles thinking, pondering, "What next?"

I felt the Sisters were trying hard to find something for me to do to help me stay upbeat and happy. I didn't like being a burden to them. For instance, Sister Florentine, who spent time to teach me. She could have trained a Sister who would catch on much faster—someone she could depend on, someone who wouldn't be taking off to go to the hospital unexpectedly for an unpredictable number of weeks.

I knew how to teach, but was confused. Years of college education and mentoring helped me become the good teacher I am, or *was*, or? The Sisters couldn't ask just anyone to take my place. She would have had to train many years before beginning serious, music major studies. The congregation had several schools needing music teachers. Only four of us in our 20s and 30s had music education degrees, and the other dozen reached 60 or older. Those haunting thoughts alone sent me to Santa Rosa at times.

Other worries alarmed me, too. I would substitute for Sister Charlene, mistress of aspirants, when she was out of town. That scared me at first. Everything scared me. When asked to help elsewhere, I felt perhaps a suggestion I should enter into another field or occupation. I enjoyed the convent library: filing books, gluing envelopes to the inside of the back covers, and typing book-signature, sign-out cards for the file—a good, necessary job.

However, after two weeks, I helped Sister Sacristan make altar breads, cleaned the big chapel inside the altar railings, and prepared for Mass. That was an honor—another job.

When I'd feel flustered and way down, I'd tell Dr. Bailey. By the time I arrived home from that office visit, he had informed Sister Agnes Ann, and she'd greet me with the news that Sister So-in-So would take me to Santa Rosa after supper.

I had no clue how many times I'd been on the eleventh floor between my various assignments, and I couldn't recall all the reasons. I knew I was better than when I first started with Dr. Bailey; but how long *was* long enough? That was a frustrating downer.

❦

Within my many hospital stays, I spent most of my day cheering up other patients, just listening to their dilemmas. Some drew to me because of my black and white garb indicating I was a nun. I reminded the confidants of my position like themselves. Listening gave me a sense of purpose. I felt God used me in a simple way to help.

I remember Rosita (fictitious name) who asked to have me visit in her room. "Sister," she began in broken English, lying in her disheveled bed, "Somebody told me you was here. I go to St. Joseph Church and help dust benches with two more ladies. We like to help what they need."

She paused—perhaps wondering whether to continue—finally, "My husband—he tell me never leave my room here in hospital. He say I flirt with men. But, Seestair, I never do such thing. I'm veddy sad—accused all the time. That's why I'm here, and I feels locked up. No visitors."

⌒

I'll never forget when I offered to edit the term paper for an Incarnate Word University nursing student shadowing Nurse Margie.

"Are you kidding?" Jean bubbled with excitement.

I emphasized, "Remember, I'm not going to check for subject matter." She laughed when I admitted, "You wouldn't want me to check for content."

"That's no worry, but I hate rules about commas, quotation marks, semi-colons, change of paragraph—all those picky things that ruin my perfect papers."

Between classes the next morning, she burst into my room and handed me a manila folder. I opened it. My pan face hid my surprise when I witnessed four wrinkled, typed pages of almost solid gray matter.

"Thanks, Sister. If you have it ready by tomorrow night, I'd really like it." No wonder she was excited—it was a challenge. With very few periods, it looked daunting, but it wasn't. I just added editing marks.

Tomorrow night arrived, so did Jean and two of her friends. Jean sheepishly tiptoed inside. "Sister, these are my nutrition classmates, Judy and Cheryl." I glanced down at the folders pressed behind their legs.

I laughed. "And they have term papers to check, too?" I reached my arm out to accept their *hidden* papers. "I'm glad to have something useful to do between breakfast and evening sleep pills. Maybe I'll learn anatomy at the same time."

The girls exhaled with relief and giggles, and spoke with nervous speed at one time. "Sister, you don't know how grateful we are." "We have so much to study." "We're doing good to gather information for our papers, and..."

My hand stopped the excitement, "Go home to study. I'll have your papers ready tomorrow evening. Jean, this is yours. It sounds intelligent, and will look a lot better with the proper punctuation and paragraphs," I teased. The three girls chatted with enthusiastic release, and stumbled over each other to leave. About six or seven term papers visited my room that week.

I recalled my own frantic moments in college. Every paper I turned in was hand written, footnotes and all. I had a poor typing foundation as an aspirant and no time to practice or teach myself in later years. The pencil copy went with me where I would write the final ink version—in doctors' waiting rooms when I drove elderly Sisters to their appointments.

There was one exception—my *last* paper. I was a Junior Sister. Sister Mary Patrice, who was one formation level higher than I was, saw the manuscript on my desk in our convent study hall. "Sister Mary Janet, you're not turning in this paper handwritten?"

"I always have. I don't know how to type. It would take forever."

She picked up my six pages and scurried over to a community typewriter, the new one with different fonts. "I'm finished with my finals, and I'm typing it for you. I'm not making any corrections in spelling or punctuation—typing it exactly as it is." She sat down, snapped in the ball with plain-font metal characters, and fed a sheet of paper around the roller.

The next day, I rushed to place my paper first on Sister Callista's desk. She didn't notice or comment. I was disappointed. The other papers piled up on top of mine; and she probably read it last. But it was typed!

PLEASE
GOD, NOT MY MUSIC

After a few months, I felt like a misfit, even though the Sisters were caring and understanding of my need for rest and rehabilitation. I tried to keep a positive and accepting attitude about what was still happening to me mentally, physically and emotionally.

I looked forward to campus concerts, without having to fill a class *requirement*. Such performances used to consume practice and study time from our intense college schedule. Thus, it was a challenge to enjoy them as a student. Now I could attend, relax and appreciate.

However, the unexpected occurred.

I asked God what was happening: *I looked forward to this recital. I thought it would be what I needed. Ann is playing so beautifully. I can't sit here any longer. I have to leave. Why did I choose a seat so close to the stage? I must go; even though we've been trained it's impolite to leave, especially when someone's actually performing. I'm going to burst out crying. I'm scared. Why is listening to this music making me so depressed?*

Since I entered the convent, I had prayed, "God, I offer myself to You completely—mind, body, heart and soul."

Was He taking me at my word? Certainly, I wasn't praying *that He would* take my body, mind, heart and soul, but *if* He ever did, I wanted to be ready to accept His will for me with all of my heart's desire. But would He take away my love for music? My nerves shook my body. I couldn't sit there another second, even if Sister Hortensia threw her daggering eyes at me. She wasn't my teacher anymore.

I deliberately grabbed my program from my lap, stood up and moved sideways, wiggling my way down our long row of seats past music majors, students, Sisters and postulants. I turned into the middle aisle. With my head down, I moved quickly toward the back of Thiry Auditorium. Everyone in the audience turned with eyes glued to me until I closed the door from the outside. So it felt.

As I rushed down the front steps, my eyes welled, but running through the pecan grove to the convent's back door, a waterfall washed my cheeks. My mind tangled with confusion.

Praying no one saw me—especially the aspirants and postulants—I doubled my pace through the first floor and a flight of steps. I didn't care if the two Sisters at sewing tables noticed as I dashed through the room toward my little cubby-hole. I rushed past without my usual greeting, faking a big hurry.

I just draped my habit over my chair, threw on my black housecoat and plopped onto my narrow bed. I buried my face in my pillow and continued bawling.

I cried aloud: Heavenly Father, my piano music is the gift I give back to You. Do you want it *all* back now? It's my special way of sharing the talent You gave me. Don't you get it, God?

I thought. I reflected. I meditated. *Of course He gets it—He's God. I'm the one who doesn't get it. What's going on here? What don't I understand?*

I was whispering aloud: Remember, God, when I taught the students. They'd remind me, "Sister, we forgot to say our little prayer before our piano lesson." Then we'd pray, "Every note we sing and play, will be for You, O Lord, today." Are You saying You want me to praise You another way? Why am I not able I enjoy piano concerts or listen to music anymore? That's the talent You gave me. Please, God, don't take away my music.

So the Sisters in the sewing room wouldn't hear me crying, I dug my face even deeper into those feathers sewn in a pillow case.

When I had no tears left, I turned over, flipped my soaked pillow and stared a long time at the twelve-foot-high ceiling. I tilted my head left to gaze out at the blue sky with puffs of Texas-white clouds. I pondered. I prayed with shallow, tired breaths.

If God wanted me to give up my piano playing, I wanted to accept that, and I told Him so. He had asked Abraham to sacrifice Isaac, Abraham's only son.

Abraham's heart must have felt torn. He and Sarah in their old age had wanted a child of their own. Isaac was Abraham's beloved. Yet obediently, Abraham took him up to the mountain to offer him as a sacrifice. His heart was old and frayed, but he knew what God had asked. After tying Isaac's hands behind his back, he laid him down on a large boulder and raised the knife to offer his gift to God. But God intervened and put a lamb in a bush for Abraham to use as the sacrifice. God accepted Abraham's willingness to do His will.

I resigned and considered: *I must be like Abraham and sacrifice my music, if that's what God is asking.* I remembered loving piano since I was tiny, giving Him and His people joy and, hopefully, making Him known through the beauty of music. *I just thank You, God, for the many years I've been able to do that. I offer my music back to You, if that is what you are asking, Heavenly Father.*

My sad tears mixed equally with joy and sacrifice: *Your will be done; but if this challenge may pass, please let it go. Help me know what it is You want me to do, and give me the grace to accept wholeheartedly and do it, always.* I fell asleep in exhaustion, but in acquiescent, confusing peace.

‌⁓

I'd tell Dr. Bailey many other depressing incidents during office visits on Wednesdays when he'd inquire of any. Often, he advised another few days or weeks of hospital stay.

Dr. Bailey was keeping in contact with my superior, Sister Agnes Ann, with my permission.

After a few months, she encouraged, "Sister Mary Janet, the public TV channel sent this brochure. A lady is going to teach classic guitar classes. You have that nice guitar your family gave you. Would you like taking the free lessons?"

"Classical guitar? I'd love it!" I almost jumped out of my shoes.

"Call for the free books and information. You may use the TV in the community room." I accepted the printed brochure as treasure, ready to examine every word.

I signed up that day and learned a new guitar strum or finger technique every week. The instructor reviewed old pieces, repeating the challenging measures. She hooked us at the end of each half-hour lesson by playing the composition we'd learn the next week. I practiced diligently every day and never missed a lesson.

"We're going to learn an impossible piece," I'd tell Sister Agnes Ann. "It sounds fun to learn." The next song was always a little more challenging, but *workable.* I was fascinated playing more than just chords. We read and played the melodies with many fascinating strums and techniques. By the end of the intermediate book, I itched to play guitar with or for someone else.

God was directing me gently with the wand of His musical hand. He was offering me a deeper appreciation for my love of music, even though I wasn't back on the piano for a long time.

Months passed. One evening at supper, I sat with four of our young Sisters studying nursing. They commuted each day to classes across San Antonio to Incarnate Word University, begun by the order of nuns who owned and operated Santa Rosa Hospital. Sister Carol asked, "Sister Mary Janet, on the way to school each day, we listen to radio songs of Peter, Paul and Mary—you know, those folk music numbers."

We laughed that folk songs with guitars were infiltrating the convents. But they were fun, clean, meaningful songs.

"We've taught ourselves several, like *Here I am, Lord* and *Kum Ba Ya.* We sing harmony, too," Sister Justin added, between sips of iced tea. "We'd love you to play guitar with us, if you like. I play the accordion, and we might ask Sister Dorcus, over in the college, to join with her twelve-string guitar. What do you think?" They eyeballed each other.

I slammed my fork onto the table. "What do I think? It sounds exciting!"

Two days later we met Sister Dorcus at the bottom of the college dorm steps—the same tiled steps we scrubbed with toothbrushes as candidates and postulants.

After huff puffing the four-story climb, Sister Dorcus led us through a long attic with pitched ceilings. She advised us to pick up one of the antique, cane-back chairs as we passed on our way to the end of the huge, makeshift room. My feet felt secure on the thick ply-board flooring.

As we traipsed, we noticed *walls* were mainly colorful sheets. They curtained small areas with old, but comfortable-looking, overstuffed chairs, and a couple of vinyl, large beanbags for reading or studying. On the squared support columns down the center of the room, a few artists had hung handmade posters with flowers and nature pictures, thanking God for His simple things. The hippie-style had hinted its way into vogue on the fifth floor!

Sister Dorcus plugged-in a small, vintage fan that sat on the floor causing the hanging sheets to sway slightly. After handing out lyrics with musical chords in proper places, Sister Students warmed up with *Puff, the Magic Dragon.*

"Wow, you girls are great! I'm impressed, and I mean it," I said. "You harmonize beautifully."

Sister Justin exhaled a big sigh. "That's a compliment coming from a music teacher! We were hoping you'd approve." Sister Dorcus reminded us to muffle our cheers and laughing.

Between us, we had two guitars and an accordion and worked on five songs. Those of us on instruments played softly the first time through until we felt comfortable.

Sister Carol had a high voice, as pure as a singing bird. "The instruments really add to the group," she said. Our first rehearsal was super successful.

Each Tuesday Sister Students had several new songs harmonized during the car's round-trips for school. They always presented Sister Dorcus and me with the chorded lyrics at the next session. We grew musically, bonded as a group—I felt more secure. Eventually we each had an organized three-ring-binder. I appreciated the goal setting and achievement.

Sister Students picked up gigs for us from interesting places. A minister/patient they cared for at the hospital asked us to sing at the dedication of his new church. His congregation labeled us on their program as *The Singing Nuns* when we entertained and were special guests during a plated-dinner at the event.

What fun we generated when our group *crashed* Mom and Dad's family Christmas after lunch! Everyone welcomed us with opened arms, especially when they eyed our guitars, accordion and binders of music. I introduced my singing Sisters, and we caved in to Mom's usual insistence of tasting her eggnog and the large selection of Aunt Tantan's homemade cookies.

I clicked Dad's wine glass with a serving fork; cheerful visiting went silent. "Mom, Dad, and all of my beautiful family, we brought you our special Christmas present—live entertainment!" Clapping and wo-o-o wo-o-o's shortened my announcement.

We grouped together to sing. It was the first time my family—including aunts, uncles and cousins—would hear us perform. Everyone swayed and joined in during two songs. Then we turned our backs to the family to fish into our big, habit pockets. Our headgear provided necessary blinders to our faces. We turned again—revealing dark sunglasses, as did Elvis Presley and other rock-and-rollers who were popular at that time. My yellow frames turned up at the outer edges.

While the relatives frenzied in laughter, we broke in and began a jazzed, but respectful *Our Father, Who art in heaven, hallow-ed be-e Thy name...and lead us not unto the devil to be tempted...hallow-ed be-e Thy name.* Dad snapped pictures, one that I knew I'd cherish forever.

Sister Wilma turned white-faced, "Hey, we've got to head back, or we'll be late for supper." While we hugged and kissed our *quick* good byes, Mom gathered a goodie-bag of cookies for each of us. We left with a *cool* story to share in the convent at supper.

I took my guitar to future stays at Santa Rosa Hospital so I could practice and watch guitar lessons on the TV in my room. The piano Dr. Bailey had put on that floor for me just sat in a corner. I knew I couldn't play it yet, but I had my guitar in the meantime.

Slowly God helped me adapt to my music at OLL. Sister Agnes Ann let me play the new little organ in St. Joseph Hall Adoration Chapel every Sunday at Mass. She also encouraged me to teach a six-year-old piano student. From the first lessons, I knew Mark was very talented, and I felt blessed to have the opportunity to shape his life, as well as the lives of many other students. I realized even more God's Hand as He continues to compose the long measures in the miraculous symphony of my own life's story.

Show and Tell Habits

After 200 years of wearing yards of black serge and stiffly starched, white-linen, how do 900 women decide on a drastically modified style of religious garb that possibly includes exposing their hair?

How do 900 women agree on even *lesser* important issues without pulling hair—their own or others'?

Would the Sisters have big divisions, big camps and preferences of fashion? True, they had modified the black and white habit several times, but we still wore a complete head covering, except for the face and upper neck. Three layers covered our arms, exposing only our wrists and hands.

By 1967 some of the Sisters had worn the old garb for 60 years. I remember that summer, the *beginning* of the *big change*—I was a member of Our Lady of the Lake Convent Community, still working in the convent office.

Any Sister could put her name on the list to be a *model*. She would wear a modified style for the entire summer—while mission Sisters were home for college refresher courses and eight-day retreat.

A special *ad hoc* committee selected names from the list. Most of the fashions exposed hair locks and required sheer nylon hose, not black cotton hose! I volunteered my name, but was relieved I *was not* chosen. It would take guts to show up the first day of summer styling.

Selected Sisters would wear and *model* a certain outfit. They were to test the care, convenience, comfort and practicality for doing the work of teaching, nursing, or working in the kitchen.

Of course, all Sisters were to consider the vow of poverty with the cost of each outfit.

One evening during recreation, my former Abilene Superior, Sister Gaudentia, rushed to grab my arm. "Look, I twisted this swatch of new wrinkle-free fabric called *polyester,* and held it tight in my hand forty-five minutes during spiritual reading." She demonstrated. "When I opened my hand, the fabric bounced open and looked just like this." It lay flat on her palm.

My jaw dropped. "No ironing? Whatever I vote for will be made of that. I can't imagine wearing something that looks ironed all the time. What easy care!"

"Yes, but Reverend Mother said it's not as cool as cotton," Sister Gaudentia added.

"But we won't be wearing yards of pleated skirts, layers of clothing and undergarments, either," I said. "We won't have our heads covered with starched fabric, some of it around our faces. I'll vote for whatever you called it—*polyester?* I wonder if my family has discovered it yet."

The next week, the models began wearing new clothes and gathered to walk in a simple, fashion *show-and-tell* in Chapel Auditorium. Sisters scurried through the halls to be on time for a good chair. The top of the U shape arrangement of seats opened to the stage where Rev. Mother, the *ad hoc* committee, and commentator of the show sat at a long table.

Sisters exhibited on the floor in front of us. Chattering comments buzzed as the first Sister Model entered in a simple belted dress. A voice behind me whispered, "Oh, I don't want to wear a dress. I'd have to wash the entire thing every day. I perspire too much."

I jotted that note into my steno pad labeled *Change of Habit Info.*

"Oh no!" "Ugh!" and similar groans greeted a modified habit with a shorter, less full black skirt, but full head piece with a shorter veil. *Not for me,* I emphasized to myself.

I sat tall and sketched in my tablet: a simple *A*-line black skirt just below the knees and a white open-collar blouse under a waist length, long sleeve black jacket. Velcro, on a pill-box hat, held a shoulder-length veil.

A-h-h's from the audience announced the majority of likes. I noted the ease of changing a blouse, not the entire suit. Sister Commentator didn't go into details on any of the garments—we had eyes to see! However, she did mention the ease of the simple suit.

After several other styles, clapping thundered the room during a *grand finale* when all live mannequins reentered the floor and sauntered between the aisles for closer looks. Sisters grouped to ask the models questions. Excitement and movement invaded the usual formality as when large groups of women—even nuns—do when new clothing is the subject of attention.

Rev. Mother rose from her seat on the stage, walked to the podium on the left, and took the mic. "Sisters!" On cue, we scampered back to our seats in silent attention.

News Flash! We were not going to *vote* on a specific style: we could select whatever outfit we wanted and didn't have to look alike any more, although we could wear similar patterns others selected.

"Sisters," Rev. Mother emphasized, "we are to respect each other's selection of new attire. If a Sister doesn't want to change, that's her choice; and we must regard her decision." We should take our habits apart and use the good portions of the skirts to make the new outfits, if possible. "Use your cotton half-slips to make suit linings before you purchase new fabric."

Sister Commentator explained, "If you make your first garment with the surge fabric of your habit, by the time you need another one, the polyester will be lower in price."

"The sewing room Sisters and their lay worker will make, or help *you* make, new items. But they'd appreciate if you ripped, washed and ironed your skirts before you took the materials to them," Rev. Mother advised. "Many of you are seamstresses and I know you will help your mission community, if possible. Only Sister Models will wear them on the missions this year. Everyone else may change next year in June 1968."

Patience was still a virtue.

⤫

How was I going to get my new outfit made? The sewing-room Sisters would be busy updating habits or making new outfits for the older Sisters. My fifth sister, Mae, a college student living at home, offered to help me operate on my old skirt and assemble a new fashion. I had permission to spend a week at home.

Mae greeted me with an all-teeth-showing smile when she opened the door and eyed the fabric draped over my arm. "Wow, this stuff is beautiful," she said, holding the top layer of washed and carefully folded yards of 60-inch-wide cloth. "It'll be easy to work with and feels expensive."

I hoped she didn't think my pattern was too complicated, especially the jacket.

"Oh-h-h, this is a great style! You'll be comfortable in it—shouldn't take you too much time to sew."

I hesitated and begged, song-like: "Mae, it's been years since I made shorts, skirts and pedal pushers back in the fifties." I shook my head, "I'm going to freak out if I have to sew this suit. How can I help *you* to sew it?"

"Yeaah !" Mae swung her fingertips to her ears, "I hate to cut and pin—it's boring. You do that, and I'll sew on Mom's old Singer."

"Done deal!" I emphasized.

We dashed to set up shop, racing from the living room to the attached cabana, three steps down from Mom's breakfast-area door.

Mae piled beach towels, pool rings, and blown up plastic balls, ducks and fish, and a floating basketball net into the window box by the door leading to the pool. I shoved boxes of chlorine, two pink plastic flamingos and various pool items to the floor of the built-in closet. Above them, coat hangers of swimsuits and caps shared space with once treasured prom dresses.

"I'll find a card table, if you want to set up the sewing machine," I said.

In an hour, that cabana hummed to the sound of a motoring needle puncturing serge. We were a great team.

Between stops to detach the skin of Mae's index finger from the machine needle, wrap a bandage on my thumb's straight-pin nicks, and inhale peanut butter sandwiches, we snipped, pinned and zipped. We energetically exchanged stories of college and convent, dating and dancing, habits and hobbies.

We finished my first, fully lined skirt and jacket. In three days we had completed the second one, using the same pattern, but with a yoked jacket with pockets. Everything was perfect. The countdown started for the big day of change of habits!

Was I *really* ready?

CHANGING EXPERIENCES

Sister Madeleine, of my novitiate group, sums up her experience on the mission with the first day of change:

> It was in the Fall of 1967 that some of the Sisters wore suits, secular clothes, or modified habits. I was in El Reno, and three of us wore suits and fashioned a small veil. The first day we wore our new dresses, we had individual school pictures taken! My hair wasn't the prettiest after being covered up for nine years! On that same inaugural day, I had first grade students and some parents wondering who I was. They didn't recognize me without the habit.
>
> We went back to the habit in the spring of 1968, and that June at Chapter (held every three years to elect new administration and to discuss the Sisters' keeping up with the needs of the time in the Church), the superiors voted that we could change to suits, secular dress, or a modified habit.

Looking back in time, I see my own first days of nervous apprehensions—to change, or not to change, and when. I met no one who volunteered to say whether she was going to modify on the first day permitted, June 1, 1968. I didn't know whether we were even supposed to *ask anyone* whether she was going to change.

I lay on my bed, with only the lamp on as I read. I glanced a few feet away and smiled in anticipation. My little new suit hung on the closet door, all fresh and pressed for its debut the next morning. Beside it hung a crisp, stand-up collared, white blouse Mom bought for me.

Questions started invading my mind like little imps. *What if I'm the only one appearing in the morning in my little suit? Am I going to be the only half-naked one showing up to chapel? Oh, Lord, what should I do? Help me, please. I can't have this weaving through my head all night!*

I wish we could introduce our new style during recreation, spiritual reading, or another less formal situation. To appear in sacred silence in chapel cold turkey—whoa! That's a biggie! I'm sure all the younger nuns will be in new duds tomorrow, but I've been here thirteen years. Even they had never seen my arms and legs or my mop of hair.

Perhaps I'll wait to see who changes, what they're wearing, and make my transformation later. No telling what my hair will be like in the morning, either. Maybe I should wait to see what the other Sisters do with their locks—those who select to let it show, if any others do. Now my stomach is dancing. I don't need this.

I jumped out of bed and turned on the big light. My jittery hand opened the closet to remove the big, bulky old habit. After shaking the day's dust, I lined it up next to the petite, new outfit. My eyes bounced between them: *wear the new one or the old one?*

I must be forgetting something. It's hard to believe this skimpy little thing is all I've planned to cover my body with in the morning. Is that simple, one-piece white slip all that will cover my bra and panties? My hands are trembling and my heart is hammering harder.

That little veil will be the only covering over my hair. All I'll have to do is plop it on my head and go.

The see-through hose on my dresser almost threw me into a panic: I lifted my pajama leggings to run my hands over my shins I shaved two nights ago. They'd do.

I've got to get ahold of myself. I'll have all night—unfortunately—to think about which outfit I'll wear. The old, big one's ready to go if I chicken out. This is ridiculous. Get to bed.

Slamming the light switch, I knelt to say night prayers. *Lord, keep me calm over this worldly decision. We have a choice to save time, money and energy with our clothing. Thank You that I'll be able to spend time doing your work more efficiently with my new little suit. Help me be the Sister You want me to be. Bless each of my Sisters and all I've promised to keep in my prayers. Thanks for all my many graces and blessings. Amen.* I fluffed up my pillow and actually fell asleep—from mental exhaustion.

The sun was peeking over the skyline of downtown San Antonio and into my room as the automatic tower chimes struck five. When it stopped, the Sisters assigned tower duty immediately pulled the ropes of the *other* bell that bonged about eight times across the campus as a wake-up signal.

I sprang from bed, prayed while in five minutes I washed my face and teeth to have plenty time to be in chapel in twenty-five minutes. I stretched the white sheet and bedspread taunt, fluffed the pillow in its case and laid it at the top of the spread—then kissed my little crucifix and placed it at the front of the pillow.

It was time for the big *clothing ceremony* all by my lonesome. I hoped many others were doing the same all over the campus. I donned undies first, then the slip, and carefully pulled up the fragile hose Patti and Joe had given me. My arms slid easily through the long sleeved blouse. It felt light and airy compared to the heavy black cotton blouse with serge sleeves and long pleated skirt attached. My heart began beating faster. I was losing seconds.

Oh no, I hadn't buttoned cuffs of blouses since I was a postulant about ten years ago. I was a five-year-old, teaching myself to get dressed; I snickered at the predicament. After stepping into the little skirt Mae made, I pulled up the zipper. I was proud of the three-dollar, plastic, flat Mary Jane shoes from the discount store. I slipped my feet into them and fastened the flimsy little buckles.

Even my mirror blushed back at me. I gulped. My fidgety fingers worked to grip a new brush purchased for this very day. I brushed back my short hair, which I hoped would have grown a couple more inches. My new little shoulder length veil—attached to a pillbox type headpiece—kept my upper, front locks lightly pulled back in place.

I had to control myself. My insides wanted to pop outside. The jacket was easy to slide into and I was dressed to leave. However, was I ready—psychologically?

I turned the doorknob slowly, opened my door and stepped through the large sewing room to its door across the room. I didn't miss the chunky heels of the old-lady-looking, black, lace-up Naturalizers. I felt a lot shorter and stood facing the tall, shiny, closed, double doors.

Yikes! I still have ten minutes to spare. I don't want to be one of the first to show up to prayer. Maybe I'll just wait until the last minute.

I peeked down the long hallway that led to the *bridge* to Main Chapel. (*Bridge* was the outdoor roof of the lower windowed atriums connecting one building to the next building on the campus.) I didn't see anyone. No one was in the hall—yet.

Maybe it's just too early. If others are still getting ready, what are they doing? They must be taking longer, because they have more to put on than I've got! If I do see someone walking down the hall with a new garb, do I smile or ignore them? Normally, we just go—always in silence—but how can you ignore someone next to you, half-naked like yourself? Maybe I'll go back to change. I'd have to hurry. I'm never late, so one time wouldn't hurt.

Don't be ridiculous.

Oh, dear, now it is late—no choice! I bravely opened the big, highly polished door and turned right. My little shoes tapped quickly, straight down the shiny, vinyl flooring. *I hope I'm not late after wasting so much time doing nothing: nothing but losing nerves.*

The hall was empty a few seconds; then I heard others behind me. I told myself to just keep looking forward and keep walking.

I opened the door to the *bridge*, and left it open for the Sisters behind me. I spanned the bridge, opened another door, and stepped into the vestibule outside chapel entrance. After dipping my fingers in the holy water, I made the sign of the cross, and swung open one of the skinny, ornate wooden doors with leaded glass.

Whoa!! The chapel was almost full! My little Mary Janes snuck me down the tiny wooden aisle that led to my double pew about midway from the front. I felt I should be wearing a big coat—or raincoat. Even wrapped in a large shower curtain, I'd have been more comfortable! My head never veered, but I could see peripherally without the side blinders I'd worn for a decade.

I didn't recognize a single person from the back. It seemed it was easier to find my assigned pew when we were all dressed alike: vacant pews were obvious. Now, I had the distraction of assorted suit styles, dresses, full habits and habit variations—and the *backs* of bobs of various shades, from jet black, brown, gray, to snow white.

My head was still aimed straight forward, but my outlying vision was panoramic. If I turned my head, they might think I was studying them. My neck moved as if in a brace. It *didn't* move!

Returning from Communion, I kept my head very low to avoid distraction and to stay centered on our Lord. I prayed, *Jesus, thank You for coming to me in Communion this morning. It's hard to focus on You. I know You are here. Somewhere!*

The quiet in chapel was eerie: there was no rattle of our long rosary beads when they hit the pews or jangled walking from Communion. No clunking sound of chunky shoes!

After Mass we seemed to float silently to the dining room—again no rosary bead sounds, no heavy footsteps.

When we descended the flights of steps, we'd automatically reach behind our legs to lift the (now *absent)* dangling long yards of skirt so no one behind us would step on them. Going *up* the stairs, we had to remember we didn't have to hold the full skirt *up* to avoid stumbling in the fabric.

My legs felt light air around my shins that I hadn't felt in years. I sensed I was featherweight. It was nice. I didn't have to sling a long veil back over my shoulders after it fell forward when I bent over.

I had begun my first day in my new little outfit—so did the majority of Sisters. Nevertheless, we still had a lot to learn.

We were content and getting used to our easy-care, light weight, comfortable, new religious fashions. Many of the Sisters used good remnants of serge from the old habits to make simple black suits. They paired them with white or pastel blouses of various styles. Most of us ten-year-or-longer veterans wore some kind of short veil, especially, when off campus. Various retired Sisters still wore the full habit, but many of those were modified somewhat. Young Sisters opted to wear more modern fashions and no veils. We all respected each other's decision.

We'd forgotten what it was like to have the winds blow through our hair or to feel the breeze on our arms and legs, even if it *was* the hot, humid breezes of San Antonio's sweltering, *mosquitoey* summers. It was nice to remove our jacket if we got too warm.

We used to mend our thick, black stockings over a wooden egg with a handle during spiritual reading, wearing them until the threads faded green from washing. Our legs loved new, sheer, nylon hosieries, but we had to contend with snags, tears, runs and replacements.

Extremely short hair had been easy to keep, except for haircuts, which we did for each other. After the change, professional haircuts and perms affected our budgets. Our longer locks required more than a couple drops of cheapest shampoo or a bar of soap. Then there were the various kinds of hair curlers, bobby pins, hair dryers and hair sprays to purchase.

To help with costs, Sister Florentine and I clipped ads and coupons for the new items the Sisters needed, along with the usual things like toothpaste, deodorants, bar and laundry soap. We kept an ample supply in the community toilet-article closet for the candidates, postulants, novices, and Sisters in the convent building.

On the first day of the ads' sales, we left to shop right after breakfast. The empty parking lot offered us prime spaces directly across from the store entrance. We were the first in line of only a few people when the doors opened, and we knew our destination. We ran directly to the hair and toilet-article aisles, and scooped up every bottle or can on our list from the shelves. Sometimes we asked a sales clerk to bring us crated boxes from the back room.

After about fifteen minutes, other customers arrived and looked for sale items. "What's the matter, haven't you stocked your shelves, yet?" we might hear. We were warts on the nose of other customers! They waited in line for us to check out our two baskets packed so well, you couldn't get a toothpick between anything. They accused the manager of false advertising for items that were not in stock.

That was just the first hour, of the first day, of the weekly sale. A sales clerk politely (but probably with a smirk on his heart) pushed our two baskets to the lot, and unloaded our tons of bargains to our trunk and back seat.

Eventually, we managed to shop different stores for the same items: first out of charity to others, but admittedly out of embarrassment, too.

∽

A few months after our big day of habit change, my superior at Our Lady of the Lake Convent, Sister Agnes Ann, entered the office when I was working with Sister Florentine. "Sister Mary Janet, your sister Patti is a model. Do you think she'd be willing to come to the convent to show the Sisters how to sit, walk, stand—things like that? I see how many of us park ourselves, and the public must be shocked."

Sister Florentine sat up straight and pushed her adding machine away. "Oh, that's a good idea. I know I'd like it, too."

I hesitated to say *yes* right away. "I know she's always booked with shows in and out of town, but I'll ask her."

Patti accepted the offer. "But I don't see how I can show you how to sit properly when I wear only mini-skirts and mini-shorts. Your skirts are great for you. You're nuns. What you're wearing now is 100% better than your old habits. I don't own anything that length. Women wear long pants that are in style now, too. I couldn't demonstrate how to sit in a skirt, when I'm wearing pants. I'll use *you* as my demo."

I almost dropped the phone. "But I don't know how sit and stand properly, that's why you're going—to show us how."

"No, no, Mary Jo. You don't have to know what to do. I need someone who will do it wrong, so I can show the correct way. You'll just do what I say. It'll be perfect."

I laughed, "Thanks a lot. I'll be perfect, because I'm so bad. Okay, I'll do it for you."

A week after Patti accepted the invitation to OLL, I greeted her at the back entrance. We chatted with anticipation, climbing the steps to the porch along the aspirancy. Sister Agnes Ann greeted us as we entered the large room divided for dining and recreating.

Sisters of all ages cheered as Patti and I entered and walked toward the chair in the middle. We faced the long semicircle of nuns.

"Wow," Patti said as she clapped for everyone in the room around her, "Ya'll look so-o-o different!" That invited laughter and applause.

I quickly introduced her for Sister Agnes Ann, who took a seat herself to look, listen and learn.

Patti was clever. She asked me to sit on the brown, low-backed dining chair facing the group.

Self-consciousness kicked in as I wondered just how to arrange my legs and feet.

"Oh, no, Mary Jo..." The group snickered at that name, and Patti responded, "I know, I should call her Sister Mary Janet, but she's Mary Jo to me, and you have to forgive me." A wave of agreeing smiles, hands and remarks relaxed the atmosphere.

"As I was saying, Mary Jo, you just sit the way you *used* to sit—when you had all of that fabric hanging from your lap to your toes."

"You asked for it." I shook my head. I placed my feet flat on the floor, at least two feet apart.

"Exactly!" Patti pointed at my position and nodded to the group. "Right, Sisters?" Hilarity bounced off the walls; hands flew up; and heads nodded in agreement.

One of the Sisters volunteered, "Often, we were so hot, we'd fan ourselves with our skirts while sitting to keep cool."

"Yes, I kno-o-ow," Patti said in singsong tone. "We saw you all the time. We didn't blame you, but you can't get away with that anymore."

Sister Agnes Ann called attention, "Look at Sister Mary Janet when she has her legs apart. We can see her white slip. If her skirt inches up much farther onto her on lap, we'd see even more!" Added laughter! I felt I was helping Patti, as she expected me to do.

After showing me how to sit properly with my knees together, one foot flat with the other crossed, she asked the Sisters to imitate. The room bubbled with delight and fun. It was a real lesson in learning.

Questions and remarks flew to Patti and to each other: "How do I look?" "Is this right?" "What do I do with my hands?" "I hope I'll remember this."

Patti asked me to walk to the door and back. My feet sauntered randomly, but I got where I needed to go.

"Now, walk this line made by the tiling on the floor." A few groans implied, *Oh no. Not me. I can't do that.*

"If you can't put one foot in *front* of the other, at least put them *closer* to the line," Patti assured. Again, the group practiced what Patti preached.

Recreation hour was fun and fruitful—we felt more confident and assured.

Walking Patti back to her car, she said, "I noticed many were dressed in the decade in which they entered the convent. I'm glad they will not still be teaching their students never to cross their legs when seated. Short skirts are in style. We should *always* cross our legs, even as we begin to sit, and always *keep* them crossed, and together."

I laughed, "Did you notice the shock on many of their faces? I know they appreciated the many hints."

Changing habits entailed many other changes: new head of hair and its needs, new clothes and their suitability, new body and its proper movements, new financial budgets. Most importantly, we learned to respect and adjust further, and to live humbly, giving thanks to God with His loving care for us.

Truth Serum and End of Life

At age about 29, after several years in and out of Santa Rosa Hospital, and many office visits, I was still having serious bouts of depressions. Dr. Bailey explained about a procedure he wanted to do to help with my *case*.

Sister Angela, director of the tenth and eleventh psychiatric floors, would be a witness. He'd ask some questions he had asked previously. A shot in my back would help me relax, and I would respond from the depth of my consciousness. (I'm not exactly sure if that's how it was worded, but that's what I understood about the procedure.) The shot was Sodium Pentothal (a "truth serum" given to obtain information from subjects who are unable or unwilling to provide it). Normally, I wouldn't remember much when it was over. It would be painless.

"When the procedure is over, rest on your back and don't move for at least twenty minutes," Doctor instructed.

I was always honest, "unzipping my soul," I used to tell Dr. Bailey. I realized holding back information slowed down my getting well, and I wanted to get on with my life. Sisters were footing the bill, and I needed to be on the missions teaching somewhere. I gave him my approval to receive Pentothal.

The next morning, Dr. Bailey and Sister Angela entered my room. "Sister Mary Janet, this is Dr. Hall. He's a psychologist and is going to be another witness."

Dr. Bailey told me upfront that not being Catholic, he didn't understand nuns, but needed to ask basic questions he asked other patients. He selected Dr. Hall, a Catholic, to help *monitor* the questions.

They went to work immediately. I *felt the fluid* going into my back, and sensed it was going into my spine. It felt a tad like carbonated fizz, but it didn't hurt. Soon I closed my heavy eyes, on the verge of sleeping. I was aware of and remembered what was happening.

Dr. Bailey started his usual, identical, familiar questions. My honest answers were unchanged.

Soon I recognized that Dr. Hall, without any warning, just started asking similar questions. I felt deceived, tricked, hurt—that wool-pulled-over-my-eyes feeling. They must have assumed I thought that Dr. Bailey was still asking the questions.

I wouldn't have minded, had I'd been told Dr. Hall was going to actually question, also. He seemed intent on selecting his phrasing and exact language. I felt he was trying hard to put words into my mouth by rewording Dr. Bailey's questions to require *yes or no* answers. Responding that way, I would have implied that my answers to Dr. Bailey were false. That didn't help the situation.

I fought sleep—was sobbing—trying to stand up for myself. I emphasized to Dr. Hall, "No! You're trying to trick me. I never implied anything like that, and I never will. It is not the truth!"

Dr. Bailey realized I had been sincere and open, and I was distressed. He pat me on the shoulder and assured me, "Sister, you did fine. You can rest. Just don't move for twenty minutes. They left.

I lay there for about thirty minutes—just to *be sure*.

Strange: when I started to get out of bed, my feet were getting very sore, in fact so sore that if I wiggled a toe, the pain increased. Not one to complain, I decided to keep as still as possible to alleviate the tenderness. I lay still all day. When I sat up for supper, I ate fast, so I could lie down and not move. The hurt was farther up into my shins.

What gave me the most psychological relief was meditating on the Crucifixion of Christ. I prayed that I would offer my discomfort, as small as it was compared to His, to His honor and glory. That alone made it all worthwhile. I finally fell asleep for the night.

The sun rose, so did I—to shower, while the aide changed my sheets. The pain had climbed up to my torso and had increased in intensity. I half dried off, half climbed into my PJs, clutched the chair, then the side table for support, folded my body over and melted carefully onto the bed.

Throughout that second day, opening my eyes or moving a finger caused the excruciating pain to increase and rise a little higher in my body. No choice—I simply lay still, didn't talk, and didn't open my eyes—just moved my ribs shallow enough to breathe. I didn't even eat.

As long as I was very still, eventually, after an hour or so, I'd have some relief. It was not that I *couldn't* move, it was just that when I *did*, the agony returned with more intensity. It was red hot, tiny irons invading my veins and muscles, taking hours to cool down if I lay perfectly still. I used every waking moment to beg the grace He was giving me to make the pain a *prayer*.

If He wanted me to endure this, then that's what I wanted. I asked God to help me keep my resolution and to keep it firmly. He was the only One I could communicate with—I didn't have to move my lips, just my heart.

Dr. Bailey would shake his head. This wasn't expected. Other doctors called in were perplexed. Not eating or drinking was another challenge.

The worst pain of all was when my parents came to visit me that evening. Obviously, Mom had been told I wasn't eating. She brought two baked, stuffed doves, keeping them warm in aluminum foil from north of San Antonio to our downtown hospital in closing-business hours. I prayed, *Oh, God, don't let Mom see me hurting.* I knew my physical pain paled with Mom's concern about me.

Mom and Dad loved us very much, and Dad always worked hard to make ends meet. As a shy child, I never let on how it burned my heart to hear my parents arguing with each other...never physical though. I'd not sleep night after night from listening to them. I'd get up for school and be able to pour my heart out to our Lord at Mass.

In my little missal that we all had, my most prayed page listed the promises of Jesus to St. Margaret Mary. Each morning in church I'd read one particular promise over and over: *I WILL HEAR THE PRAYER OF THE LITTLE CHILD.*

I just know things will get better, because He made us that promise. After all, I'm a little child. I'm praying so hard to Him; surely He'll hear my prayer. Besides, I'm not praying for something unimportant like wanting a new toy or something like that.

Many nights I had my hand on the knob of our front bedroom door. (They had no door; they were sleeping in the dining room for a bedroom.) I even creaked it open a little. I was trying to get the courage to say, *Just say you love each other and go back to sleep, OK?*

I always looked back and wondered how I would have been as a parent with so many kids in that small house and no washing or drying machine. Washing all those diapers on a scrub board by hand whether it was hot or cold outside: Mom did that. I know other families had less than we did, but it was a matter of being able to cope. Some are able to handle conditions easier than others. I never held it against either of them, but always prayed, as I do today. I pray for the situation, place it into His hands and that He'll take care of it. He always does. Each time it turns out *better* than if it had turned out the way I had thought was best. I constantly forgave and still forgive my loving parents.

During their visit to the Santa Rosa Hospital, I put on a façade. I sat up in bed, forced the corners of my mouth to rise a little, and made efforts to talk while enduring the most excruciating agony I have ever endured in my lifetime. My mask hid my grief from Mom, but I wondered whether Dr. Bailey had told her of my suffering.

There was no way I could eat those doves. "Mary Jo, they are delicious and have lots of nutrition," she coaxed with a sad, pleading smile—her eyes on the little warm, silver, package.

I was afraid the doves would upset my stomach, and that would be worse. Trying to be cheerful, I managed to speak. Even whispering increased the torture: "Mom, they look delicious. I know you went to a lot of trouble, but I can't eat them right now."

Mom lowered her head in disappointment and worry about my nutritional needs. But Dad perked his eyes, when I suggested, "Dr. Sheehy across the hall—the man here with a broken back—he's a hunter, remember? He'd love these doves; he has no family. I'm sorry, Mom." She and Dad delivered them to him.

When they returned, hoping to give the conversation a positive turn, Dad beamed. "He devoured every morsel, and the bones were whistle clean. We always like to talk hunting and fishing!"

After my parents left, I dissipated into the bed, weak and exhausted. My body was like a horrible, hot bruise.

Lord, if this moves up to my neck and into my head, I'll probably go insane or even die. I beg You to relieve me of this. I know You want us to pray for our needs, but I firmly resign myself to Your Will. My agony is excruciating; it doesn't begin to compare with Yours.

No one knows Your anguish when You wore the Crown of Thorns. Mine is nothing like that. You were tortured and beat with no one to care and comfort You, except Your sweet mother and a few others. Please, I beg. Give me Your continuing grace, to keep accepting Your Will to my end. If it is Your will, please help me get well. But if I must suffer and leave this earth, I want only what You want.

All my being from my toes to the top of my head—is dedicated to You. That's why I'm on this earth: to give glory every second of each minute of each hour of each day. Every breath and movement of every muscle for Your honor and adoration. I prayed all night, never sleeping, repeating the same prayer.

Night lingered and gradually passed. Pain subsided after a few hours, as long as I didn't bat an eye. But the dawn brought nurses to poke, prod and test—more moving, more throbbing. Puzzled doctors interrupted any stillness. Every breath was competing with the unbelievable. Was I being introduced to the rest of my life? Or was I to enter my new, eternal, life?

Jesus, You prayed in the Garden of Gethsemane to Your Father in heaven: 'My Father, if it is possible, let this cup pass by. Still, let it be as You would have it, not as I.' You knew what suffering You were going to have to endure, and You still accepted Your Father's will. I want that prayer to be mine with the deepest sincerity of my heart. Please be with me—in my simple agony. Is this the end of my life, too? Will I awake in heaven soon?

Those thoughts and prayers were in a loop in my mind every waking moment.

⁓

A group of Sisters from OLL campus came the next day. I was elated and greeted them as best I could speak. I was like a rag doll. They lined up along the left side of my bed, along the row of windows.

I barely whispered each one's name, which surprised them. Even Sister Elaine, my piano teacher at the university, came. She seldom left the campus. Sister Margaret Rische, my former superior/principal from Lawton; Sister

Pacifica from the kitchen, and Sister Emil from St. Henry's: their visit uplifted me, but suffering had no sympathy.

That's all I recall from that long day. I was exhausted. I know I slept.

⁓

At about one o'clock in the morning, I awoke with absolutely *no pain* whatsoever! Was I in heaven?

No! But I felt like it! I sat on the edge of my bed with my feet on the rubber-topped metal stool next to it. Gingerly, I held to the side of the mattress and stood tall. I smiled, turned to the dark windows to the heavens. With outstretched arms, I whispered loudly, "Heavenly Father, thank You. I praise and glorify You! How can I ever give enough thanks?"

I hadn't been up in several days. I hadn't moved my head to notice the mail stacked neatly in piles along the window sill, on my side table and on the rolling stand in the corner. Not wanting to disturb patients in the other rooms, I pulled up the chair after mounding the envelopes onto my bed as a table.

Cards were filled with personal prayers, some pretty, some with cartoons others with prayer cards. My face needed to rest from the big smile that was hard to relax. My room was still dark, except for a small light from somewhere. After a while, my door opened, and a flashlight shined on my back. "What are you doing?"

I jerked around, "I'm opening all of these cards and letters. Look, there're all over the place. I feel just fine. I'm catching up on things."

Night Nurse: "I'll be right back." No other comments.

I was still sitting there about forty-five minutes later when in shuffled tired, bent over Dr. Bailey, wrinkled faced, whisker stubs, and a few long hairs standing crooked on his baldhead. His coat hung over his shirt and his well-wrapped tie. Steaming coffee shook in his large cup and woke up the closed scent of my room. Night Nurse had alerted him.

His sleepy eyes opened wide, deepening the furrows in his forehead, "When did you start feeling better?"

"I just woke up and didn't have any pain. Then I noticed all these cards and letters. Look!" I scooped up handfuls toward him. He just pat me on the shoulder, turned, and shuffled out of my room with his tall shadow.

A few days later several Sisters said the congregation had prayed intently for me. They thought I was dying. One who had visited remarked, "You looked more dead than alive."

∽

A year passed. I asked, "Dr. Bailey, you know how honest *I've* been with you about my health." He nodded a firm *yes*. "Please, please, tell me what was wrong with me. I can handle whatever it was. Now *you* be honest with me."

He leaned forward, put his elbows and clasped hands on his desk. He looked to me eyeballs to eyeballs, "Honest to God, Mary Jo, I...DO...NOT...KNOW!"

Only God knows. I know I learned to resign myself to Him once again, with another faith-filled experience.

Walking Papers

I would be the last person ever to believe that I wouldn't be a Sister for the rest of my life. On my calendar, I had struck through three weeks of New Year, 1969, when Dr. Bailey came to my hospital room. He flipped on the light after hanging something on the outside door handle. He appeared to be ready for some important meeting later—with a new tie, crisp shirt, and fresh splash of Old Spice like Grandpa used. Even the few hairs lay smoothed on top of his shiny head. He pulled up the extra chair that Nurse Margie brought earlier that morning for some reason.

"Sister Mary Janet, we've had three years together. I've been consulting with other doctors and with your superiors. How do you feel about your recovery?"

I sat taller in my own chair, laid my pen on my stationery pad, and turned toward him, "Oh, Dr. Bailey, I know I've come a long way. You have been a gold *mind* in my life." I said.

He chuckled, but continued, "You've been one of the most honest and open patients I've experienced in my many years as a military psychiatrist and many years since. I know you want to sign me out, and I'd like to see you do that, too."

That was a confusing surprise. "I don't think I'm quite there yet, Dr. Bailey. Why do I keep coming to the hospital? When can I stop taking the Valium? Am I ever going to be myself again?" I pleaded.

He continued, "Well, my colleagues and I feel it would be good for you to have a year of just rest and relaxation," he paused, "out of the convent."

Silence fell, except for, "Dr. Hall, please come to the nurse's station."

I felt my face whiten, and I stared right through him. My stomach tightened. I lost my breath.

I flew out of my chair, put my hands on my hips, and bent over to his face, "You have to be kidding!! What are you talking about, Dr. Bailey?"

He whispered, as if to hint for me to lower my voice, "I see you're upset, Sister Mary Janet."

"You and your colleagues! You already admitted you don't know that much about nuns and religious life. What do your so-called colleagues know? I'm taking up for myself!"

I grabbed a folder and jumped from the bang when it slammed the floor. I felt better. I was distracted for a few seconds.

Embarrassed, I sat down again, but eyed the lined trashcan at my feet. When I kicked it, wadded tissues and tiny, pleated-paper, pill-cups scattered frantically under my high, hospital bed.

Dr. Bailey's eyebrows rose, and his eyeballs bulged. "Well, I was going to ask about your feelings—but you just did. Any more thoughts?" he asked in my moment of *silent* perplexity and rage.

"Yes, I *do,* Dr. Bailey! You know how much I love being a Sister. Leaving has never entered my mind, even with my challenges. I've enjoyed my missions, especially the Sisters, community life, sharing, working and praying together. You know that!"

I got up to go nowhere, except for about three feet from the side of my bed to the door and back, not saying anything for a long time.

"It'll be embarrassing when I run into students and their parents, and they recognize me. They'll feel awkward, too. We won't know what to say. I don't even want to think about it. I'm confused and can't see how running away from the situation will help."

"You won't be running away. Remember, you'll be able to return. When our bodies and minds run out of energy, we have to give them a break to heal. It will be your medicine for the year, like the military personnel need—R and R—rest and relaxation.

"Sister," he continued, "you'll still be a full-fledged nun the entire year. You can go back to the convent. I've spoken with your superiors—you know that I keep in touch with them. They agree, too, and say to do what we all think is best for you."

My volume rose a few notches. "You can't be serious. I have to wrap my mind around this—it's making me dizzy."

His eyes followed the *dizzy* steam from his coffee cup. "Why do you think you're here?"

Besides my volume, my speed also increased as I stumbled over my words. "I got sick because I was naive and didn't realize I could've spoken up for myself. I didn't say 'no' to all the work I was asked to do. It wasn't the Sisters' fault, but it wasn't my fault either. I thought I was obeying, and I was. We inherited the religious formation many of the Sisters brought from the old country. They'll think I blame them or that I don't appreciate all they've done for me."

He sat pan-faced and waited, so I fumed on.

"Dr. Bailey, I only know how to teach music. I'm not ready to teach in *any* school yet, private or public. Besides, it takes a long time to build a group of piano students. You don't just hang up a sign—PIANO LESSONS—and quickly gather enough students to support yourself. Even if I had a piano and pupils, I have nowhere to live, no money to feed myself. I don't even know how to punch a cash register."

He showed a little life, when he nodded.

"But really, what will I do for a job? Where will I live? I don't own a penny. I can wear this black skirt with colored, printed blouses, but I'll need lots of other clothes, shoes, food, an apartment and transportation—so many other things."

This time I waited for him to break his silence.

"Your family will help you," he said. "Your parents won't make you live on the streets."

Short seconds of quiet were long minutes of unbelief. He looked up from a steam-bare cup, but said nothing. Both of us were still a long time. "Doctor Bailey, how on earth am I supposed to *act*?"

"Live as if you were not a Sister."

In the middle of talking about something serious, I asked, "So, you're saying I can be free to do *anything*?"

Dr. Bailey actually blushed and shook his head. "You know what I mean. Sister Agnes Ann says you won't be expected to say your required daily prayers, things like that. Go on dates, as any young person would. You're beautiful and will have many romantic offers. Behave yourself, of course. Travel. Have fun."

"Oh, yes, *have fun*! Thumb a ride across the country. I do have lots of fun in the convent with the Sisters. You really don't get it, Dr. Bailey."

He shifted in his chair and ignored my expletives. "I haven't spoken with your parents yet. Thought maybe you wanted to tell them."

"Oh, no! Oh, YES! I have to tell my parents!" My palms gripped my cheeks.

"I'll probably feel worse when I have time to think about it and let it settle in my mind: when I realize I'm not dreaming and think about all it will involve."

"Like what?" he prodded.

I got up and walked to the window, watching passers-by, a long few minutes. I grabbed a handful of tissues and bawled uncontrollably, like a newborn.

His eyes never left me. He let me think and deliberate. I had no choice. They had all agreed; that was it. However, I still had many questions.

The furrows on Dr. Bailey's face hung like runs of over sprayed paint. He was as wilted as I; but I spoke slowly, "I'll be counting the days to go back; I know I will."

I do not think he understood what I really felt.

He tilted his head left and right slowly, as if he were wondering whether I would be as *free* as I should, if I were counting days with determination to return. Maybe he thought I'd return to the convent, even though I might come to realize I shouldn't, for whatever reason.

Dr. Bailey just looked at me, but I read his eyes. He knew he had just laid a heavy—one I knew would always be with me. He stretched his long legs, rose, pursed his lips, and walked to the big, metal door. Its slam echoed the sound of my heavy heart. I was his important meeting that day.

ANOTHER NEW LIFE

I had to calm myself after the fiasco with Dr. Bailey, when he convinced me to leave the convent for a year of rest and relaxation. Our conversation haunted me all night.

However, I sheepishly grinned when he showed up early the next morning. "Dr. Bailey, you know I want to get well. I'll do my best to live just as you're asking. If I don't use this year the way you say I should, I'm just prolonging my situation. I'd better call Mom myself. I know it'll be hard for her to accept, but I know that she and Dad will make the transition as easy as possible. I'll call her tonight."

Dr. Bailey nodded. His eyes teared. I knew he understood how hard it was for me to accept these walking papers. He knew I was resolved to take all of the new *medicine* he was prescribing for the entire year. God was sprouting a new, long limb in the tree of my life.

I prayed, *Lord, if this is what I have to do, I must resign myself to Your word.*

I had many questions. How would I tell Mom? What would I say? What if Dad answers the phone? What if they get upset or quiz me?

I remembered having questions like that when I wanted to ask them to *enter* the convent about thirteen years earlier. I had taken months to gather the courage, ended up writing to tell Aunt Sister Clair and let Mom read the letter. She had said they expected it. That was then—this was different. I had just hours to pull myself together to announce I'm leaving temporarily.

I decided to call before Dad got home from work. No time to get flustered, just pick up the phone, and let God take over. I did. I tried to calm my quivering voice, and hoped she didn't hear my heart thudding against my ribcage.

I remember the exact words—short, sweet, to the point: "Mom, Dr. Bailey, thinks a year of leave from the convent would be good for me."

"Le-e-eave?"

"He says I can go back at the end of the year. The Sisters agree. I know it's last minute, but he says maybe in two days?"

"That soon?"

"I don't want to interrupt the house, but is it okay to go home for a while?"

"Uh, sure."

"I just have a small suitcase, and I can help out grocery shopping, cooking, cleaning, taking Grandma Ahmama to the doctor—things like that—until I find a job and get my own apartment."

"Oh, I see," she said quietly. I pictured her staring at the phone, biting her upper lip. She continued with more perk in her voice, "Mary Jo, that'll be fine! We'd love to have you home. We'll have a place for you. Two days—Friday. I'll be there by check-out at ten."

I did it. I told Mom. I knew she would assure me.

⁓

Dr. Bailey came again, after his shift.

"I told Mom, Dr. Bailey. I needed to get it over with, so I didn't talk long. Now it'll be on my mind all night." He prescribed a stronger sleeping pill. I conked out that evening.

Early the next afternoon, my two sisters, Jerri and Patti, made efforts to awaken me from my deep sleep. I was still trying to overcome the sleeping meds. My mind was wondering around in its sleep. "Mary Jo, Mary Jo," they called, shaking my shoulders as I lay on my back.

I barely opened my eyes to behold two faces peering over me with heavy stage makeup, including long, false eyelashes. They had just held a brunch-fashion show at Frost Brothers a few miles away from Santa Rosa Hospital. I hardly recognized my own sisters. My *own* eyes radiated redness and sandy gunk.

"What are you doing here?" I asked with effort to gain *cognizant*-consciousness.

They took turns calling out: "Wake up! Hurry! We can stay only a short time. Mom told us about your news. We have a proposal. We're excited. Come on, girl. Wake up!"

Both yanked to help me sit on the side of the bed. I folded over like a tall, barely stuffed giraffe. "I'm still groggy from the strong sleeping pill I got last night. Seems like it's the middle of the night. I had to go back to sleep after breakfast." I flopped to one side.

"Oh, Patti," Jerri belted, "she'll be perfect with makeup and a good haircut. She has a Geoffrey Beene bod."

"Hey, whatta ya talking about?" I slurred. My tongue and my mouth hung open like a drunk.

They pulled over the wooden chair to share, but kept a determined look-up at me.

"Mary Jo, we've been discussing since last night. We have something for you," Jerri said. "We need another good model at Frost Brothers, and we know you can do it. You have the chiseled face, and you're tall with the high-fashion-model figure."

Those words slapped me awake; my gunky eyes glared wider. I sounded a high-pitched, piercing, "You've *got* to be kidding! No way. N-o-o-o way!"

"Wait! Wait!" Patti stood up, interrupting my freakish expletives.

I upped her volume a level, "What do I know about clothes, hair, and makeup—other than black and white and religious garb?"

A long sound of silence. Eventually, I rattled, "This makes me nervous. When I get nervous, I gotta pee. Gimme a minute." I wobbled off the bed, left them alone and staggered into my bathroom. I could hear them talking, but I couldn't understand what they were saying—my heart was pounding too loudly.

When I reappeared, Jerri whispered, "Mary Jo, just *listen* to what we have to say, okay? We're going to help you."

I politely shut up, but drooped to one side again.

"I'll train you, Mary Jo," Patti low-toned.

Jerri assured, "We're not going to let you work until you're ready. We wouldn't *want* you to do that."

"Just take time to think about it, Mary Jo," Patti said. "You'll be great. Just relax. We must get home. Kids are getting out of school. We'll see you tomorrow at Mom's." They left.

I lay down, rested my lids, and inhaled. I needed to breathe again. I reminded myself that Jerri *was* the fashion coordinator of Frost Brothers, and I knew that any model would desperately aspire to work at Frost: that was the highest level a model could attain in San Antonio. My eyes popped open—that thought didn't help; in fact, it was daunting.

And Patti? She had reached the pinnacle as *the* top high-fashion model in San Antonio. She far surpassed the other models. With her picture on the cover of *Vogue* Magazine, she had hundreds of photos in local newspapers, and had lots of TV experience. She and Jerri worked for just about all of New York's and many of the world's finest designers. Jerri even owned her own modeling agency. They certainly were successful, seemed sincere about helping me, and believed I could do it. But it wasn't me!

Back to thoughts of realities: What other jobs could I do? Maybe help Dad at Barbera Sports. I could dust, sweep, greet customers, fold or hang sporting clothes. I could even wash the huge windows facing Broadway and the side windows on McCullough of that enormous place. Yet, they wouldn't have enough work to pay for my financial needs.

What kind of life would the nuns think I was living? I wouldn't want them to see me in all that makeup. I couldn't keep it a secret. They'd find out, when I'd visit them and Aunt Sister Clair in the summer. They might not want me back after being a model.

Worse yet—what if my students saw me in fashion shows, in the papers, or on TV? My former students and their parents from St. Mary's and St. Henry's were scattered all over San Antonio. I remembered the student I taught, who worked as a candy striper right there at Santa Rosa Hospital. She took me in a wheel chair for my psychological exam. I can't hide.

When I was a teenager, Mom pointed out a woman in St. Ann's Church parking lot. "The lady getting into that blue Chevy used to be a nun." People will talk about me; but I'll stir up *more* gossip: "That model was a NUN! ERRRRR!" I sat up in bed.

I couldn't leave for a year and be relaxed. What was Dr. Bailey thinking?

Burying my head in my pillow, I deafened my thoughts with my yells. I didn't need that. If I didn't live in San Antonio, it would still be hard, but not *as* hard—no one would know me. Modeling was not even an option—I had to get my head out of the sand—of this pillow.

What do I tell men who take me on dates, when they ask, "What do you do?" That is a *perfect* icebreaker! Everyone does something—except Mary Jo!

Would I say, "Oh, I'm a piano teacher; I just don't have any students?" We would have great conversations. My dates would have a hay day with questions!

Dr. Bailey says to relax! I am going to be stressed, but in a different format: a walking *sandwich board* of conversation! How could I be so naïve? Dr. Bailey was right when he said he doesn't understand religious life. I wonder if it occurred to him that I'd be waddling out into the world in stress—up to my ears.

The rest of the day, I stayed in the Sisters' chapel on a patient-pass. I had had it about a year for *being responsible by checking out and back at the nurse's station.* I sat a few pews from the altar gazing at the familiar peace in the large, dim, Gothic setting. Tall candles, with flames pointing praise to Heaven, directed my thoughts upward. I needed no words. I just sat—with Him. He knew my every breath and requests. Time ticked, ticked and ticked. There was no need to go or do.

For several hours, I prayed, *Thank You, Heavenly Father, for my long stays here on my road to recovery. Should I open my mind, humble myself, and accept the generous offer Jerri and Patti are extending to me, even though I would be on stage for all of San Antonio to see, exposing myself to gossip? You know it is not my cup of tea. I have no desire to model and be perfection with hair, makeup, and clothes; but I do love and trust my two sisters. I appreciate what they're trying to do. Please be with me.*

I sat. Paused. Then I continued. *Help me know what to do when I leave tomorrow and start a new life.* I rose slowly, genuflected on my right knee, and walked serenely back to Room 1109. Tomorrow would come too soon.

Friday arrived on time. Mom knocked on my door exactly at ten. She wore her special navy skirt, gray blouse with small ruffle at the neck and at the end of the long sleeved cuffs. Her pearl necklace draped below her usual big, beautiful smile. I wore my black, knee-length skirt and white blouse, no veil, and five-and-dime Mary Jane shoes with plastic soles, and a grateful smile.

"The family's eager to have you come home!" she greeted. She must have been on the phone all evening, and have been exhausted. Knowing Mom, she worked to have plenty of food, to perk up the house and to have a bed ready somewhere. We hugged a long time before I picked up my tattered, small, black cardboard suitcase. We tried to be relaxed and chatted calmly all the way home.

My life was beginning once again.

PHOTOS
CONVENT

Family – Day of Send Off to convent: L to R: Mom Winnie, Aunt Tantan, Daddy Joe, Mary Jo, Grandparents Danny and Ahmama Osborn, sisters Jerri and Patti. Front L to R: sisters Peggy, Candy and Mae

Unloading trunk at Our Lady of the Lake (OLL) Convent , San Antonio, Texas. L to R: Imelda (my assigned angel), Patti, under trunk Candy and neighbor, Mary Jo, Jerri and Cynthia Vollmer (my school chum).

Home and car on Huisache and Breeden two blocks from
grandparents and Tantan's home.

Mary Jo, freshman picture in
Providence High School uniform.

Mary Jo praying at outside station of the cross in
pecan grove at OLL.

I studied often on second floor porch of aspirancy watching
for family cars on visiting Sundays.

Mary Jo (back row, far right) is captain-for-the-day for aspirant basketball team game.

Senior class in aspirancy. Mary Jo back row, 2nd from left.

Family on Conventual steps on
graduation Sunday.

Mary Jo (age 16) high school
graduation picture.

Top of Cross Mountain in
Castroville, TX, at Moye school
for summer credits needed to skip
junior of high school.

I'm in the pink formal Mom
lovingly made. I wore the
layers of gathered net tulle,
edged with many yards of
thin pink ribbon, during
multiple piano recitals and
programs as a sophomore in
high school.

At grotto at Moye on visting Sunday.

Mary Jo, Aug. 1956,
front porch of home
on Huisache.

Postulate in background.
Mary Jo's angel Mary
Catherine.

Annual Christmas picture
Mom Winnie designed,
drew, assembled in home
living room.

Sister Ann Joseph with new postulants on Cape Day. Mary Jo in top row far right.
(Frances Ann, her music buddy in far left of same back row.)

Mary Jo, postulant, at altar preparing for daily Mass in Conventual Chapel at OLL.

June 1958. Postulants are dressed as Brides of Christ before Investiture Ceremony. Mary Jo is in front row, second from left. They erased their big smiles, just before this photo was shot, when Sister St. John said, "This is not the time to advertise for toothpaste."

Little Mae shares a double pew with Aunt Tantan
and smiles at her biggest sister Mary Jo.

Mary Jo is front forward with her "bundle," just before the group heads to a room upstairs to get their hair cut and return dressed as novices in the habit in white veil and receive their religious names.

Investiture Day, June 1958, bottom row, L to R: Aunt Nancy Osborn, Grandma Nona Barbera, my godfather Uncle Pat (Nancy's husband) holding Ann, Candy (behind Ann), mother Winnie, Jerri, new novice Sister Mary Janet (formally Mary Jo). Back row, L to R: Aunt Sister Clair Osborn, Patti, grandparents Danny and Ahmama Osborn, and dad Joe.

Aunt Sister Clair Osborn with me,
a new novice named Sister Mary Janet Barbera.

Final Profession of vows for life (after five years of yearly vows), received gold ring with triangle and eye of Providence, wore wreaths for the day.

On her first mission assignment in Abilene, TX, Sister Mary Janet teaches a class unit on orchestral instruments to seventh and eighth graders at St. Joseph Academy for day and boarding students.

Grandparents first in family to own a television set, years before any TVs were in homes: Charles F. Barbera, Sr., and wife Nona (Mary Rose Giovannazzi), with Mary Jo's sisters Mae and Peggy.

Little sisters grow up. L to R: Mae, Jerri, bride Patti, Sister Mary Janet, Peggy and Candy. Latest wedding fashion.

Filligreed, fancy fashions and eyeglass frame of the time! Mom Winnie, Candy, little Peggy, Sister Mary Janet, bride Jerri, Aunt Sister Clair, Patti, Mae (front).

JF Kennedy picture in motorcade in San Antonio. Day before he was killed.

After years of annual vows, Bishop John L. Morkovsky says "Sister Mary Janet, receive as His spouse the ring of faith..." Aug. 2, 1965.

"Go the Mass is ended." Sister Mary Janet, eyes closed in deep emotion and love for, and devotion to, her life as a Sister of Divine Providence.

Picnic with family after final vow ceremony.

ESTELLE AHMAMA IN BACK   SR. MARY JANET   SISTER WILMA   SISTER JUSTINE   SISTER CAROL

Rock-a-Bye, Baby, Rock, Rock. Sister Mary Janet (with guitar) and part of her singing group surprise her family at Christmas 1967.

Inside Sacred Heart Conventual Chapel in 1955 on Our Lady of the Lake (OLL) campus for daily Mass, community prayer, and all formal ceremonies.

Sister Mary Janet in new change of head piece and mid' 60s-fashion eyeglass.

THIS OLE GREAT POSE WON TWO PRIZES IN NATIONAL PHOTO CONTEST

"Captain" Sister Mary Janet at the wheel of her dad's boat!
This ole' great pose won two prizes in national photo contest.

Perpetual Adoration Chapel in 1955 where the Sisters rotated 24/7
in the presence of the Blessed Sacrament.

Sisters' Orchestra - Sister Mary Janet plays clarinet. Back row, 2nd left.

The Singing Nuns – The young nurses obtained several off campus gigs for us.
I'm with the guitar on the right.

CATWALK

Before and After

Ding. Ding. Ding. The doorbell rang repeatedly. From across the living room, I could see my sister Patti through the large mirror that extended from Mom's built-in, four-foot high planter just inside the front door.

"What a surprise!" I opened the door. "I have to get used to these nice, unexpected visits if I'm going to be home for a year." I was thinking, *Gee, after thirteen years of my family making an appointment or having specific days for family visits, this is a big adjustment. What if I have other plans? I'm embarrassed to ask them to let me know when they're coming.*

Patti's face was Dresden-doll-flawless—attention-getting from her eyebrows, eyelids, eyeliner, and long, mascaraed eyelashes to her lightly tinted cheeks and chin, and outlined, painted lips. Her dyed, red hair completed the look with a *Vogue* knob on top.

After we exchanged kisses, Patti stretched out both hands and gently presented me with a coat hanger covered by a long, white, plastic bag. "I made you something." She tilted her head and smiled lovingly. "I hope you like it and especially hope that it fits!"

I held the hanger above my head, while she carefully lifted the covering. Patti put her hands under the plastic bag, opened it into a wide tent and ducked her head inside. She removed the precious garment and bestowed it on me with both hands. Taking advantage of standing in the center of the large rug in the living room, she had a perfect opportunity to make a dramatic presentation.

"Oh, Patti, the colors are beautiful. What is it?"

"Mary Jo, long pant-suits for women are hitting the scene—very high fashion, dressy or casual. They will go everywhere—home, shopping, restaurants, parties, and even to church." My smile shrunk to a slit as I raised my eyebrows, which she did not detect—she was studying the outfit, and continued. "These are the latest colors, too. They're called avocado-green, loud pink, and purple. I especially like the tropical flowers and leaves on the white background," she said.

I stood frozen. *She expects me to wear those? I never wore clothes that loud as a teenager. I'm almost thirty years old.*

The pants go to church? Well, they are pretty. I exhaled my deep breath.

"Patti, you *made* all of these? They are gorgeous! I love the colors. It must have taken a long time to sew." I hugged her again. My frozen body began to thaw—somewhat.

"Well, you know I'm not a seamstress. Someone else would have done it faster and better. These new zippers are easy to sew, not like the ones we dreaded as teenagers. Come on, let's go to the back bedroom and see if everything fits."

"This collection is called a mix-and-match," she said, as we walked down the short hallway to the flocked-red wallpapered bedroom I shared with Mae.

I stripped to my undies and pulled the long, pants up my legs, trying to keep them from wrinkling. The unfamiliar cloth felt different from our serge that rumpled at times. Obviously, she had pressed it carefully.

Patti helped draw the sleeveless, stand-up-neck tunic over my head. It hung about eight inches past my waist. She unwound a two-yard length, six-inch wide, avocado green sash. "Now, Mary Jo, this is another, highly fashionable, trend— the long sash. See how I picked up the avocado green in the print fabric to make this sash? You may wear it in your hair or around your neck." She wrapped the band tightly around my waist and knotted it off-centered to my left.

I stepped in front of the floor length mirror. "It fits perfectly, Patti!"

"Yes, it does. I can breathe a sigh of relief now," she said. "But wait, there's more. Where are the shorts? I know I brought them."

"Shorts?"

"Yes, mini-shorts."

"You're kidding, right?"

"Don't worry. I didn't make them as short as I wear mine. Now, Mary Jo, you do not want to wear those things we wore in '50s, you hear? Those shorts are outdated. You'll get used to mini-shorts, when everyone else starts wearing them. I am always ahead with the new trend. When everybody's dressed in the latest, I like to jump to the next fad."

"Oh, here are the shorts under this plastic bag," I said. My thoughts gasped, *Oh dear, they are short! What am I getting myself into? My head's spinning. Maybe I should have left them under the bag. I remember thinking I was half-naked when I showed up in chapel the first morning we could change from the big, serge habit to the simple little suits. Now I will be half-naked!*

Patti interrupted my thoughts, "Good. Let's see how they fit. Leave the tunic on."

I felt rushed.

They were perfect too, although I knew I'd feel better when the fashion had become popular, and I was among others wearing them that short.

"Now, Mary Jo, we need to get you some white shoes with heels."

"Oh, no, not heels! I can just feel myself stumbling."

"Yes, heels! You do not wear pants with flats. Heels are chunky ones. They are going to be the rage and will be in all our shows in a few weeks with spring fashions. They are comfortable and easy to wear. Besides, you will be wearing all kinds of heels in fashion shows.

"We need to go to Solo-Serve. We love that place. It's two blocks away, just past church on San Pedro. Bobby Grimm is the manager. Remember the Grimms, Mom and Dad's favorite couple?"

"*Do* I? I went to the senior prom with his brother, Cacky, when I was a freshman," I reminded.

Patti laughed as she helped me undress. "How could I forget? I'll re-introduce him to you. Sometimes he lets us know when a big shipment of clothing comes in from the better-ready-to-wear stores, like Frost Brothers. We have to look for possible flaws. Sometimes items have the wrong size, or the garment has a label upside down. It costs too much to retag, or rip and re-sew many labels. Solo-Serve sells everything about 50% off."

I was distracted, apprehensive about Bobby Grimm. *What if he welcomes me with a loud voice and asks about my leaving the convent? What if other customers overhear him? He always sees Patti dressed in the future upcoming styles with lots of makeup. Then he'd eye me dressed as I am. Embarrassing.*

Mom's large grandfather clock struck ten. Stores were opening.

"Okay, Mary Jo, you're heading out with me now. I'm all excited. We have lots to do today. Spring shows start in three weeks. I'll be busy working with Jerri, and I've booked myself solid for our busiest season. I want to have time to teach you the ropes.

"You'll be in all of the shows and do the floor modeling at Frost Brothers. Jerri is depending on you. We have lots to buy: makeup, shoes and much at Solo Serve. I'll take you to lunch while we're out."

My mind felt pressure, rush, bombardment. *Whoa! She has to be kidding! They didn't tell me I had to start so soon.* My insides were rumbling again.

I scooped up my little black zippered-bag that replicated a cheap bank purse. Patti eyed it, probably wondering whether I really needed to bring such a thing along in public. I didn't blame her. I'd be self-conscious if I were in her fancy, stylish shoes—with heels!

I inhaled. *Am I doing the right thing, this fashion show, modeling stuff? Can I actually pull it off? This is overwhelming. Why did I let Jerri and Patti talk me into this? They said I would be perfect, but never told me all these details. They were kind, but smart!*

I only have the hundred dollars the Sisters gave me. I didn't want to bring it from the convent, but now I'm grateful. I don't know what I don't know about this modeling. Is there more? I can't afford much else until I get enough students to teach piano. That will take forever!

Patti knew all she had to do in a very short time. She wasn't bossy, just doing what was needed—matter-of-fact. I needed it—to be guided and pushed for now. I took advantage of the free oxygen and filled my lungs.

What a contrast—from convent to catwalk! I had just stepped into another new life. I felt hit between the eyes with the speed of reality. I still trusted Jerri and Patti. I prayed, *Heavenly Father, I trust You, too.*

I exhaled. My day had just begun, and in new, bright colors!

◦‿◦

After Solo Serve (Bobby Grimm was not in the store), we drove the speed limit to the mall in Patti's faithful Ford. I sat captured in the front passenger seat. We raced into the closest parking spot outside of Beall's department store. I followed her as she zoomed past racks of clothing and carpeted areas of shoes, directly to the cosmetics counter.

Patti immediately started picking up little packages of eye makeup to study the colors; then she reached for shades of blush.

"May I help you lovely ladies?" the clerk asked. She directed her next question to Patti, "You look like you know just what you prefer. Your face is beautifully done."

"I'm the BEFORE—she's the AFTER," I blurted out. They burst into laughter. The ice was broken, but I hoped she would not inquire about my appearance. I examined and fiddled with a few items with no clue what they were, or their purpose. What else was I to do with my hands? I felt like a roll of toilet paper propped in the middle of a banquet table!

I kept my head down, hiding for all to behold, and hoping she would not ask if I had just escaped a penitentiary—or a *convent*, God forbid! I looked as if I had just crawled out of bed with my wacky, self-cut, hair-do that looked the same whether it was combed or not. The little veil I used to wear had covered my hair, except for the front. My face? All I did this morning was wash it in the shower.

Patti collected an assortment of basics. "I have a set of better-quality false eyelashes at home. You can have them," she said. When the cashier read the total, Patti quickly handed her some bills for the payment. I smiled at her in sad appreciation. She was not obliged to pay, but I had no choice. I also knew there would be many more expenses to come.

Patti's financial contribution made me feel as if she were responsible for me. *I needed to start modeling months ago, and I cannot begin until I get training. Then I probably will receive pay weeks after the work.*

Heading for the car, Patti said, "Mary Jo, I'm picking up a bucket of Young-blood's chicken. We can go to my place to eat and have more time doing your face. You'll feel better trying on clothes after your hair's cut and when you're wearing makeup."

"Yeah, I'm sure I'll be more comfortable then," I said. "And I haven't had fried chicken in years. Thanks, Patti." I dotted the tears in my eyes.

After detouring to pick up her son, Joe Jr., from Holy Spirit Elementary and waiting in line at the drive through for the large bucket of Youngblood's, our tummies growled at the smell of peppered, seasoned, hot chicken. By the time we reached her home, we had inhaled our chicken wings in the car and had enough left for other meals. We had plenty of time to decorate my face.

I studied instructions of each little item as I pinched and scraped to remove its cardboard and plastic wrapping while leaning on one end of the black, Spanish-style, padded bench in Patti's family room. Even opening the package was frustrating. Would I ever know what to do with those paints and powders, brushes and pads?

I still had to learn to dress, fix my hair and walk a ramp. I was feeling queasy again and sighed, *Oh, God, what are all of these things Patti has bought for me?*

Patti beckoned from down the hall, "Okay, Mary Jo, come to the bathroom where the lighting is better. Here's a basket for your makeup." She laid it on the marble counter under bright, round makeup lights surrounding three edges of the large mirror.

I radiated a smile with my good idea: "Let's start with the lipstick and blush. I can do that." I picked up the metal tube and plucked off the lid.

"Oh, no, Mary Jo, those are the *last two* things you put on your face. You have to prepare the canvas before you paint." Patti asked me to wash my face. "Every single morning, for the rest of your life, put moisturizer on your face. Makeup dries your skin. You're already twenty-nine, and you don't have one wrinkle, because you haven't had anything on your face for thirteen years."

I shook my head and dropped the little tube into the basket.

Just the reminder I did not need to hear: it's been a long time since I've had any practice. I'm out of style. It has all changed. My skin is going to wrinkle in the process of making it look good enough to model. In the convent, we were not concerned about getting mountains and valleys in our foreheads and chins. She handed me the large jar of white creamy moisturizer.

I applied the magic potion on my face as she insisted, "Just pat it on and always only with your middle finger, gently. Don't rub—pat."

Frustration set in, *This already consumes more time than I want to spend putting on* all *my makeup. I do not look any better! Moisturizer, drats! However, I will be faithful, since she insists.*

The next hour was a blur of techniques: plucking brows, applying foundation, powder, eyelids with three shades in different places, eyeliner under and over, mascara, false eyelashes, shiny, white under the arches of eyebrows. Finally the "last two," as she called it: the blush and lipstick—and she actually *outlined* the lipstick!

Then Patti stood back, looking at me in the mirror. She asked with a big, proud smile, "Now look at your eyes. Don't they just *pop out?*"

I stared into the mirror and giggled inside. They popped out all right: Wide! I was not myself. Her question sounded as if it were supposed to be a compliment. She had worked patiently a long time: I had to agree, "Uh." I swallowed hard. "Yes, but, I don't know what to put on where, and in what order."

"It takes time to do it correctly," she assured, "but it will go a little faster when you get the hang of it."

My stomach churned again, but not from hunger this time. *I'll need at least an hour to get my face ready for a show. In the convent, I washed up, dressed in full habit, made my bed, and walked over to chapel in twenty-five minutes; and I finished thirty minutes of meditation—all in the span of an hour. I have not even learned how to fix my hair, and Patti said I might need different hairstyles in one show.*

I still had the majority of training to endure, but I knew I would always be grateful for these first days of her loving kindness and dedication to help in my *new life*—before to after.

Walking with Rules

In February, only one week into my leave of absence, Patti started *working on me* in her home on the days her husband, Joe Sr., worked out of town. I slept in her guest room. We worked late and began early the next morning.

In her small dining room with a full-mirrored wall opposite the ceiling-to-wall window with same length, soft, sheer drapes on each side, we shoved the table to a corner and put the chairs in another room. We needed the longest possible *ramp* length to walk fast without having to turn around. Walking straight from one corner of the room to the opposite diagonal corner gave us that yardage.

She began demonstrating, while instructing, "Keep your eyes directly ahead of you and your face forward, Mary Jo. Take long strides, one foot in front of the other, stand tall, shoulders relaxed, and let your arms swing freely." She constantly repeated those words while I walked alone. "That's the basic we'll work on a long time."

For greater strides without stopping, I shadowed her from the dining room, through the short hallway, through the small family room, the eating area, kitchen, back to the mirrored dining room. We retraced the circle repeatedly, making grooves in the carpet. She stopped to put the needle down on the large vinyl record of Tijuana Brass with its quick, up-beat rhythms, similar to the speed we would hear while modeling. Again, we floated the circles until I was a dizzy zombie.

"Keep your eyes looking straight forward. Stand tall. Relax your arms. Stay up with me."

"Oh, Patti," I panted as I collapsed on that long-padded bench in the family room. "It's only February, and I've worked up a summer sweat. How do you keep up? This is exhausting. You call this the *basic walk*? Are you sure I can do this?"

We laughed until our ribs were sore.

She went to the kitchen. I closed my eyes and draped myself over the bench.

Minutes later, she sauntered over to me with two malt-shaped glasses. Tall spoons stood between scoops of vanilla ice cream floating on top of root beer that hugged striped, bent-over straws.

"Wow, I haven't had a Black Cow in years!"

"You need some energy food," she said as she raised a hunk of ice cream on her spoon and sat on the other end of the bench with me. "We're just starting. You're doing fine. I'm glad we did your makeup again this morning. You look more like a model, and you walk more like one when you feel like one. You're going to do a pivot and the back-to-back with me when we're finished our snack."

I thought we were finished for the morning. I had forgotten I had makeup on, but I didn't tell her so. I sat tall and stretched my neck to peer into the wooden-framed mirror across the room. Yes, I did look different. "So explain what a back-to-back is," I said between sips of Black Cow.

"Two girls are on the ramp walking toward each other. When they meet in the center of the ramp, they pivot halfway around until they are back-to-back. Then they return to the ends of the ramp. They turn and walk back to the center of the ramp. But instead of doing a back-to-back, they *pass* each other and continue to the *opposite* end from where they started," she explained and demonstrated in the middle of the room.

My heart was pounding. My stomach felt it was *riding* that Black Cow. "Oh, no! It sounds complicated, Patti. How do I remember all that?"

"You practice it until it comes naturally. Mary Jo, you're doing a crash course. This is just your first day. You don't have much time to practice on your own while you're at my house. I'm using this valuable time to show you what to practice at Mom's in her long den. It's better than my small dining room. She has these same musical recordings. You'll get it; I know you will. We have to be ready in a few weeks."

I did not want to think about chickening out. I had to stay as positive as Patti. She and Jerri were depending on me.

The next day, we sat in her breakfast area on high stools around a tall, round table enjoying our invented concoction of toast with melted American cheese topped with mashed avocado.

"Now, Mary Jo, there is still much to learn, but I'll show you as we go along. There are rules to remember."

I was surprised and reflected, *I know all about rules. I lived rules in the convent for thirteen years. More rules!? What am I getting myself into?* I grabbed a pencil and the roof-repair door-flyer next to me on the table.

Patti sat on the tall stool, crossed one knee over the other, and clicked her long, painted, pointy fingernails on the high table. She paused. Then she looked up and read, as if from her mental script:

1. First, and foremost: I don't care if it's a gunnysack. You love it! You model it as if you adore it. You *never* let on, especially to a designer, that you don't like a garment, bag, coat...anything!

2. Never sit in a department store dress or trunk dress. Neither Frost Brothers nor the designer tolerates a model wrinkling a garment.

3. Never eat in the dressing room or have food and drink around the clothes. Crumbs attract mice, and drinks destroy clothes.

4. Always be on time, even early, with full, stage makeup applied. For a show, arrive with your hair the way Jerri or the designer requests: slick, teased, casual, long or short. Have wigs or wig-pieces ready. We have to get those for you, too.

5. In just about every show, we model the sporty, the lunch-wear and the formal eveningwear. Sometimes we show beach or lingerie.

6. You are a coat hanger—a mannequin. When a designer has a trunk showing, we line up in a semi-circle, only in our panty hose and bras in the Frost Brothers dressing room. He brings mainly dresses, pants and coats, and assigns them according to the body-shape and look of each girl. It saves lots of time to see what he has to work with. Get used to that.

She got up, her forehead a little furrowed, her teeth biting the side of her lip. "I guess those are the main points. I'll cue you in if I think of anything more."

Was she joking? I waited for the punch line, but it never showed up.

My mind circled: *I don't have anything to hang a bikini on! How will I get out of those shows?! I don't care if they tell me they don't want me in lingerie events.* I tried to quell the angry flames my eyes burned in the wall across the room.

I wrapped my sweater around my body from February's cool air. Perhaps I was cold from the idea that my bare body could be standing in just my bra and panty hose in a room full of models, and a male or female stranger.

Patti adjusted the central heating unit.

"You must display the outfits beautifully," she said. "The dressing room behind the stage for shows is another story. I'll help you the first times, but I'll have my own station to set up, so you'll have to be on your own soon."

Whoa! Now I really wanted out. I wanted to tell her so, at that moment. *Shh!* I told myself, *Just trust her and remember the rules—and the paycheck. You can do this. You need to do this.*

⌒

Eventually, with diligent practice, I learned the choreography of the ramp, but the hair was different. When I was a teen, stylists loved my hair because it had what they called "great body and easy management." That was *their* experience. I did not know what that meant. I thought they liked it because it was pitch-black and shiny.

I was not out of the convent a full week, and my concern was hairy. Where would I go to be styled reasonably? How would I have it cut, knowing I might need various flairs within one show? I could wash it, but I didn't know what rollers to use or how to use them. Were the new hot rollers quicker and easier than a blow dryer? Where would I go for a crash course in hair styling? Of the many challenges I faced, hair seemed the most daunting.

Lying in bed at night, I quizzed myself. *I do not want to ask any family member for help—they will think I'm looking for another handout. Lord, I place this mercenary situation into Your hands. You've provided me with a clean, good job. Now, please help me with such an earthly challenge.*

Night awoke with the sun and an early phone call from Patti.

I yawned with my eyes still closed and put the receiver on the pillow next to my ear. "Hello-o-o?"

"Mary Jo, get up! I made you an appointment with Robert, my hairdresser, in forty-five minutes. Wash your hair so we won't have to pay him for a shampoo..."

While she was racing on about something, I popped out of bed, began unbuttoning my PJs with my free hand, and grabbed my undies. "...I'll pick you up in thirty minutes." CLICK. BUZZ. BUZZ.

I slammed the phone down, held my undies close to my body and snuck quickly, hopefully unseen, to the bathroom. I didn't want to wake Mom when passing her room.

I yelled quietly to myself the entire time. *Okay, I can do this. I have had thirteen years of experience washing and dressing fast. This is my* forte. I rushed into the shower and yanked the curtain.

My sudsy washcloth circled my face and reached higher to bubble my hair. I finished my eight-minute shower and deodorant soap shampoo, bolted out, dried off, and wiped the steam from the mirror. *My face! I have to put my makeup on all by myself. Not today! Not in this mad hustle!*

I towel-dried my hair, slew underthings on, grasped the towel close to my front, and tiptoed back to my room. I was glad Mae and Peggy were in school, and Dad was at work—no challenge for privacy from them.

A sudden decision seared my brain. *What do I wear? I don't have time to ask Patti. I haven't made a decision like this in thirteen years.*

I took that last thought back: I recalled having to decide in the convent whether to change from my black habit to the little black suit—*half-naked: my hair would be showing!!* If I waited a day or so, I'd see whether many other Sisters had changed. A hard decision then—old habit or new one—seemed easy now when selecting from a closet full and be stylish.

I stepped over a pile of laundry and slid the door open on my side of the closet questioning, *I have these lovely hand-me-ups from my five sisters that Patti gathered and brought last night. She assured me they were all perfect to wear, not outdated. She said she had told them to give me only things they would still wear, but hadn't worn much anymore.*

I selected a warm, button-down, light blue sweater with a brown skirt from my sister Candy. I held it up and smiled. No time to reminisce. I had to put on my face.

I grabbed the clear, zippered cosmetic bag with its goodies and flew back to the bathroom for better lighting—as if the light was going to help me know what to put where and how?

The grandfather clock warned I had ten minutes until Patti's arrival. Breakfast wasn't important!

Moisturizer! I knew that was first, and I promised to use it. She'd be proud of me and she'd ask if I had dotted it on properly.

Panic attack made me dizzy. I stared at the other stuff: no time for foundation. I opened the dark brown eyelid stuff. Did it go on the lid or on the *crease* in the lid? I don't recall where I put it, but it went somewhere on my eyes, so did some lighter brown. I didn't have time to tackle eye liner.

Mascara—it just goes on my eyelashes—that should be quick and easy! But I must hurry. Only five minutes left. I had forgotten that when I untwisted and pulled the lid, a little stick came out, too, with a brush loaded with what looked like tar.

I poked the little brush toward my eyelashes and jabbed my right eyelid. My eye blurred. I felt nauseous with panic. What to do with that hunk of junk around my eye? I couldn't believe it. I snatched a fistful of tissues from the little box on the counter. Trying to remove it just schmeered it worse. I glared into the mirror, *Yikes!! I look like someone socked me in the eye! What do I do?*

Makeup remover! I added a few drops to the tissue, rubbed ferociously, and thought I'd gone blind from the layer of tar and oily mixture on my eyeball. I frantically repainted my right eyelid with the same shades of brown on my left lid. Circles of blush put life into my pallid cheeks. My twitching fingers scooped up all of the items, chucked them back into the clear, zipper-bag, and dropped it into my shoulder-strap purse that Jerri gave me.

DING.DING.DING. Patti was at the door. I scurried to greet her, and hoped she'd be proud of my efforts to dress, to apply moisturizer and face paints, and to recover my accident with the mascara.

"Your skirt and sweater look nice," Patti said. I felt good. I'd passed my first test. As we headed directly to the car, I said, "Thanks. I did my makeup, too!"

She looked from the corner of her eyes at my face again and nodded politely.

Minutes flew by, and so did we. Patti pulled into the small lot at Robert's simple, but efficient salon.

"This is Mary Jo, a new model for Frosts, so you'll be seeing each other often," she said. I didn't yet know why I was supposed to see him *often*. Robert pointed to the large barber chair. He studied my hair while he and Patti exchanged tidbits about what she wanted him to do. Robert ran his fingers through my locks, fluffed it up and under. He slid it between his fingers, "Very nice body, but you need a better shampoo."

I stared. I hoped he didn't ask why my hair was wacked and bent out of shape, or what shampoo I used. I squirmed in the seat and wrapped my fingers around the ends of the barber chair's arms.

As Robert clipped, Patti sat in the vacant barber chair next to me, bent forward with a pad and pencil, and explained, "Robert, Mary Jo has dark hair, and the fuzz over her lip is dark, too. I don't want her to shave it. Would you mix some of your bleach and powder for facial hair? I'll pay you."

My body went numb, except for the skin on the back of my neck that rippled—I hoped he didn't notice.

Robert stopped clipping and stood in front of my face to examine my upper lip closely. "Yeah. Remind me before you leave." Everything was matter-of-fact and nonchalant: I was a mannequin.

I left with a teased hairdo, one black eye of stubborn makeup, and bleach for my moustache.

We climbed into the car.

On the drive home, Patti explained that Robert also worked in the Frost Bros. hair salon. After Jerri booked us for a show, we could make an appointment and tell him how Jerri wanted the style—sleek or puffed. He would cut, color, and/or style for us. We'd sign a voucher and leave a tip.

At last, I felt there was something I could live with.

Patti worked with me almost daily on weekdays and overnights when Joe Sr. was out of town. We crammed speed walks, turns and pivots. We struck single and group on-the-spot poses for ramp shows and finales, and for newspapers. We drilled head turns and footwork, serious and fun looks.

I learned what to do with arms and hands, and how to open coats from bottom to top—my hands would be in place to remove the coat and drag it carefully. I practiced how to hold a bag over my shoulder or arm so it didn't detract from the dress.

Was I still missing something? I would find out soon enough—too soon, if we started work in a couple of weeks.

On Live TV

I picked up the phone. Jerri sounded hurried, "Mary Jo, tomorrow night Frost Brothers is providing five models for the local annual TV Awards Ceremony. You're to be at Channel 5 Studios in full stage makeup..."

"Hey Jerri, wait," I dropped my half-eaten sandwich, sprang from my chair and shouted, "I'm not ready to model yet. It's been only ten days since I left the convent, and you said I wouldn't start..."

She interrupted, "Just stay calm and listen. You will not be modeling, just handing trophies to managers of the TV channels. Managers will present the trophies to the winners of their station."

That put my mind at ease, somewhat, but my heart was speeding. What I had eaten of my sandwich wanted to return to the plate. I grabbed a pen and pad, but my fingers shook so vigorously, I let Jerry continue her lecture.

"Patti said she's on the way over to you to help select your clothes."

"You mean I have to wear my own?" I asked. I sank back into my chair.

"Patti says you have some outfits you bought from Solo Serve. I have to call the other models. Patti will fill you in on details. This is exciting. See you tomorrow evening. Don't worry, you'll be fine."

Jerri hung up—I hung on. I peeled my frozen fingers from the receiver thinking, *Oh, this is just great. My first event is on live television. All of San Antonio's viewing audience will watch me be a clutch!*

I gulped what remained of my sandwich.

DING.DING.DING. Patti had wasted no minutes.

"Now, Mary Jo, I know this is unexpected, but we got the perfect combination of clothing yesterday." Her voice quivered a bit from the last-minute rush. "You can do this."

We raced down the hallway to my red-flocked, fleur de leis papered bed-room. The closet door banged as Patti slammed it to slide right. She yanked my short, front-pleated, blue skirt—with high waist and large, false buckle—off the hanger and threw it over her arm.

She grabbed an organza white blouse with the large puffed, long sleeves and the wide cuffs. It was a pullover with a V-neck and wide collar. The outfit was one of my favorites with my new black patent leather, two inch, chunky-heeled shoes with a two-inch flap across the top.

Despite the preferred, chosen selection, I felt wiped out from frantic stress and still had an entire sandwich in my stomach waiting to make its way up and out.

∽

Morning tore through the night. Patti picked me up early for a hair ap-pointment with Robert downtown at Frost Brothers. While there, we took the elevator to the third- floor Ladies' Better Ready-to-Wear. I would model there in a couple of weeks. I met Carmen, the couture buyer originally from France, and Mr. Harris, one of the vice presidents also a buyer.

Jerri's office was just off the large, carpeted department and was smaller than I expected. It was mainly a larger dressing room with a small desk and enough space for eight extra bodies for pre-show fittings.

We did not stay long. We had to rush home to dress, apply full stage make-up and get back downtown to Channel 5 an hour before the award ceremony.

Several hours later, Patti arrived at our home with long, curled-pieces snuck into her own mounds of hair, her Dresden-doll-flawless face, and displaying her soon-in-style flowing, wide purple pantsuit.

I exhaled with her compliment, "Your face looks good," but handed her my false eyelashes and glue for help.

When we walked toward the front door, Patti stopped short to demonstrate how to carry and hand the trophy to the host. "You are not important, just a necessary item, so don't attract attention to yourself. Only smile gently. Go to the host area quickly, but not rushed."

After Patti adjusted my long, gold neck-chains, thin, round, gold bracelets, and large, loop gold earrings, we sped in her Ford back downtown to Channel 5.

When I observed the huge, familiar logo I had seen on the TV screen above my head on the small edifice, my blood felt like soda fizz. I wondered, *Why am I a body of nerves? This isn't going to be difficult! All I have to do is walk out, hand an item to some man, and walk back. I'm not even important.*

Obviously, Patti was familiar with the place. The receptionist greeted, "Hello, Patti, you look fabulous, as usual. Meet in the same dressing room. Others just arrived. Another pretty model?"

"Oh, yes. This is Mary Jo. She works for Frost Brothers. See you later," Patti said, nudging me toward the hallway. Her hand to her mouth, she whispered, "Mary Jo, I forgot to tell you. You are not new. You are just a new model working for Frost...Okay?

"You're hired because you have the look of high fashion and are good at modeling, not because you're our sister. Eventually, everyone is bound to find out, but no need to advertise it until everyone sees how good you are. Tell yourself you *know* what to do. Show your confidence."

That was a shocker. Now I can't claim my sisters. She surely has confidence in me. 'Sure. Fine,' I mouthed back.

The plaque on the door read *Room 3*. Patti hurried into the room. I shadowed her. Girls hovered over wide-opened, large, modeling bags of every kind holding worn cosmetic pouches, combs, various hair and makeup brushes, hair pieces, mirrors, shoes, half-slips, bra inserts and lifters, Tampons, small bottles of notions and potions, extra packages of panty hose in assorted shades and textures.

With room for only two chairs in the small area, girls stood or knelt over their containers.

This event did not seem to stress the other girls: Joanne and Gail, who had come directly from floor modeling at Frost Brothers, were standing in bras and panty hose between changes, gabbing about kitchen recipes. Why was my heart reminding me it was in my chest?

Patti laid her big, loop-handled, straw-like bag across the room in a corner, and left some room for me to lay my pocketbook with compact, hair pick and meager set of makeup. I pretended I was in control and watched Patti from my peripheral. I had no such collection of items. I surmised that after years of working in the field, things accumulated in those bags, as does a woman's large purse. You just grab and go, and all the extra sometimes-needed stuff goes along for the ride.

Girls turned their heads to Patti and me as we settled in.

"Everybody, this is Mary Jo. She'll be working with us now," Patti said. Girls introduced themselves.

I didn't need to hustle to do anything, I thought. I was dressed with makeup and hair ready. Patti pulled an eight-inch, makeup brush from her bag and began to powder her nose. I nonchalantly reached for my purse and drew out my brand-new mirror-compact. I was afraid I would mess my makeup, so I faked touching up by gently dotting here and there at my face. Patti grabbed another huge brush and swept the tops of her cheekbones. I mimicked with my barely used Cover Girl little brush to my own face.

I seemed to be the only one studying what everyone else was doing, and hoped I was doing it inconspicuously.

Everyone was dressed, made up, and hair-ready, when a Channel 5 assistant tapped on our door and asked us to follow her. We wound through the familiar hallway and down another that led to a large table with tall, shiny, gold trophies standing in formation like military soldiers during inspection.

Lady Assistant gathered us around, "The awards are aligned in the order to be presented. You do not take the trophy from the table. I will hand one to you."

I listened intently, asking my heart to control itself. The seasoned girls nodded a boring *yes, we know.* Lady Assistant seemed to focus on me with my pop-eyes attending to her every word and the trophies.

As she continued, she motioned to hanging drapes around the mic *stage* area. "You walk out and stand to the right of the host, who will receive the trophy when he is ready. You always go out in the same order. Any questions?"

No one responded. I certainly was not going to ask any questions. I was to be experienced. If I had questions, I would have cornered and asked Patti.

Patti discretely motioned with her finger over her shoulder to have me line up behind her—I could observe and study her.

Clapping from a small audience broke my nervous silence. The announcer blared out something I did not pay attention to, and the show began!

Patti lined up first and sashayed out with a small smile, handed her trophy to the host under the spotlight and glided right back.

Lady Assistant handed me my trophy with its back facing me as Patti had described just before leaving home. I gripped one of the four long columns with my right hand and supported the base with my left. Either it was much heavier than it looked, or my arms were nervously weak.

I prayed, *Lord, don't let me drop this monster. I have to remember not to get attention to myself. Get out and get back.* I mimicked Patti outwardly with my slight smile, but my insides did their own routine. I was glad the few bright spotlights blinded the audience from me.

We lined up, walked out, handed the trophy, and lined up again, repeating like wind-up dolls. Surprisingly, the event went rather quickly. I survived unscathed. *Much ado about nothing.*

On the way home, I fired quick, high-pitched questions and comments: "Patti, could you tell I was shaking? I thought I might drop the trophy; it was heavy. You all didn't seem a bit nervous. You looked so relaxed. I didn't expect the lights to blind my view of the audience. I wish we could have taken our pictures..."

She cut me off! "Mary Jo, we don't take pictures of ourselves. That's a real sign you're a beginner. Do not even mention it. If a newspaper, a television, or other professional wants it, that's great; but don't shoot one for yourself."

Patti continued her lecture, "You'll have lots of pictures taken for newspapers, believe me. You performed really well and looked fabulous! Channel 5 likes your look. This was a good opportunity to get a little feel of the dressing room, the lights, makeup and hair, even though you wore your own outfit."

I looked out the window. I felt all dressed up for my first day on the job, but no photo-reminder.

We talked all the way home. She dropped me off. Mom, Dad, Peggy and Mae were having supper. Mae looked up with a big smile, "Wow, you look good." Dad whistled with his lips curled as only he did, while Mom brought me a plate. They shared my first *formal* experience.

Peggy beamed with big eyes and asked, "How do you feel about being a model after being a nun?"

"How do I put it into words?" I paused. "I feel like Cinderella after the ball. Patti's been my main fairy godmother, with all of you being the helping, little mice—sharing the house, the red-flocked bedroom, bathroom, so many lovely clothes—all those many things."

I joshed Mom and Dad, "You're loving parents, not like Cinderella's."

Mom lowered her head, no teeth showing, but corners of her mouth were up a little. Dad teased, throwing his chest out.

"Tonight I was all dressed and danced at the ball. I enjoyed it, but now I'm taking off my new shoes, tons of stage makeup and false eyelashes, and my new clothes. My fancy hair-do will be washed out soon."

Peggy laughed, and blurted, "Yeah, that's a good comparison. We know."

Mae grinned with a strong nod.

I took off my two-inch heels, "What do you mean, *you know?*"

"We model sometimes on Saturdays and in summers when school's out," Peggy said.

Mae commented, "You'll be going to lots of *balls*. You'll spend hours getting ready, come home, and take it all off. A month or so before each season, you'll show the new, upcoming fashions. Some weeks you won't have anything to do."

I jolted. *What did she imply? No work means, no pay. This kind of work is spastic—very busy, sometimes not busy at all.*

Peggy continued, "Be ready. It'll get hectic. Patti's constantly on the go. Jerri is, too. We get exhausted hearing them talk about it."

That was all I needed for my decision: *I am grateful. However, I will play Cinderella and dress for the ball until I get enough piano students to be on my own.*

BROADENING HORIZONS

Patti and I took a break after getting up early to refine poses for newsprint and to finesse fake-eyelash-gluing in her small dining room. The ceiling-to-floor mirror reflected the huge window on the opposite wall with the Texas Mesquite tree dancing to February's cold winds outside. We snuggled in our big sweaters at her shiny glass and wood table, foolishly enjoying our Black Cows of vanilla ice cream and root beer, instead of cups of steaming hot chocolate.

"Mary Jo, I've made an appointment tomorrow with Ms. Vincent, who owns Military Models (later named Mannequin Models), to broaden your horizons for modeling experiences," she announced.

"Oh no! I don't want to work for anyone else yet. You and Jerri know I'm new. Why can't I wait until I get more experience at Frost first?" I stirred my ice cream and sucked the root beer furiously through the skinny straw.

"Once we start showing spring fashions, I'll be helping Jerri with the big shows and won't be able to go with you," she said. "Ms. Vincent has work available that's very nice and in other places such as Sears with tea room modeling in Luby's cafeteria in Central Park Mall. She does ramp shows for other stores with luncheons at San Antonio's four military bases and the Tower of the Americas. You will have newspaper shoots before and after many of them."

Patti opened a large drawer in the buffet nearby and gingerly spread a set of large manila folders in front of me. I watched as she opened one with a zillion pictures, some newsprint, some glossy—all of her—in modeling shows or striking poses.

My jaw dropped. I stared at her picture on the cover of a *Vogue* Magazine. She wore a fitted neon-pink, knit short dress. She sat sideways on a large round box with her knees raised to her chin. Her arms hugged her long legs with matching pink hose and heels.

My little sister amazed me. She was patient with my clumsy efforts and limited knowledge of fashions after thirteen years in the convent.

I noted the gentleness given to the priceless items. She reached for another folder. "Ah, this is what I need. These are some of my works for Ms. Vincent," she said as she fingered through the assorted sizes of photos and newsprint in color or black and white. She spread them out across the entire table under the black wrought-iron chandelier in the small dining room. They doubled in quantity reflecting in the ceiling-to-floor mirror on my right.

"Oh, Patti, I had no idea. You're so talented—no wonder you're the top model in San Antonio—you have so much experience." My hands framed the sides of my face. "This huge collection is beautiful. Each one has a different pose." I rattled off questions as they tossed in my mind. "How did you know what position to strike for each garment? You said *table modeling*. What's that?"

"Whoa! Slow down." She flung her thin arms. "Use your judgment: fun outfit for fun posture and formal position for evening wear. Ms. Vincent selects dresses you model during lunch hours at Luby's Cafeteria for Sears. Walk around each table to show-and-tell a brief description of the outfit—the fabric, care and price. Be sure to say it's from Sears, right next door."

My stomach started its dance. My head shook with quick jerks as I spread my arms above my head. "But how do I find all that information? I don't know much about fabrics. Do I have to memorize it for each ensemble?"

Patti laughed and started placing the treasures back into the folder file, "That petrified me, too, before my first experience. While I walked from Sears to Luby's, I simply read the information from the tag on the dress, or I read it in the dressing room. It's easy to remember info for one outfit at a time."

That helped...a little. "That's really different. What kinds of *rules* do I have to obey for table modeling," I asked with a hidden tremble of angst.

She turned the heat up, sat down, rubbed her cold hands briskly together and then placed them under her armpits. I mimicked the idea.

"First, since there are only two girls working," she said, "make sure one of you is always modeling at the tables. Do quick changes in the dressing room back at Sears. Ms. Vincent has few accessories for each selection, not as many as Frost provides. She and her assistant, Ms. Staples, replace things on hangers so you can relieve the other model at Luby's as soon as possible.

"You provide your own hose and shoes, unlike at Frost, where we advertise their foot-wear for each item."

I stopped sipping my Black Cow, pounced my feet onto the floor, and wrinkled my brow at Patti.

She tilted her head, "I know. You don't have a shoe collection now. I'll help you get some basic colors for the summer fashions we'll be showing soon. Avoid pure white—it glares too bright with some outfits. Go for off-white or cream. Sandals and your chunky black patents will go a long way. Always have extra panty hose on hand in case of snags."

I slapped my knee, "Now I know why you models have those big bags. I have that gray baggage with a zipper, and pockets on the sides."

Patti agreed and continued. "Remember that Luby's diners eat out, most for special occasions. You do not want to interrupt if they appear involved in deep or business conversation. Walk slowly so they see you coming. If they do not acknowledge you, just walk leisurely to the next table. Be natural and wear a smile. Some will ask questions. If you don't know the answer, just say so.

"The models almost always get to eat in the lunchrooms for Ms. Vincent shows. Luby's cashier will recognize you from working the tables and give you a receipt."

We rose, put our soda glasses into the dishwasher, and ventured back to the dining room table. Sitting opposite each other, we gazed quietly out of the ceiling-to-floor window to our side.

"Oh, I forgot." Patti slapped her right cheek. "Jerri doesn't take out her agent's 20% fee from you or me, but Ms. Vincent will deduct her fee from your paycheck. I don't have time to work for Sears anymore, with all I do at Frost. I appreciated the work I did with Ms. Vincent. She's very considerate and knows you're my sister."

I considered, *It sure will be nice when I get a paycheck. I won't see one for a month after I work for Frost or for Ms. Vincent. I've never made a dime in my life. Surely no one realizes that. When I babysat, Mom said it wasn't right to take money from our friends. In the convent with our vow of poverty, we never kept a penny from teaching or from gifts from friends or family.*

I want to start giving Dad and Mom something for rent. I don't know how I will ever repay my sisters. Patti buys so much for me. Jerri doesn't deduct her commission from my paychecks. Then there's the one-hundred dollars I want to return to the Sisters and...

Patti interrupted my thoughts, continuing to clue me in on working for Ms. Vincent. "She has many more models working for her, so you won't want to cancel Frost bookings to work for her.

"Get your schedule of monthly work from Jerri before you sign up for Ms. Vincent, since Frost hires only about eight very high-fashion-look models, who are usually professionally trained to do New York-and Paris-type shows. Frost Brothers rates as the pinnacle, the highest level in modeling in all of Texas."

"I have something for you." She rummaged in her big purse on the floor and handed me a pocket calendar with a field of Texas bluebonnets under a baby blue sky dotted with fluffy clouds. I opened it carefully. It exposed a year of months in one-inch squares. "This is your daily commitment book—your most valuable possession. Lose it and *you're* lost!

"You don't make a booking unless you check this little calendar. Write in it immediately. Never leave home without it!" We both laughed. "Check it carefully to be sure you get paid for your work each month. Mark the squares very carefully."

I immediately marked my Texas bluebonnet book's appropriate little square with "TV Awards," and placed it in the side pocket of my gray modeling bag.

"But, Patti," I asked. "Why are Frost shows more high-fashion than others?"

She explained: "Jerri attends all the New York shows, brings her creative ideas back to Frost—clothing, model walks, looks, stage back drops, all of it—and immediately mimics it in our shows. Designers love to come to San Antonio for the professionalism. Girls would do anything to model at Frost," Patti said. "If you cancel often when asked, you won't be called again."

I gulped. My legs almost osmosed into spaghetti as we put on our coats to take me home. *Did she need to tell me all of that? I hope I don't let Frost down.* Again, I felt the responsibility of doing my upmost for Frost—especially for Jerri and Patti, who were investing much time and effort. I looked forward, but with my usual trepidation, to meeting Ms. Peggy Vincent soon.

The next day, dressed in full makeup, Patti and I strolled through Sears to the women's dressing rooms. Ms. Vincent and her assistant, Ms. Staples, were at the end of the little hallway with curtained rooms on each side. Piles of garments were on a bench, along with jewelry, bags, hats and scarves.

They set CHECK-OUT-CLOTHING-FOR-MODELING paperwork onto chairs by the long mirror at the end of the hall and greeted us with wide hugs. "Patti, we haven't seen you in ages, but you impress us with your work on television and in the paper frequently. We miss you and still can't figure out how you have time to do all your work at Frost Brothers." They turned immediately to me with dancing eyes and white-teeth smiles.

I introduced myself and assured them I was looking forward to working together, "I'm not hurt if you need to correct me. I want to do things right. I'm used to Patti's pecking and training." They laughed at the tease.

Ms. Vincent continued to match garment to accessories, writing on her clipboard as she spoke, "All you Barbera girls are beautiful! Would you like to work Luby's on Thursday, Mary Jo? Marge is modeling the mature woman's clothing, but little Betsy just called in coughing and sneezing. We know if Patti trained you, you are ready! We're pulling garments now. If you want to stay about an hour for your fitting, you won't have to make another trip tomorrow."

I felt slammed from the back with fearful joy! I looked over their shoulders with surprised questioning to Patti, "It's up to my chauffeur."

Patti jumped at the offer, "Ms. Vincent, you're known for being so accommodating. That's perfect. I have shopping to do and will be back in an hour. I need to look at off-white shoes, sandals and many other things." She nodded a smile at me as she turned to leave.

I dropped my handbag on the seat in one of the dressing rooms, feeling everything was happening too fast: I was riding a carousel and couldn't get off, but I could use the money.

"We're excited to have you work with us, Mary Jo," Ms. Vincent said. "We have many shows planned for spring and summer garments soon." Quiet Ms. Staples smiled and nodded a big approval.

"She's a tiny size four or six," Ms. Vincent said. Ms. Staples quickly left for the clothing racks and returned with a pantsuit and a dress over her arm to get started.

My mind was screaming, *I'm not prepared for this at the last minute. I need to hide my hands. They're shaking. I don't think well under this much pressure. Can't let on I'm nervous. I can do this. I have to—and fast.*

I was standing in my stocking feet in my undies, ready to jump into the clothing. Ms. Staples helped me unbutton, un-zip, un-belt and remove the jump suit from its hanger in the little dressing room with angled mirrors so we could see from all views.

She tiptoed to help slip a feather-soft, Easter-perfect, one-piece dress of pastels over my head. She stepped back with her hand to her chin and examined me. She wrapped a long, light weight scarf around my waist and tied a square knot to let it flow with wisps down the side front. I slipped back into my shoes.

Moving into the little hallway, I posed and did a complete turn with my hands down and out a tad for Ms. Vincent. She removed her glasses so they hung on their gold chain on her bosom, "That was a speedy dress. You look fabulous, Mary Jo. It looks like a different dress."

She handed me a glossy clutch purse and carefully strung several long costume pearl strings over my head. She eyed me top to bottom and added a wide, matching stretch bracelet and earrings.

"Ahh, the perfect hat!" She presented me a dressy Easter bonnet—lavender straw and wide brimmed. She adjusted it low on my forehead, tilting it slightly to the left. "No wonder they want you at Frost. You'll stun diners tomorrow and you'll love working with Marge."

Both women made me feel comfortable, but that was the dressing room. The test would be on Thursday.

Thursday arrived, hauling along more excited butterflies. I borrowed Mom's Buick to drive to Central Park a couple of miles away. I parked and zipped directly to the familiar dressing room.

"Mary Jo?" an unfamiliar voice called from one of the little curtains. "I'm Marge. Ms. Vincent asked me to watch for you. She and Ms. Staples are pulling some accessories for us. Your changes are in this room next to mine," she said pointing.

"Oh, finally I get to meet you," I said. I dropped my large gray bag onto the floor by the mirrors, and removed my new, off-white sandals Patti purchased for me the previous day. I began stripping while we chatted through the walls of our little cubby rooms.

She asked, "You're lucky to work at Frost. You have that look. How do you like it?"

Thank goodness she did not see me look up and freeze with one leg into a pantsuit. "Everyone is very nice. We just did the TV Awards Presentations." She didn't know it was my first and *only* job! I quickly changed the subject, "Got any clues for working at Luby's today?"

"Normally one of us goes ahead to get started, but we'll go together, so you can get the feel," Marge suggested.

"Are you kiddin'? That would be great. Thanks, Marge."

Ms. Vincent and Ms. Staples arrived with bags, scarves, "necks" (necklaces) and earrings. Ms. Staples tied a lime 48" scarf around my neck to hang down in the back over my white and yellow pantsuit. She wrapped my neck with a handful of long yellow and lime-green beaded "necks." She topped my head with a white, straw fedora with a turned-up brim.

"You look striking. We'll be waiting for the crowd to follow you back here," she teased as she handed me a long, shoulder strap, white bag. I hung it on my left shoulder with my palm resting on the top of the shiny flap.

Marge emerged from her curtained area to examine herself at the end-of-the-hall mirror. She carried her stately, mature figure well—head and shoulders tall, but relaxed. Her full face radiated with fresh colors of soft, fresh, spring pastels around her sparkling blue eyes with a touch of mascara appropriate for her expert age. The touch of gray in her round, teased coif framed her face. The matching soft-flowing, two-piece ensemble of light pinks, blues, lavenders, and a touch of lemon gave her a delicate elegance above her cream pumps.

We studied the removed tags and tucked them into pockets in our garments. Mine read: Washable. Double-knit Polyester. $9.99, Sears. Women's Sports.

Marge entered the wide, opened entrance of Luby's cafeteria. The deep maroon, vinyl booths around the walls, décor of black, wrought iron fixtures, and shiny, dark brown table-tops formed a half circle around the food-serving area. Marge walked majestically on the dark red carpet as if she owned the place. She smiled gently and nodded as she glided to the back to work her way to the front of the eating area.

I did the same, taking the opposite back corner. I noticed little signs pinched between clips at the top of tiny stands in the middle of the tables that read: MODELS SHOWING GARMENTS FROM SEARS. I relaxed, *Wow, what a break. Patrons know why we are wondering around in this dining room, smiling, with all of this face paint and false-eyelashes!*

Eager eyes turned and followed me. I heard many comments among the clientele: "That outfit is cute. Wonder how much the entire ensemble costs. It looks so together."

"Love the bag. Look, a new model. Super pant suit; I need to get one. It's the new fashion trend. Let's walk over to Sears when we're finished."

◦◦◦

I stopped at the table in the corner, "Hi, I'm showing a polyester, completely washable suit from Ladies' Sports at Sears for nine, ninety-nine." I did a slow, full turn with both feet close together thinking, *Wow, Patti would be proud of my pivot!*

"Beautiful. Thanks," the two women responded. However, pride comes before the fall, and my head got too heavy. I jerked to move to the next table and slammed into the man getting up from his seat with his tray in his hand.

Utensils rattled and banged against glassware as everything slid from one end of the tray to the other.

I glared at the mess, then up at him, "Oh, I am so very sorry. Please excuse me," I begged.

My thoughts shot like lightening-bolts. *Just what I need—get food spilled on my white suit, and have to buy it myself with all the money I don't have. First day on the job and I'm in arrears before I start.* Then another idea flashed—maybe I would have to pay for this rich man's suit to be cleaned or possibly purchase another. On top of it all, I assumed Sears would fire me and I could never model at Luby's again.

Everyone in the cafeteria was watching the fiasco—at least 100 witnesses against me. I hoped Marge wasn't looking at the circus I was causing.

I bent over to help the gentleman do whatever I didn't have any idea he needed to have done. "Are you all right? How can I help you? Did your handsome suit get soiled?" I asked.

"Oh, sweetie, I'm perfectly fine. Don't worry about anything. Thank you for being so gracious in asking," he comforted.

The other two men at the table asked the price of my garment. One of them knew his wife would love the entire collection for her birthday on Saturday, especially the "long scarf and cute hat."

I had fallen quickly from my perch with my heavy head: I was not parading around in that big room looking pretty all by my lonesome. The important people were the diners at Luby's. I should have learned that lesson right from the front door, not the hard way in the back of the room.

The rest of the day went smoothly, Marge didn't even know of the incident. The four of us strolled back to Luby's for our free meal together. With a rapid, higher pitched voice, Marge turned to face Ms. Vincent and Ms. Staples, walking backward for several steps, "You should have seen Mary Jo. She had ease and friendliness when I glanced over to her at the tables."

Inside Luby's, the crowd was thinner. I followed the other three to the serving area and pushed my tray on the little metal ledge. My stomach gurgled at the stronger, more noticeable warm smells and displays of the huge selections under bright lights: assorted entrees from fried catfish to Mexican foods, from ground meat to prime rib, from creamed spinach and broccoli to carrots and corn, buns, muffins and cornbread. There were pies of pecan, lemon meringue, cream, chocolate and coconut. Cakes lined up like rows and columns on a grid. Selections and decisions made me drool and feel dizzy.

I reflected: *Wow, the others are already looking for a place to sit. Either they are used to the selections and choose quickly, or they just don't eat much. I'd better hurry. My tray has too much already, like that poor guy I bumped into with his tray of empty glass and utensils.*

I was famished but I chose my meal with the least expensive Salisbury steak and thick mushroom/onion gravy, mashed potatoes, carrots and peas, long stick of corn bread, and the "most requested dessert" (so the little sign next to it said) of butternut brownie pie with a tall glass of milk. I held off on the luscious looking salads to conserve expense on the free tab. Besides, I needed something to stick to my ribs.

The cashier grinned at my full tray, but nodded, "Enjoy your meal."

Where were they sitting? I was embarrassed walking to my right, then turning to the other side of the food line. I froze: *Oh, no! They're at the table where I crashed into that rich man in the fancy suit! I'm like a criminal going back to the scene. No one suspects me, the criminal.*

I spied my group and studied their meager meals. I felt for Marge, Ms. Vincent, and Ms. Staples who feasted on simple, low-calorie, mounds of rabbit-food salad and no dessert. They ogled at my full tray. Marge put her coffee cup down. "How do you stay so thin—when you eat like that?" Our two agents gaped for an answer, too.

"Our parents are both small and thin. My sisters and I probably get it from them. We all eat lots of everything," I said. I couldn't tell them of the 20+ pounds I lost in my last years—in the convent and hospital—that left my tall 5' 9" body a mere 105 pounds.

The conversation was upbeat, reviewing the day's success, with compliments to Marge and me. No one questioned my pandemonium.

My mind quizzed, *Maybe I should confess to Patti. But then, some things are better not said if not necessary. I can't wait for my first paycheck next month!*

GEOFFREY BEENE

I had been home on leave from the convent for only about six weeks. I was alone on Mom's pristinely well-kept French Provincial piano attempting Chopin's "Waltz in G Flat" for the first time in several years, and with slow success. About fifteen minutes into my practice, I jumped up to answer the phone in the breakfast area.

Jerri sounded hurried, as usual, calling from Frost Brothers. Anyone listening to *my* end of the conversation heard, "Jerri, who is this Geoffrey Beene, who's coming to town?"

"Mary Jo, you don't know who Geoffrey Beene is? Honey, he's one of the top designers in America. He studied in New York and Paris and has a fashion business in New York since '62." She rattled so loudly and fast, I looked at the receiver. "I want you and Patti to do pre-show photos for newspaper ads."

I slid onto a high stool at the bar dividing the breakfast area and the terrazzo-tiled, large den, feeling weak.

"*The San Antonio Light* will shoot gobs of photos at the Hemisphere Convention Center in his fashions from our department. The pictures will be with the story advertising Beene's huge, black-tie fashion show soon. This'll be one of our biggest events of the year. Isn't it exciting? And you'll get to be in on it all."

She had to be kidding! Upset I banged my knee with my clinched fist, but tried to convince myself it would be easy. I felt the blood evaporate from my face.

"Thanks very much for asking me, Jerri," I lied. "I'll call Patti." My thinker asked, *Why do they ask me to do last minute things I am not ready to do? The first time was the TV Awards Presentation. Then when I went to meet Ms. Vincent, she invited me to stay for a fitting to work two days later. Now these big photo shoots!*

Numb, I was afraid if I slammed the phone down, I would break it; so I disciplined myself to set the receiver in its cradle gently. I zombied over to the piano and mashed my palms on random dissonants all over the keyboard, until I was calm enough to call Patti for the particulars about some famous *bean*.

"Mary Jo," Patti said, "I'll pick you up tomorrow at nine. Wear your fullest stage makeup. Carmen, our high fashion buyer, and Mr. Harris, a VP and the merchandise manager, will meet us at the Convention Center with our clothing. Bring everything: makeup, hair pieces, variety of shoes, hose, anything you think you might need."

Five minutes later I yanked my gray suitcase with the looped handles from the closet, opened it wide, and plopped it in the middle of the bedroom floor. I stared into its empty cavity. Patti had said, "Bring...anything you might need." *Like I know what I might need?! I'll pack everything she named and anything else that fits in this bag. What doesn't fit does not go.*

I did just that: zipped and un-zipped the bag to check, re-check, add, or take out, until tomorrow came.

Ding.Ding.Ding. I raced to the door. Patti rushed me back to the pink bathroom, with a large Sears paper sack in her hand. She lined up hairpins and bobby pins between her lips, plopped a jet black, puffed, curly hairpiece on top of my head and started to work.

"Ouch! Are you nailing it to my skull?"

Ignoring my cry, she quickly arranged my own hair to blend in *naturally,* "You're done. Let's go."

I lugged my bag with both hands again and slammed the front door after us. It was only March and I was sweating jellybeans by the time we reached Patti's trunk. "You said to take anything I think I might need." Patti rolled her eyes, shook her head, but laughed.

We sped south on San Pedro to HemisFair Center in the heart of the city, about two blocks from the San Antonio River and the Alamo. She knew where to park. We charged into the new building, looking like we'd be checking-in that night after a hustling day in our *street-girl*-heavy makeup and hair-dos!

Carmen and Mr. Harris had arranged for us to change in a small, office space just off the huge new area with vintage vehicles in the Confluence

Museum in HemisFair Plaza. As we entered the arena with sparkling automobiles, my eyes grabbed a gold-filigreed, tall stand with a large, elegant poster:

March 9th, 1969

**Witte's Transportation Collection moved
from Brackenridge Park to New Confluence
Museum-HemisFair Plaza**

March 28th

**Gala Benefit Supper
Featuring fashion collection
of Geoffery Beene of New York
$15 per person to the Museum's Annual fund**

Reservations limited to 500 persons

Thinker figured, *Wow! Fifteen dollars! Good thing we don't have to pay admittance. We only make twenty dollars for a show, and nothing for the fitting the day before. How does Patti pay for those two days of parking and baby sitter?* Patti re-introduced me to Carmen. I had met her only once when we went for hair styling with Robert at Frost Brothers for my first (and only, so far!) job—the Local TV Awards Ceremony.

We immediately prepped for photo shoots. I undressed while petite, mid-aged Carmen held her arms high to reach inside a clear plastic bag with the light blue logo, *Frost Bros.,* printed diagonally across from top to bottom. She kept her eyes on the prized dress, then slowly handed me the hanger loop.

"Mary Jo, you'll wear this," she said with Frost-pride, French accent and great confidence.

"That?" The first dress I would model for Frost was familiar: *black and white—*convent colors! "I'll love wearing this, Carmen. The linen is gorgeous." It was elegant and above-the-knee short: white-on-top with three white self-buttons that met the black, high-waist, attached skirt. A perfect, sleeveless, dinner dress!

Carmen spread a large, blue sheet on the office floor, un-buttoned the top of the dress with her white-gloved, small fingers. She opened the garment, forming a hole, and set it on top of the blue sheet. Balancing with my fingers on her bent shoulders, I cautiously stepped my stocking feet into the expensive gap before me.

When I thought it could not be prettier, her short arms spread out and removed the lid of a white, four-inch high, Frost-labeled box that was lying on the floor on the sheet. She tenderly removed layers of white tissue.

"Whoa...that's heavenly!" I whispered to her.

She presented a self-lined satin, large-tied, flat bow and attached it at the top of the garment under my chin. The two wide-flowing ends of the bow rested on my small bust. All of this was in softest baby-pink.

I slipped my feet into Frost's two-inch, curved, chunk-heel, baby-pink, satin shoes. I noticed about store-shoes: masking tape covered the soles for protection.

"Wait until you see what I have next!" Carmen warned. She opened a small bag and lifted out a tissue-wrapped something in the palm of her left hand. Gently she exposed an elaborate set of pierced earrings with Florentine gold loops from which dangled nine strands of diamond-like, dancing-sparkle stones and a matching wide bracelet.

My heart sprinted. "Ahhh," I inhaled, asking myself, *Will I be showing these kinds of gems in Frost shows?* My fingers trembled as I toiled to replace my ten-cent studs with the long chandeliers.

She adjusted the bow and stood back, "Mary Jo, you look stunning. Geoffrey Beene will love it."

Mr. Harris' voice echoed through the offices toward our little cubby area, "Mary Jo? Patti? We're ready when you are." I don't remember what Patti wore—I was absorbed in my own efforts to be in the here-and-now of luxurious fashions, and hoped to show them with ease, far out of my comfort zone.

"Mary Jo, you show off your Geoffrey Beene and that 1933 red Duesenberg parked next to the shiny, light tan Bentley," Mr. Harris directed with open arms.

"Show it off?" I asked. "You mean I can touch it?" I stiffened. I had not a clue what to do with that monster.

He grinned with pursed lips, as if I were joking. Patti noticed and interrupted to help me in an exciting, loud tease behind him and the photographer, "Yeah, Mary Jo! Get on that beauty and act as if you love it. Show off! You know how. Act like it's yours!"

I teased seriously back, so they all heard, "You asked for it. Here goes!" I measured my steps slowly and elegantly toward the red monster glaring at me with its two large, unlit headlights. I gulped a big knot.

Thinker recalled, *Mom treasures her piano. We never touch the cabinet or put anything on it except the music books. This beautiful car is 36 years old. What if I dent or scratch or get fingermarks on it?*

I sheepishly placed one foot on the wide running board, forced a smile, and peeked into the passenger window with my hand on the long, door handle. CLICK-CLICK. Every time I moved, CLICK-CLICK.

A little fortified, I ran my clinging hand around the treads of the spotless, shiny black, spare tire at the front of the running board, as if it were my honey's shoulders. CLICK-CLICK. CLICK-CKICK.

"Great, Sweetie! Keep going!" encouraged Camera Man.

I know I should not get inside this car. The dress would not show off, and Patti said never sit in a fashion because it would wrinkle. Keep moving fast, strike many poses. Every movement is important. Constantly—face, arms, legs, and garment—always camera-ready!

A few tourists in the museum were gathering, "Mommy, look, they're taking pictures of that pretty lady on that big red car."

You do not need distractions, Thinker scolded. *Keep focusing.*

The big headlights on the front were tempting. I hugged one of them, running my fingertips under its *chin* showing *him* off toward Camera Man, yet conscientious that my hands did not hide the dress. Dress and car were fighting for center stage. CLICK-CLICK.

Mr. Harris spun around and slapped his thigh. He and Carmen hooted and laughed. "Way to go, Mary Jo."

I dashed again to the running board! Camera Man rushed back with me.

With my rear to the passenger door, my left arm stretched out with my fingers standing up onto the hood, directly below the windshield. Right hand stretched back and over the convertible's black top. CLICK-CLICK.

"Oh, yeah, Baby, that's a winner," Camera Man yelled. CLICK-CLICK. CLICK-CLICK.

"Take FIVE," Mr. Harris laughed. "Great shots! When we get back, we'll shoot by that 1840 yellow and red stagecoach." He gestured to the area across the room by the front door.

More tourists wandered and gathered behind Camera Man's area waiting for the *show* to begin again.

And it did! I posed in the same lovely Geoffrey Beene dinner dress with the large, baby pink bow and matching, satin Mary Jane shoes, my big, tall curly hair piece, full makeup, and million-dollar, fake, sparkly earrings and matching wide bracelet: "Stagecoach Fashion." In that pose, I was *conversing* with the president of the Horseless Carriage Club about the upcoming gala benefit supper. Those shots were snaps!

We finished after many other shoots. In our Cinderella-after-the ball-clothes, Patti and I repacked our bags.

All in my first day's work on a photo shoot. The *big, exciting,* as Jerri called it, ramp show at the convention center and in-store floor modeling experiences were yet to come!

Only 322 more days until I can go back to Our Lady of the Lake Convent and my music. I'm a fish out of water.

FITTING AND
SHOWING BIG BEENE

We were standing in our undies and high heels waiting for the two men from New York to enter the small room, about two months after I left the convent. I heard comments such as: "I wish I could wear my girdle." "Your new diet must be working." "Look, here's an exercise I just started that's supposed to reduce my thighs."

I was in the corner next to my gray modeling bag wearing my new padded-for-up-lift size 34B. I felt like a pencil standing on its pointy end—my teased hair was the eraser on top. I tried to be suave and calm, thinking, *Oh, if the nuns could see me now!*

Eight exclusive Frost Bros. high-fashion models were in the medium size dressing room for one of the most important ramp shows of the year. Patti casually introduced me to the girls, not mentioning that I was her and Jerri's sister, nor, especially, that I was new. The three of us hoped no one offered any interrogations. I had met several of the girls at the local TV Awards ceremony.

I decided to avoid *new girl* questions by reading highlights about the show in the newspaper article on Jerri's bulletin board:

Geoffrey Beene, the brilliant and distinguished couturier, just-announced winner of the National Cotton award...has brought his entire collection to Frost Bros. third floor downtown for you to select from...the "Geoffrey Beene fashion gala"...with the presentation of the collection at the opening of the Witte Confluence Museum in HemisFair Plaza...informal modeling of the collection on Tuesday and Wednesday...with fashion expert, traveling envoy, Henry Ginsberg to assist with your selections both days...See, among other fashions, the importance of the big pants story, in linen, gypsy print and sophisticated silk for evening wear...he creates high quality clothing for women and men in subtle colors and simple design.

Mr. Beene studied fashion in New York City and Paris. In 1949, he began a career noteworthy for unconventional design even before he started his own New York Company in 1969.

Jerri, fashion coordinator, swung the door open, clasping her two-inch-thick, red booking-calendar in her hand. She looked over her shoulder as she backed into the room with her other hand clinging to the rods of the large wheeled hanger with Geoffery Beene's clothing. Her assistant, Cathy, was pushing from the other end.

"Hi, girls! Are we excited around here! You remember—I met Geoffrey Beene and his assistant, Henry Ginsberg, at the last Fashion Fair in New York this past year. It's their first visit to San Antonio. We want to make a big impression on them so they will come back again. We're happy to have Mary Jo start working with..." THUMP! THUMP!..."us."

Jerri turned to acknowledge the Thump on the door next to me. Mr. Harris stepped inside for a moment, bowed his head and motioned for the two men to enter. We were their eight, in-undies-only mannequins, standing in a semi-circle (wearing more makeup than clothing) and smiling pleasantly.

Their eyes spanned from left to right and studied us quickly. We were just additional, boring necessities to endure and to dress in splendor and magnificence for their upcoming and luxurious, big splash! They were like gynecologists five minutes before quitting time—greeting the last naked woman after a long Friday before Labor Day!

Without hesitation, Henry Ginsberg reached up to the wheeled hanger to remove the first dress. A few girls gasped and whispered observations and remarks: "I can't wear that. It's too tiny." "He needs to give it to that new girl... Mary Jo?" "I told you I needed to wear a girdle. I should have started that new diet long ago." "I should have been doing those exercises more often." "Patti can wear these—she can fake anything and look fabulous."

Jerri spoke up and suggested, "Give it to Patti?" Geoffrey Beene nodded when he saw who *Patti* was. Jerri opened a folding chair, sat and began writing the assignments on the long paper on her clipboard.

You could hear sighs of relief as the girls threw frightening glances to each other and waited for the next parcel and assignment—and there were about 40 more on the wheeled hanger!

This time, a tall, two-piece, wide pantsuit made its debut.

Giovanna stepped back a tad to be less conspicuous with her cups-that-overfloweth. Jerri's eyes widened, too, "Mary Jo? On the end by the door?" she recommended. I reached out with both hands, accepted the beautiful, paisley, gypsy-print with matching babushka. *Oh dear, I'll probably have to wear this and mess up my hair. I will look a wreck for the next outfit.*

A sense of frustration enveloped the room, although I was too green to notice it at the time. Most of the garments were for toothpicks like Patti and me. Each girl eventually had a few garments to wear, but Patti and I got all the remaining articles.

I had no clue what was going on then, but on show night, it would sink in—big time!

We fitted and refitted, exchanging garments, until all of the styles found a suitable human coat hanger. We packed our big bags, returned three blocks to the cheaper parking lot farther from the heart of downtown, and drove home. I felt disheartened, knowing today's efforts were not going to be reflected in my paycheck at the end of the month. There was no pay for days of fittings!

Patti seemed more concerned—anticipating procedures in the *dressing room* at the big night's gala—than I was with my very first ramp walks.

We arrived two hours early at HemisFair Center on Friday, and available parking lots were already shrinking. Initial guests were entering the museum via a colorful canopy. Mariachis entertained in black suits, peppered with silver and red rhinestones, and fitted pants tucked into their tall, fancy, Mexican boots.

Brimmed, studded, black hats edged with red tassels danced to the Latin rhythms of their fat-bellied, Mexican, acoustic, 12-stringed guitars.

Our parking lot led us through the entrance door to the "Corral of the Comedians," the former Spanish Pavilion, where the Mexican buffet-supper was setting up. We dashed past vivid colors of reds, greens and yellows with replicas of the famous Mexican flower boats of Xochimilco.

Suddenly between huffs and puffs, I called out to Patti who had raced ahead and was holding another door open, "I hear music—music like that lively Tijuana Brass recording we've been playing to practice my ramp walks!"

"Yep, that's us! Kenny Fisher's accordion and his players are here warming up. You'll hear a lot of him. He knows the kinds of music and speed we need for our fast walks."

"Oh, my gosh!" I set my bag down, spread my arms out and did a 360-turn inside the Transportation Hall. "This place is beautiful." The 1933 red Duesenberg I had done photo shoots on and the light tan Bentley tucked themselves artistically around the room with the center reserved for the show.

Our four-foot high temporary stage offered tall greens in pots on each side of a curved trellis of spring flowers and ivy. It all glistened in the spotlights. The narrow T-shaped ramp, with its foot extending from the stage, edged itself with golf-ball size, intense lights and was twice as long as I expected. It shot out among five hundred white chairs perfectly lined up on three sides facing the T-ramp. My insides were too frozen to feel my heart beat.

Jerri greeted Patti and me with her clipboard in the dressing area to the left of the temporary stage. "Glad you are here extra early. You're at these two tables closest to the stage. You're going to have many fast changes, since I had to assign you two most of the garments."

She handed us each a 22-inch long paper with our names in the upper corner. A grid divided it into rows and columns.

Rows across read:

GARMENT.HOSE.JEWELRY.SCARF.
GLOVES.HAT.SHOES.HAIR.OTHER.

Columns under those headings identified the particular items.

A neatly stacked pile—jewelry, hose in packages, scarves, hats—was in the middle of my table.

I had never experienced a dressing room for a show, so I had nothing to compare with the set-up there at the museum. Patti stood still to observe the situation. "We can do this. We have to."

I looked around. "What's wrong, Patti?"

"This is a make-shift dressing area. St. Anthony's, the country clubs and most other places have a more professional dressing room. Actually, this is not bad—just more of a challenge—and you're new. I have to focus on how we're going to set up." She examined the individual, plugged-in, makeup mirrors, the pile of accessories on our tables, and the wheeled hangers with our individually assigned clothes next to our tables.

I imitated as Patti taped her paper-grid at eye level to the pole of the wheeled hanger next to her table. She read the grid, placed Garment 1 first on the wheeled hanger and the other garments in sequence behind. She gathered the specific pieces of jewelry for Garment 1, removed the tags, and opened necessary fastenings. Then she placed the set to the far left, lower right, on the table with the *tags* in a group just above. She separated the remaining pile of jewelry in sets and lined them up sequentially for each garment left to right on the table. I followed suit at my station.

My back was stiffer than the table I was bending over as I lined up my jewels, but my insides shook like a pile of Jello. Time flew by as we concentrated. The cool room began to get warmer and warmer as other models crowded in with their large bags. Each entered, studied the situation, and focused on setting up her own area.

"My neck is already sore." Patti messaged, before she opened the proper package of textured panty hose, tucked it in the neck of Garment 1 as a reminder to change hose before donning that next fashion. Scarves hung carefully over their costume. Shoes lined up in order left to right under the table. At the back of the table, she stacked hats. The last one we would wear was on the bottom.

My finger quivered as I stepped back to re-check my layout against my grid sheet. I ran a forwarding-tape, mentally throwing on each set of eight garments.

Some girls sat in undies in front of their mirrors layering surplus makeup, applying more glue to eyelashes or over-smiling at themselves to check lipstick covering their pearly whites. The volume of nervous, excited murmuring climbed up a notch. I wilted on my wooden, rickety chair, wondering if anyone else could hear it rattling to the beat of my pounding heart.

Jerri struck her clipboard loudly with a ruler. "Girls, here are Rosie and Sylvia, our dressers tonight. And this is your fifteen-minute warning."

Everyone scurried to their wheeled hanger to begin their routine of dressing.

"Dressers?" I whispered to Patti.

"Yes. Our first dressing is easy—we have plenty time. But when we come back after working the ramp, time darts by, depending on how many girls work the ramp before we go out again and how difficult our next set of clothing and accessories are. If you need, call out *help* or *quick change*."

We pulled up our panty hose, rose and removed our first clothing from the wheeled hanger. She continued, "I like to let the dresser know just what I need done, like pull up an awkward zipper, help pulling over or stepping into something, get the hose ready, or hook the jewelry around my neck, or hang up my outfit or tie my shoe strings while I fix my scarf. They help to hang stuff back up, too."

"Wow, that's great. I'll take one home with me," I joked.

Patti kept a no-time-for-jokes face and said, "I'd rather get dressed by myself, if possible. Sometimes dressers get jewelry mixed up or get the wrong thing I ask for. We have to be sure to keep things organized, or it is a real mess toward the end of the show. Sometimes someone else needs a dresser more than I do, too. Just use your judgment and think ahead. Focus the entire time you are back here. I've appreciated the dressers at times though."

Did I need this just before the show started? Now another decision—do I, or don't I, need a dresser?—and just when? Here goes. I tried to pull my wits together, and prayed I could do it.

The room was rocking with movement, so was the thermometer—up, up, up!

Hose first. No snags. I was on my way. My first garment was the colorful paisley, gypsy pantsuit, with large white loops dangling on my ears, peeking from under the triangular babushka with a large knot tied to the right under my chin—and rows of white and silver bracelets.

◦∼◦

Patti and I stood behind a temporary, maroon curtain to the left of the stage. Jerri had her clipboard under her arm while lining the other girls in order, occasionally adjusting a hat or scarf. After the announcer welcomed the crowd and introduced Geoffry Beene and Henry Ginsberg, Jerri gave Patti a gentle *go-nudge*.

Familiar Tijuana Brass music from Kenny Fisher's accordion and players echoed through nicks and crannies of the huge room of crowd and cameras, vintages, lights and ladies. Patti had opened the show as she dashed out to the bursting round of applause. All I could see was the stage. She pivoted under the flowered trellis covered with ivy and sped out to the end of the T ramp.

Pulling my babushka a tad over my left earring, Jerri said, "You look great. Go out like Patti, do a back-to-back with her in the middle of the ramp, but do not do a back-to-back with Myrna. Just pass her at the middle of the ramp."

Jerri was the only one allowed to peek through the seams of the maroon curtain toward the T ramp. I felt my *go nudge:* we never left without it.

I reminded my mind: *back-to back-with Patti, but not with Myrna who is after me. Just pass by Myrna.* Taking a big breath, planting a slight smile, I walked out to the trellis on stage.

Instantly I struck a still pose like a mannequin. With both hands on my waist and with outstretched elbows, I fanned-out the long, full, paisley-print tunic top. My legs, spread far apart, showed off the wide-bottomed, matching pants. In the same instant, I profiled my face over my left shoulder to display the back point of the large babushka and large knot. I stared behind the opposite side of the stage past Jerri and the other girls.

I froze: *Oh, dear, with my head turned due left, I can't see when Patti reaches the end of the T ramp, and that's my cue to start walking down the ramp.* That was one of the last rules: quick pose, then stone-still. My fingers stiffened with fright.

The crowd burst into applause. I figured, *Patti had to be at the end of the ramp showing off her outfit. All eyes had to be on her. I had to do something while no one noticed. If they did see, they would think we planned it.*

Like the twitch of a butterfly's wing, I snapped my head forward, staring directly down the ramp. Timed to a T at the end of the T ramp! Patti was taking her first step toward me. I took my first step toward her. We paced our speed to meet half way. I spied Mr. Beene, Mr. Ginsberg, Mr. Harris and

Carmen in the front row of chairs facing the ramp on my left. They were clapping with their hands high, almost hiding their big smiles.

Suddenly...*Oh no, these shoes are too wide for my thin AAA feet. I hope I don't stumble. Can't look like I'm scared.* I reminded myself, *Keep your smile, Mary Jo. You can do this.* The long pants hid my altered, slightly shorter steps, but I had to take more of them to keep up my pace to meet Patti in the center.

I kept scanning the audience close by, far back, and by both side exits. Patti looked at me with confidence as we met. I could not blow my first back-to-back. Seemed we had done it a jillion times in her dining room and hallway.

With this full tunic, I can't meet as close as we practiced, I calculated. Weight on left foot, right over left, pivot turn halfway around. Shift weight to left and step forward with right. We were back-to-back, facing opposite directions: I sped to the T end of the ramp for my second turn alone, she to the stage for her last pivot and off stage. Loud applause encouraged.

Myrna was on the stage waiting. When we passed, my full tunic swept her slightly.

Happy Thinker: *Wow, I did it. I'm on my way. Modeling's not so bad. I know I can do this.* I disappeared behind the maroon curtain where other girls were waiting to go onstage.

Jerri grabbed my arm and talked like a tape recorder on fast speed. "Great, Mary Jo!! Few girls on ramp before you're out again, usually seven. Extremely fast change. Patti, too. Take stuff off on your way. Get right back here. FAST!!"

I ran to the dressing room, tearing off the babushka, snatching the earrings and bracelets. "Fast change!!" I yelled. No need to yell. No one was there. Just Patti and two dressers. She—almost dressed to go out. I'd be right after her.

Not thinking, I plunged the white earrings and gobs of bracelets into the middle of the neatly separated-by-garment rows of sorted jewelry. What had I done? I looked on my grid and read: GARMENT 2. Mentally, it did not amount to a hill of beans. I grabbed the next garment on the rack. Its scarf fell onto the floor. That was a no, no!

Rosie put her dark hand gently on my arm, "Mary Jo, I have your dress here. You need to take off those hose and put these on. That's the *third* change. You're dressing for the second change."

I panicked, *She must think I'm out of my pea-pickin' mind! This is only my second change and I'm a nervous wreck. I have six more changes after this. Both dressers helping me, and I don't know what I'm doing.*

Sylvia put the not-needed-yet Garment 3 back onto the wheeled hanger.

I snatched the hose off my legs and tugged to draw the next, very-textured ones up my sweaty limbs. Rosie helped me into Garment 2, which I hardly recognized through my blurred eyes. I grabbed a tissue to blot my forehead. I had sense enough to remember not to shift my mile-long eyelashes, hoping their glue didn't melt in the heat emanating from my feverish skull.

Jerri poked her head in and yelled, "Patti, you're on next." Patti checked her grid, grabbed her proper set of jewelry and rushed to the exit. Jerri continued, "Mary Jo, you're after Patti."

Rub it in, why don't you? If my heart would leave my esophagus, I could breathe. No time to breathe.

My fingers dangled uselessly, like spaghetti from spaghetti tongs. I fumbled to wire the tiny holes in my ears with earrings and wondered, *Why didn't I have my ears pierced with a screwdriver instead a thin needle?*

I was in my dress and the scarf. I worked my numb feet into some sandals, which Rosie buckled for me as she shook her head up at Sylvia. I did not have time to decipher the body-read. Sylvia handed me a fedora and I headed toward Jerri.

My head! My hair! I hadn't even had time to think about the rat's nest after tearing off that @%!* babushka like a wild woman!

"You're here?! Gimme that hat." Jerri swished her fingers frantically through my hair, forced the tilted fedora down a tad onto my forehead and rearranged some locks close to my face. "Patti's out now. Pass her on the ramp, work the top of the T with a turn at the two cross-ends." She peeked out at Patti. "Mary Jo, how did you dress so fast? I told Patti to work the ramp a little longer to give you extra time. How did you do it?" she insisted.

I hesitated. I thought. I shook my head, chalked it up to the unexplained and slowly whispered, "You *really* don't want to know!"

She *go-nudged* me. The ramp was easy. Walking a tight rope would have been easier than the dressing room. It was a nightmare.

Somehow, the show went on and on and on. The ramp was always the easy part after that. I felt comfortable. The crowds never bothered me, even in some scary moments later on. I didn't know the impact of work Patti and I had done until that first big show.

If folks really wanted entertainment, they should focus cameras in the dressing rooms!

NEW YORK FLOOR MODEL

Jerri, my sister and fashion coordinator for Frost Brothers, rushed over to me. "Mary Jo, Geoffrey Beene loves your look. Henry Ginsberg says Beene wants you to be his floor model Monday and Tuesday."

I had just completed my first ramp show, one of the biggest for Frost Brothers, and we eight models were in the museum dressing room sorting our accessories that Jerri had to return to various Frost departments Monday morning.

My ears kangarooed. "Oh, no, Jerri," I demanded. "I've never done whatever floor modeling is, and this is the third time out of three that I've done last minute assignments for work."

I had told myself, *No more last minute modeling again*—this time I meant it!

The power of my words was obvious: she immediately wrote my name in her red, thick booking book. "Be in my office by nine on Monday. You'll be on the floor right out my door. I'll clue you in while sorting stuff from this show. It will be perfect. Wear all your makeup, as you did tonight."

Unfortunately, I could not make the week extend longer. Monday arrived on time. So did I at the bus stop—two blocks away from Mom's house—with my bulging bag of assorted shoes, makeup, hairpieces, bra puffers, combs and brushes. I wore my ever-ready, short blue fitted skirt, and the sheer white, puffed long-sleeved, three-inch cuff blouse, lots of gold costume bracelets and necklaces.

My hand gripped a crumpled dollar bill. *I hope my two dollars will cover the round-trip bus fare. Weird how no one in my family knows the cost of a bus ticket. In the convent, we had a complimentary shared bus pass. I'll miss the parking permits we used at the many A-1 Parking lots—if I ever can afford to buy a car. An apartment is my first goal, but I'd have to eat peanut butter all the time to afford rent.*

I appreciate using Mom's and Dad's cars for short jaunts, but keeping it downtown all day wouldn't be right.

Cars were racing past. I wondered, *Why does almost every driver stare at me? Is it unusual to ride a bus? Dad thumbed rides on the way to work and school with four of us. We thrilled riding in police cars and ambulances. There goes another gawker. Sheesh! I'm just going to work. Whoa! Maybe they think I'm a prostitute! Good gosh! I have to buy a car. Wonder how much they are? This is embarrassing.*

The San Pedro bus pulled up at eight-fifteen. I lugged my heavy bag up the three steps, dropped it next to the driver and handed him my crumpled bill. *Thank goodness—he handed me eighty-five cents change.* I turned slightly toward the scattered passengers, but spoke to the driver, "I need to get off at the closest stop near Frost Brothers, please." *Maybe if they realize I'm dressed for legal, decent work, they'll know I'm not a streetwalker or whatever.*

I sat next to the back door to avoid more attention from new passengers when I got off.

We passed all the familiar streets, homes and businesses I had grown up seeing. Half way to town the bus stopped at our old home street of Huisache where we started our ride for school, town, or church since my sixth grade. I wanted to yell to the passengers, "Look! That's where I lived as a kid—on the corner of that block down the hill. I lived there until I went to the convent!" However, I dared not.

I savored every smiling moment. I sat tall in my seat and reminisced in quick flashes: Laurel Theater still across the street, gas station and Handy Andy. Up Huisache was St. Anthony's School, where our Sisters of Divine Providence taught Patti, Candy, Mae and Peggy. I tissued my eyes through *tiers* of makeup and false eyelashes.

The bus escorted me back in time. I didn't care whether the other passengers watched me. I was a child: children look, wonder, capture and smell the scenes.

After about ten minutes, the bus jerked to a stop. "Frost Brothers!" the driver hollered.

"Oh, yes! Thanks for the ride!" I called back. As the bus passed, Frosts appeared directly across Houston Street—the largest store in the block, three stories high. With no car in sight, I jaywalked.

Before I entered, I laid my bag down to gaze at glass encasements that displayed very suave, high fashion, *Vogue* garments covering thin mannequins—each with a stone-face expression. I felt as immobilized and stiffened as they did: petrified. *Here I go again.*

My arm bounded back as I reached for the door's large, filigreed brass handle. Automatic doors! I could have entered the first department with my eyes closed and known where Carmen and Mr. Harris spent part of their pay-checks. I smiled, closed my eyes and inhaled deeply.

I passed the glitz and glitter of shiny golds and diamonds, obviously heavier than most of my family and friends' pocketbooks. Sales people, removing white cloths off their displays, planted their eyes on me as my bag and I headed to the filigreed, arched, metal entrance and doors of the elevator and punched *TWO*.

❧

The familiar large carpeted area led me toward Jerri's office. I gulped and inched to the dressing room where we models had been mannequins—for Geoffrey Beene to dress—several days earlier.

"Great, you're early," Jerri said, moving aside the hanger of Beene's clothes from Friday's gala for my bag and me. "Beene and Ginsberg will arrive soon. Change in here today so I can be in touch."

I removed my shoes and undressed.

"Put on this silk black and white. Go to people on this floor and try to draw them over to his clothes. Talk about the garment as you did at table modeling," she said.

We walked to the section of hanging garments for Geoffrey Beene along the opposite wall. I eyed his name in fancy lettering high on the wall.

"A new model, Jerri?" We both turned to see Saleswoman A, a mature, short, stately woman. "I just called a client. She wants to meet Mr. Beene and see his clothing. Will your new model show them for her?"

"Yes, this is Mary Jo."

Sales A returned to make more phone calls to attract more clients.

Elevator doors opened. Mr. Beene and his spokesperson, Mr. Ginsberg, walked toward us. After introductions Beene strolled to his line of clothes.

262

Mr. Ginsberg turned, "Mary Jo, Geoffrey says the silk looks fabulous on you."

I didn't know whether to say *thank you*, since it was their dress. I said, "It's a beautiful dress."

Elevator doors opened wide again and a group of excited, high-pitched, Spanish-speaking women dashed toward our better-ready-to-wear department.

"Oh dear, they're here already." Jerri showed her welcoming smile and spoke hurriedly to me: "They're a bus of wealthy patrons from Mexico City. The sales women invite them to the big designer trunk showings. They fly up here to shop."

"Welcome, ladies!" Jerri said in high voice and with wide opened arms. "How are you?"

"Muy bien. Very well, thank you," came from assorted pitches reflecting eager-to-shop energy.

"This is Mary Jo. She'll model your Geoffrey Beene selections." She motioned to the hanging area with the fancy printing over Beene's line.

Salespersons floated from Carmen's office across the plush white carpet to greet their individual clients. High-back chairs with cream-colored and gold-metallic thread cushions formed a large semi-circle.

Mr. Harris introduced the two celebrities. Geoffrey Beene stood behind Henry Ginsberg a tad to one end of the section of walled clothing. Rapid, refined Spanish resounded as each lady introduced herself and shook hands. Chatter rattled as they turned to find and finger the new styles.

While excitement persisted with tossing fashions on and off the rods to their sales person, Jerri said, "Mary Jo, they're picking garments they want you to show. The sales people will take turns speaking for their clients. You will have many, all quick, changes."

Sure enough, Sales A stepped toward me with a dress draped over her arm. "Mary Jo, please show this. My client is the one already sitting down." I ran slowly over to the Beene line and found my size two. No clients were searching in that section. I thought, *Goodness, dressing for each of them seems confusing and time consuming.*

I dashed to Jerri's office and ripped off the dress I was in, zipped into another and sped back again. *Oh, no! All of them are sitting now. I don't remember which client wanted to see this one.* I walked toward the group. Sales

A immediately directed me toward her client.

Everyone *oh'd* and *ah'd*. Sales A took over the sales pitch. Client nodded. The two conversed in Spanish while Sales A wrote up a retailing ticket and exchanged it for a wad of cash from Client. Sales A disappeared to a cash register.

Immediately, Sales B showed me the paisley pantsuit and dreaded babushka I wore in the show Friday.

After more *oh's* and *ah's* I was dizzy from many changes, but sales women were orderly, professional and certainly knew their clients' desires and body—as well as pocketbook sizes!

I observed, *Whoa! What are these ladies doing? Those stacks of bills: they don't even try on the clothes. This is a different world. We saved money in the convent by mending the same clothes repeatedly.* Clients bounced to and from chairs to the hanging clothes for more selections each time I showed another fashion.

Sales C begged in a whisper, "Sweetie, show this to my client. She hesitates purchasing new trends, but is easily convinced." I grabbed my size of the black, silk, evening outfit with flowing wide pants, undressed, blotted my forehead, arms, and armpits with a tissue, dressed and rushed back to the group.

"AIEE, NO! PLEEESE, I want for evening. No long pants!" cried Client in broken English. I directed a big yes-smile, pivoted slowly to display the elegant, new style of eveningwear and nodded assuredly.

Sales C standing next to her, bobbed approval, bent and whispered, "Oh, yes!"

Client shrieked, "Jes? Pants for evening? Jes? Oh...okay. In my size?"

Sales C walked to the wall of clothing.

Layers of beams, excitement, and Spanish dictums intermingled from all chairs. "Pants? Evening? AIEE. I wondair what my husband weel say?" Three flew out of their chairs to return to the hanging rack to review more choices again.

I felt I was meeting myself coming back, dashing back and forth until all the women felt their long, expensive flight, cab fare, hotel, meals and purchases had been worth their trip from Mexico City once again.

Constant Spanish buzz and business came to a screeching halt as Elevator slammed its doors.

Whew! What now?

I stood in the middle of the carpeted area to let sense and sanity slowly absorb into my fluttering being.

Jerri rushed to me, "Mary Jo, while no customers are on this floor, go to other departments. Show-and-tell the dress to shoppers. Draw them into our better-ready-to wear on the second floor. When you get back change to another Beene fashion and go out again." I read my tag and headed for the Elevator.

As the door opened, I knew the beauty salon was on that floor: I followed my nose to the right and around a corner. "Mary Jo!" Robert called. "How's it going?" His eyes circled my face, glancing at my hair, but he continued working with stinky fluids and tiny papers on Mature, Dishwater-Blond's head.

I answered him while eyeing his client, "I'm showing a fashion by Geoffrey Beene—his first time here from New York, and he's on the second floor." I pivoted quickly. She drooled at the reflection in the mirror over the counter. Robert politely turned her chair around with his foot, for a full-length view of the fancy pantsuit.

"It's stunning, but seems dressy for pants," she remarked.

"Pants are *in* for anywhere now—church, shopping, entertaining and for evening," I assured.

Robert's other client on the left rammed her hair dryer up, "Geoffrey Beene? I read all about him and his big show at Hemisfair last Friday—and look!" She yanked back a few pages of her *Vogue* magazine, shoved it under my face and jabbed her finger repeatedly to a picture: "Geoffrey Beene's ad! He's still here? Robert! Hurry, my hair is bound to be dry. I want to get down there right away. My neighbor will be so jealous!" she said in an air of teasing.

After twenty minutes working on first and third, I returned to the second floor. Vogue Magazine Woman was radiating from ear-to-ear, changing positions in front of the angled mirrors—in the black and white size 12 evening pantsuit with bell bottoms draped on the floor. I assumed her salon-set hair encouraged her to shop. I passed Alteration Lady with tape-measure necklace and pincushion bracelet heading toward Vogue Magazine Woman.

My stomach growled for grub. I went to Jerri's office, undressed, put my arms into my own blouse backward for temporary modesty, opened my little brown bag and removed one of six, round Hi-Ho peanut butter sandwiches. I carefully put the entire treasure into my wide opened mouth, mashed my lips together so no tiny crumb dropped to the floor, chewed and swallowed all six rounds, one after the other. A handful of grapes helped wash them down.

I felt drained after only half of my first day of floor modeling. Since Jerri was down on the first floor, checking items back into their departments, I lay flat on her office floor. I inhaled a deep *breath* which I hoped did not meld into a deep *sleep*. I could feel my muscles relax for 20 minutes until the door swung open, hiding my corpse behind the door.

An unfamiliar man's voice announced to another someone, "Oh, Jerri's not back yet," and slammed the door. I bounded up with fresh, new energy—so I told myself. In five minutes I was back on the white carpet in the gypsy-print, pantsuit and the dreaded babushka.

⌒⌒

Beene and Ginsberg were whispering by the counter beside Carmen's office. I surmised, *They must have been the two unfamiliar voices.* I smiled, began my little speech about my outfit to a woman walking from the elevator's closing doors and directed her to the fancy sign over on the wall. Geoffrey Beene greeted her, but Henry Ginsberg lowered his head with his raised eyebrows on me. I heeded the beckoned call.

"Mr. Beene would like you to bring your portfolio in tomorrow. Who is your agent?"

My frozen body sweat jellybeans. Split seconds blasted hundreds of questions: *Portfolio, what is that? Agent? Should I have one? Did I do something wrong? Are those good or bad questions? I know I've heard those words before, but I can't remember why. I think Ms. Vincent is my agent, but not for Frost's. What do I say? I wish Jerri would hurry back. I'm scared I'm going to say the wrong thing.*

"Oh, okay," I said to Ginsberg and added, "but I forgot. I'm supposed to be downstairs," I lied and scurried toward Ever-ready Elevator to exhume Jerri from the first floor.

Jerri scared me when she jumped up from her chair behind the counter.

"Wow! Portfolio!? Agent!?" She began wrapping her skirt around the piles of little jewelry in her lap and frantically asked, "Why did he want your portfolio?" She dumped the mounds of jewelry and tags into a bag and handed it to the sales lady who was helping her behind the counter." I have an emergency. Please check these into your department for me." She grabbed my arm and pulled me toward Faithful Elevator.

I explained my big, get-away lie. "I didn't say anything else. I didn't know what to say, or not say."

"You did well. By the way," she insisted, "*I'm* your agent, you hear? I'm going to find out what he wants."

I peeped like a chicken, "I'm going to work the other floors. You all can talk."

Jerri left the elevator, but I took refuge in other departments: beauty salon, men, jewelry, sports, children, shoes and bags. I could show, tell and hide in Beene's outfit.

I had to return, but hoped I didn't disturb Jerri's important conversation. Managing a mouthful of breath, I punched Elevator's button. In a few seconds, I was on second.

"Mary Jo," Jerri burst, "I've been all over this floor, up and down on the #$%^&* elevator looking for you." Blood from my face flushed into hers. "The guys are gone for the day. Ginsberg says Beene wants *you to replace* one of his two New York models. He loves your look, your walk, the way you talk and handle the customers. You're exactly the size and shape of his other model."

"Jerri, this is insane. Why doesn't he take Patti? She wrote the book on modeling."

"He loves Patti's modeling. She's married. They can't move to New York. Joe has his job, little Joe is in school. Mary Jo, you're single. It's perfect."

We collapsed in Jerri's office. Jerri was throwing both palms up, talking fast and loud.

She was right! I did not understand. I felt I was drowning in information, decisions, change again, questions, and no money to my name. Besides, I had not talked it over with a *sane* person yet.

I asked, "What's this portfolio he wants to see?"

"You don't have one yet. It's a resume: collection of your modeling photos, newspaper articles and pictures, including your list of experiences." Her voice got more insistent, "Don't let him know you're new and inexperienced. He likes you. Patti trained you well. We'll start taking pictures right now, right here, in his outfits. I'll tell him we'll send your portfolio later."

She left to borrow Carmen's new camera that Jerri called a "Polaroid that prints out a picture in a few minutes."

I wilted onto a chair by the long mirror, tried unsuccessfully to wake myself up from the nightmare and mooched around in my gray bag with numb fingers. I had to salvage what was left of paint sliding with perspiration from my face. The mirror stared back at me with a muted expression—paint sliding off the image in it, too.

Am I supposed to be excited? Maybe it's easier up there in New York. Where's Patti?

Jerri boomed back into the room with the camera and insisted I hurry.

"Jerri..."

"What? Look! Wear this black and white dress. He'll love you in it—it's one of his favorites." She looked into the camera for an angle in front of the long mirror. "Come on, Mary Jo. Using the mirror, I can get full-length poses of the back and the front at the same time."

Jerri viewed through the camera. "Oh, dear, I've got a reflection of almost the entire room in the mirror—my desk with all this junk, the chairs, that wheeled hanger, your bag, my bag—everything. Come on, let's move everything."

"I'm too old for this, Jerri. I'm twenty-nine."

We continually pushed and pulled stuff; she viewed through the camera repeatedly.

"Ah-ha! Okay. We're ready. CLICK. A picture slowly emerged. She pasted a backing on the three by five-inch color photo so it wouldn't curl. It wasn't like Patti's pretty, large black and white, glossy prints, but Jerri assured me they were good enough.

"Mary Jo, you'll make oodles of money and be a New York Model!" she claimed.

I posed with more appreciation and enthusiasm.

We worked several hours. Jerri drove me home, pumping me up about the fun, advantages and great experience of fabulous New York. I felt she was aiming up to the moon, or at least to the top of the Empire State Building!

I tore through the house to my red bedroom, yelling, "Mom, Geoffrey Beene wants me to be his showcase model in New York. I need to call Patti."

My gray bag banged the floor. I kicked off my shoes, changed into my housecoat and flopped onto the bed with the phone receiver in my hand.

I spoke so fast, Patti just listened as I drew a picture with mixed words: Ginsberg, Beene, portfolio, agent, Jerri, New York, showcase model, Polaroid, posing, doubts, assurances, confusion, more doubts and, finally, "what do I do, Patti?"

"Mary Jo, I'm fixing supper right now," she said gently. "Take it easy. I'll have to call you back."

Mom tiptoed through my opened doorway drying her hands with a kitchen towel. "Mary Jo, I know you're excited. I don't know all of what you're talking about, but you might want to think about whatever it is and talk with Patti before you sign anything. It's all new to you."

Quietly, thoughtfully, I sat up and looked at Mom, "I know. That's what I thought, but Jerri seems to think I should go—once in-a-life time chance while I'm still single."

"Just don't rush into it. Supper in ten minutes." She tucked her kitchen towel back into her apron.

I watched as she left the room. *Here's Mom, cooking for all of us and I'm not home to help as much as I thought I could. She always has meals ready. Dad comes home famished, and Peggy and Mae do homework. Ms. Vincent is lining up work for me. We models don't make as much as people think and there's no pay for fittings. If I had enough piano students, I could stop modeling.*

Next morning: DING.DING.DING. Patti was picking me up. We had fittings for a show soon at the St. Anthony Hotel a block from Frost Bros.

"Mary Jo," Patti chose words carefully as she turned onto San Pedro, "New York is expensive and modeling up there is a challenge for anyone. You think you're busy here. You'd be on your own with no money yet. Geoffrey Beene doesn't know you've had only one month of experience. Many girls up there are nice, I'm sure. But some very serious models can be jealous of each other, back jab and detest the new, pretty girls.

I shifted in my seat, staring into space. She paused—maybe to let me digest that much information or maybe to gather more thoughts.

Patti continued, "Sure, you could say you'd modeled in New York, but would it be worth it? On your own you'd have to find a place to live, get yourself to work by bus, subway, or taxi and walk with your heavy modeling bag. You'd be exhausted and look a mess by the time you arrived at wherever every day.

"You'd go all over New York, depending on your bookings. If you decline they won't call you back. No one is going to help you—you'd be their competition. You'd be isolated. We love you, Mary Jo, and care for you here."

I said nothing.

We were driving yesterday's route, which I'd welcomed from the bus windows. I had re-lived my teen years in ten minutes. Here again I smiled at these familiar places.

Suddenly I saw crowds of people tramping silhouettes of towering brick and windows, racing to red lights, waving at passing cabs, disappearing into subways and appearing as field mice all around me—all from unfamiliar, maybe unsafe, corner curb—watching it all, wondering where I was, and why.

Patti turned to me, "Mary Jo, in this business, you have to watch for yourself. Sometimes men want us because we're pretty. Your job might even depend on catering to them. I know you don't want that."

"You're right, Patti, I am naïve. I had no time to think. Jerri didn't think, either. She was sweet to help me, but I bet she's having second thoughts today. Modeling is a challenge here—how would I survive New York? I thank God every day for you all. I'll always remember how you both give of yourselves. Thanks for being honest just now. I'm going to floor model today, but I *am not* going to make a special effort to run into Beene and Ginsberg."

I relaxed as I inhaled and exhaled this time.

MONEY'S IN MY NAME

In San Antonio, just about everyone knew the name Barbera. Barbera meant the sporting goods business, success, money, honesty, service and dedication to work at church and school. Dad with his Italian temper was eager to live up to those standards. It also meant having to spend every working day with his family of the same Italian temperaments—his father, brother and his nephew. Unfortunately, the pressure came home with him.

My parents had been supportive in January when I left the convent for my year of leave. Mom was the mainstay of my readjustment in their home. Seeing Dad getting up early for work and arriving home at six-thirty, I began to realize the stress of his work and what it meant to be a Barbera girl.

Spring sprang in 1969, several months after leaving the convent. We had a few shows for summer fashions at Bright Shawl luncheons and at the historically famous St. Anthony Hotel's Anacacho Room. I had been working with an ideal stage, runway and dressing room; the month had ended and I needed to get paid.

I retrieved two legal size envelopes from our mailbox—Frost Bros. and Mannequin Modeling with Ms. Vincent. Finally! Paychecks!

I dropped the other mailings onto Mom's large couch and ripped the parcels at their end.

My mind raced: *Wow, total of $119 in my name! What do I do with this? That's a crazy thought. I'm used to endorsing and laying gift-checks on my superior's desk. I'm 29, and I've never earned a single penny in my life! Mom always told me, "We don't take money for babysitting—they're our friends!"*

I sat down on the couch staring at the two checks. *How do I cash these things? I've needed money for three months.* I grabbed a pencil stub from the side table and began a list on the back of the Frost envelope:

NEED MONEY FOR:

*Sisters - $100 they gave me when I left.
*Church – 10%
*Mom and Dad at least $50 a month, rent.
*Summer shoes – dress/casual – for modeling/personal use
*Summer clothes
*Hosiery
*Second bra for work/other undies
*Many toiletries depleting soon - hair, face, bathroom
*Bus fare

I didn't need a mathematician. I gulped. *Thank You, God. At least it's a start.*

That evening at supper, I asked Dad if he'd cash my checks at Barbera Sports. "I suppose I could. *This* time." I smiled big, but wondered why he hesitated.

Then I asked if I could walk the mile after work and hitch a ride home from his business. "I get off at five and you close at six. I'll be glad to help while I wait—dust, sweep, anything. I can save bus fare."

Mom just shook her head and gazed at her supper plate.

"If you wanna hear us yelling back and forth about the business—your grandpa, Charlie the second, and Charlie the third—okay. You might as well find out how we fight to get along," Dad blared.

I didn't ask questions and didn't want to interfere. Why spoil a good meal? I'd be a happy passenger and ignore anything I heard at the store. Besides, I'd have to carry my heavy bag wearing my good shoes. There was no rush to get there to wait until closing. I'd converse cheerfully with Grandpa Charlie, unless there was serious talk between the guys. My potatoes mashed into my blurred meat patty on my melamine plate.

⚬⚬

After a couple more months of work, and cashing checks through Dad, he came storming into the front door while I was putting away piano lesson books.

He was *hot* at the collar, "I can't mess with those little checks anymore. I sell the high ticket items in that store—all the boats, inboards and outboards, the mini-yachts, fishing boats—motors, hiring and firing to keep us in business. And guess who has to take care of our end of reporting sales and expenses. And make paychecks! It takes too much time to sign your little checks, write it in the book, take out the cash, put it into an envelope hoping I don't misplace it and remember to bring it home." He handed me an envelope and wiped his face and neck with his large, white, wrinkled handkerchief.

"I'm sorry, Dad. Thanks for doing it all this time." I slid the little check my student had just left on the piano under a crocheted doily.

He raised his volume up a notch. "Go to my bank a few blocks from Frost Bros. Tell 'em you're Joe Barbera's daughter and you wanna open a checking account. I just hope they don't get your credit mixed up with ours. I have enough stews at work without a mix-up like that."

I contemplated, *Sheesh! I didn't know it was going to be a problem. I know banks make mistakes from past experience in the convent, but Dad's getting huffy.*

Mom stepped out from the kitchen and waved her wooden spoon for him to cool it, but only I noticed.

He frowned and fumed. I got a sermon about my precious checks. I certainly didn't want a mix up either; I didn't need more challenges.

I saved my money frugally; after all, I had a vow of poverty. I weighed every dime. Eventually, I purchased only what I needed, paid the Sisters back, paid Dad a little rent, and was proud I had some left in my purse.

⟳

I soon got an eye and ear opener as I waited for my ride home from Barbera Sports after work. There were no formal offices, just two areas on the south wall, and each had a desk, cabinets, a chair or two, papers and books piled at random. Some framed hunting-pictures hung diagonally in Grandpa's area. A few boat racing trophies (that had no room at home) haphazardly acted as paperweights in Dad's area.

Both cluttered sections displayed mounted animal heads supervising the disorder. A photo dangled from one of the horns with fishing line. I don't remember what, if anything other than junk, divided the two makeshift *offices*.

Dad tried to concentrate on his paperwork. Between puffs of smoke from a pipe or cigar, Grandpa ranted and raved. His rough voice went down Dad's neck constantly, as well as down the necks of customers in the store. Of course, Dad did not let Grandpa have the last word!

Why would an employee want to work in such atmosphere? Dad complained to me that an employee would not work on a Saturday unless he got overtime!

When he learned we always paid time-and-half for every 15 minutes over 40 hours a week to our lay people who worked for us in the convent, he raised his eyebrows as if it were news. I understood why they had constant turnover of good employees.

 ⌒

I arrived at the bank the following week, early before work, so I didn't have to spend bus fare for a *bank only* trip. I opened the tall, leaded-glass doors and basked in the cool air-conditioning after waiting at the bus stop in the hot sun.

I dropped my heavy gray bag at my feet and flexed my left arm. My purse hung on my right shoulder. As usual—from the top of my highly-teased hair, to my painted face with long, false eyelashes, to my puffed blouse, to my short skirt and down to my shiny black heels—I felt I looked like a hooker. I waited and observed.

Bank personnel, who had been scurrying with last minute prep for the day's work, took second looks. Re-stacking orderly papers, raising wondering eyebrows and shoulders, they offered each other the *honor* of waiting on me.

After my own body-read of them, I walked to the nearest unoccupied desk with a metal plaque: NEW ACCOUNTS. I gently placed my priceless cargo of shoes and modeling-junk next to the desk's brown, low back chair facing the rest of the room of employees at their desks.

Caged tellers along the walls hugged the entire area. I beamed gently and waited again.

Forcing a smile, a brave gentleman approached, "I'm Mr. Bradley, bank manager. May I help you, young lady?" The room heaved relief, went back to work, but eked oodles of curiosity.

"Oh, yes, thank you, Mr. Bradley," I said with a smile and just loud enough for cocked ears to overhear. "I'm Mary Jo Barbera, Joe Barbera's daughter." Heads with pursed lips popped up, pencils snapped on desks—all screaming an air of *Bradley gets all the big accounts*.

"I'd like to open a checking account."

"Oh, yes, of course. Open an account!" Brave Bradley said. "Let me get my paperwork."

He scampered over and whispered to a few employees. Slowly a couple wandered over, bowing and scraping, almost to a fault: "Welcome! Coffee? Cookies? Anything?" Miss Pris sashayed quickly to the snack area just in case.

Brave Bradley dashed back to the chair behind our desk and offered me coffee again, which I declined so my lined lipstick wasn't washed off my face. "Oh, no thank you. I don't want to be late for work at Frost Bros. I have an in-store show at ten."

He wrote my name, address and phone number on the proper lines. "And how much would you like to deposit, Miss Barbera?"

My thoughts jerked, *Miss Barbera*.

I was familiar with *Mary Jo*, but I had never been addressed, *Miss Barbera*. It felt final, but he did not have to know I planned to return to a convent in a little over half a year.

My confident fingers reached for my purse, unzipped the little pouch on the inside and unearthed my valuable savings to hand over to Brave Bradley, "The bank will take care of it and I can write checks when needed."

I drew my wad of cash out, as the ladies from Mexico did when they purchased their expensive Beene fashions. But I gripped mine with more care and attention and handed it over the desk saying, "Forty-five dollars for now."

Slowly, he laid down his fancy, long, brown pen.

Silence. Motionless. Stares face to face. I mashed my teeth together behind pursed lips.

Thoughts persisted: *What did I do? Did I say anything wrong? You say something, Mr. Bradley, please! Am I supposed to talk?*

He leaned over his desk, perhaps embarrassed knowing the employees would ask, and whispered, "Miss Barbera, the usual minimum to open a checking account at our bank is one hundred dollars. I'm sorry. You may come back when you're..."

I interrupted quickly, but careful of cocked ears, although I felt the women had dissipated into their work, "Oh, but by the end of the month I hope to have enough to add up to that. I'll be more careful with my spending." I didn't know how I'd possibly spend less, but I was determined to do so.

"I'm sorry. That is our bank's rule."

Disappointed, embarrassed and nervous, I apologized for his time, grabbed my faithful gray bag and disappeared out the front door to Frosts.

At dinner that evening, I relayed fine details of my banking experience as *Joe Barbera's daughter*—from the first impressions exchanged, to the meager amount of money, to the sudden apology, to the decline. We all knew Dad coveted his reputation as an honest, honorable-in-everyone's-eyes, best-in-the-business, award-winning Barbera Family salesman and business owner.

He needed affirmation: "You told 'em you were my daughter? You gotta be kidding!"

The beer in his frozen mug burped onto the table when I answered his emphatic, "You had *how* much to deposit?" He rolled his eyes and hit his forehead with his palm. He was redder than the meat patty on his plate was twenty minutes earlier, and his bank knew I was a Barbera Girl!

Mom and I got up to clear the table.

RAUCOUS DATING GAME

Recall I had left the convent in January to recoup from extreme overwork. It was still early summer, but even spring can be humid and hot in San Antonio. My sister Patti and I stopped at the food court in North Star Mall after selecting economical, cooler clothes for me.

"Mary Jo, when Dr. Bailey asked you to take a leave of absence, he wanted you to relax, live, and date—like a normal single woman."

"Yes, but I don't know anyone."

"I understand. It's tricky. These first months have been hectic, and it's been new for you."

"So how do I meet reputable men in their 30s, willing to go out occasionally and only until next January—with an undercover nun?"

"Joe and I have known Ivan for years. He's a confirmed bachelor, Catholic, and has many other good friends. We're invited to Paul and Carol's condo to swim on Saturday. Ivan's invited. They're all eager to meet you."

"That sounds like a good idea," I said, although a little apprehensive. I hadn't dated since I was sixteen.

Saturday Patti, Joe and I arrived in our swimsuits under our loose beach tops. Patti introduced me to Paul and Carol; then Ivan bounced through the pool gate right after us. He was physically fit, curly haired, blond, jovial and personable. Tall, hand-planted palm trees hovered over us to shade the pool.

The six of us had the area to ourselves. Joe, Paul and Ivan constantly teased, even elbowed each other into the pool. "Hey, buddy, watch out! I'll get you back after that one!" On and on—shooting water or water-soaked foam balls at each other.

We enjoyed playing Marco Polo as if we were kids, or aiming a foam ball into a floating water tube.

Carol served simple cold drinks and the three guys had a beer each. Soon we were into fun that was more rambunctious: splashing each other, popping water from clammed palms and trying to outdo each other with the creativity of getting each other wet amid the amusement and active arm swinging.

Disaster approached.

Ivan went under water and motioned me to climb onto his shoulders so I was higher than the others were. I did. He held my legs over his chest until only my feet were dragging in the water.

It was a balancing act: I had nothing to hold onto except Ivan's head, hair and ears. I tried to avoid mutilating him.

Disaster happened!

I swooped up a tsunami amid yells of hilarity as I flanged into the deep water behind Ivan. He turned around as I popped up for air. My eyes—even with the edge of the water—did not want to believe what I saw.

Everyone howled as I stared at two, foam, swimsuit falsies bobbing back and forth on waves between Ivan's bulging eyes and mine! I fought to grab them, but not being a swimmer, I was hanging on to Ivan with one hand. With the other I jabbed erratically as falsies floated in opposite directions. Eventually, the little monsters zigzagged the white capped waters to where I could touch bottom on my two big toes.

I water-danced a frenzied tarantella to the accompaniment of loud cries of laughter.

What was I to do, except to snatch the defiant little items, drown myself in humility under water for replacement, come up for air again and join the amusement? I needed a wake-up call from that dream, but even our deafening ricochet of hilarity didn't end my nightmare.

That's how I met Ivan.

Ivan and I went out often and I dated some of his chums. However, on Sunday at Blessed Sacrament Church the same month, I read a bulletin announcement:

> The Catholic Alumni club invites practicing Catholic, single, college graduates, twenty-one years or older, to meet with members after Sunday Masses today in the parish hall for information and refreshments.

In the hall, members welcomed me, "We have no dues and you can attend as many or as few get-togethers as you like. We meet at restaurants, in our apartments for parties and for drinks and dancing at respectable nightclubs. Sometimes we meet at clubs on the San Antonio River. Here's our June activity calendar."

Although it was like dating in a fishbowl, we all had great times and I became very active, even working actively in the community to gather foods for the needy from stores, entertaining with my guitar while singing in nursing homes, and dating many wonderful men. Most of us attended weddings of couples who met through the organization.

To make up for little summer modeling work, I was teaching several piano students in Mom's home and at Sim's Baldwin Piano Company in North Star Mall. Although I had as many students as I could handle, 40% of my income went to Sim's Baldwin. I looked forward to having enough students at home so, eventually, I could drop modeling. Besides, I had only until January to hang in there and be *normal*.

At the same mall, two miles from home, was the new Frost Bros. *North*, where we could depend on modeling every Saturday in the summer around the indoor water fountain. The water feature was just a few yards from the inside entrance of North Frost in the large rotunda. A two-foot high runway with vanity lights along each side was set up extending from North Frost to blending into the circle around the decorative tiled wall of water. It stretched out another eight yards into the open mall.

For two months, posters in the mall read:

**MISS AMERICA, JUDITH ANNE FORD
in FROST BROS. NORTH
FOUNTAIN FASHION SHOWS
July 4, 1969
1 o'clock and 3 o'clock p.m.**

The week before the show, Jerri called to book me, adding, "Mary Jo, this'll be exciting. We seldom hire male models, but Ivan (yes, the Ivan from the raucous pool incident) will be in these big shows. You, Patti and Miss America will also do the downtown, in-store fashion shows on Monday and Tuesday."

Saturday Patti and I showed up at North Frost on July 4th for the special productions at the mall. Several hundred extra chairs sat around the fountain and runway in the huge rotunda. Runway lights were bright, and Kenny Fisher's accordion was attracting early birds an hour in advance. Merchants bustled with customers flooding their stores before the one o'clock event.

During the show we all drew crowd-handclapping, but Ivan and Miss America won the well-deserved, loudest applause prize!

After the first production we were famished. We quickly changed into our own clothes, and decided on lunch together before the next performance—a challenge with shoulder-to-shoulder people. We lost precious time checking out fast food places to accommodate eleven.

"I just reserved the Branding Iron," Ivan called. "They're moving tables for us." We flocked together and rushed back to the nice little restaurant with black and red décor. Our table extended from the cash register to the back of the room. Ivan sat at the head, I to his left and the only vacant spot was across from me.

We were studying our menus when a voice called out, "Hey, Ivan! What's going on?"

Ivan looked up. "Hey, Chris! Good to see you!"

Chris beamed from ear-to-ear as he scrutinized the painted faces with fancy hairdos at Ivan's *banquet* table. He was a tall, handsome hunk with fair skin, was about Ivan's age, and was dressed in a uniform I did not recognize yet.

"Come on, Chris! Sit down here," Ivan said. Chris didn't hesitate. Ivan explained our quick lunch between fashion shows. He introduced me as "his girl" and pointed out Patti, since we were the only ones Ivan knew.

Adrenalin was high. Models with excited, high-pitched voices, had been chattering about the two shows. Now their eyes bounced between Chris and me. I was the only single girl besides college-age Gail. Even I noticed Chris had no wedding band!

Chris was on his lunch break from an upstairs workshop with other Braniff International Airline employees. I tried not to stare, but he was sitting directly across from me, and the other girls were engaged in their own chitchat.

I studied, *He has beautiful blue eyes and a sweet smile, but his light brown hair doesn't take up much real estate on that large head any more. I wonder how old he is. He is a friend of Ivan and Ivan knows we're just dating. Besides, Patti says Ivan is a confirmed bachelor. I wonder if Chris has been married before, maybe not. I have no intentions on marrying anyone, but maybe he'd like to date sometime before January. It wouldn't be right to ask Ivan for Chris's phone number. I don't even know his last name. I couldn't call him, anyway. Girls don't call the guys.* In 1969 it wasn't proper.

Soon models were paying bills at the cash register. We had to rush back to Frost Bros. to change for the next show and refresh our makeup.

Leaving Branding Iron, Ivan offered me his arm—and so did Chris, on my left side. I was elated, but we talked about little nothings during those few seconds. Would I see him again? Small chance.

A new crowd had started to gather around the fountain for the second show. All eyes turned toward us as we approached. Cameras, intended mainly for Miss America, got bonus shots of us. We couldn't ignore their clicks, so we smiled pleasantly and dashed into Frost Bros.

We began unbuttoning our own duds as we neared the dressing rooms. Through the thin area dividers and curtains, the models came alive and squealed like teenagers: "Mary Jo, who was that gorgeous guy? Did he give you his phone number? Did you like him? What was his uniform?"

He seemed like a nice person, but I did not care for this hyped-up attention and these questions. I hardly knew more about him than his Braniff Airline uniform and his physical appearance. I hoped men would not be interested in me only because of the way I dressed, where I worked, or because God made me pretty.

DESIGNERS AND EXCUSES

I needed the perfect dress for the lowest price San Antonio had to offer, and our faithful Solo-Serve, a block from home, was my only necessary stop—right from the box to the rack, and waiting for me. Ivan was going to Europe. His friends were giving him a party in the HemisFair Tower and I was to be his date.

Ivan picked me up that Saturday night. He, nor anyone else, had ever seen me dressed as I was. When he entered the living room, he stopped short with raised eyes, accompanied by a jaw-lowering approval. Even I was impressed with my daring, pink, light weight, short, dinner dress and soft, evening makeup. I did not need an excuse to leave those long, false eyelashes at home.

From the front, the fashion showed a one-inch, stand up collar. It was sleeveless—three inches away from the edge of my shoulders—had a slightly gathered bodice, high waist of two-inch satin ribbon and a slight A-line very short skirt. I wore white patent-leather shoes, slightly pointed, with low heels and a thin strap on top. Dangling pearl earrings and a small, white pocket purse put finesse to the ensemble.

"Whoa!" Ivan exclaimed with both arms curved forward and a small bend forward at the knees.

He thought he'd seen it all, until I smiled and did a slow, dramatic 360-degree pivot in the middle of the living room to expose my *bare back* from the stand up collar to the waist. A six-yard, costume pearl necklace Patti had given me when I'd left the convent, was looped in cascading small to large layers around my neck, down across my bare back to my waist. My very thin, tall bod loved the built-in little falsies.

I knew Patti would be happy with my comfortable creativity. She was, "Mary Jo, you are so clever." I thanked her for the training to be original and innovative.

Patti and Joe, along with many of Ivan's friends, were sitting as we arrived and made our way around the tables in the large circular tower to greet, introduce and give thanks. I felt "highly uplifted," overlooking the historic, lighted, downtown San Antonio River, the Alamo and miles of panoramic and picturesque views below.

There he was at one of the tables—the Chris I had met at Branding Iron between the two July 4th fashion shows at North Star Mall. The arrangement of tables in the tower allowed only visiting at the assigned table, so I didn't see him the rest of the evening. Nor did I see him before he went with Ivan to Europe. His work with Braniff Airlines allowed him to travel as often and where he wanted, as long as he showed up for work.

While Ivan and Chris were gone, I was lost in work for fashion designers once again during the last months of summer, especially, for Helen Rose Fashions of California. Sitting on a plush couch in Frost Bros. while posing for the photographer, she asked, "Mary Jo, show that lovely gown with me. Be creative. Have fun." I swished and turned to show-off her designed long dress of bright colors with several full petticoats. The photo was not only in the newspaper, but also in her tri-fold, color brochure.

My little pocket calendar squeezed in bookings for designers like Valentino, Oscar de la Renta, Bill Blass, Emilio Pucci, and Pricilla of Boston. There was a full page, color, newspaper ad with Ann and me announcing a charitable ball at Oak Hills Country Club with *Vogue* Magazine styles like Malcom Starr. Every time I showed up for work at Frost Bros., models asked whether I'd seen that man, Chris, whom I'd met at the Branding Iron Restaurant on July 4th. I did not need an excuse to avoid answering anymore.

Mannequins in store windows displayed fall clothes at North Star Mall, when there he was again. I almost ran into Chris from the side. I was rushing and already late for my piano lesson at Baldwin Piano Company. My legs were weak from running, and now they were limp from excitement.

He remembered me. "Oh. Hey. Hi. Got time for coffee and pie?"

"Uh. Oh! Yeah! I mean"... *what do I tell him?*

"Good, how 'bout..."

I interrupted nervously, blurting in staccatos: "No. I mean yes. I mean. No. I gotta go. I'm late for a piano lesson. Gotta go. No pencil, paper to give you my phone number, either." I must have sounded like a big bag of excuses.

"A piano lesson? Here at the mall?"

Sheesh! He does think I'm making up excuses.

"I don't have a pencil or paper either," he said.

My thoughts overlapped each other: *Now he's making excuses, or does he really want to go out? Can't let him go. Waited too long to meet him again. Now I'm really late.*

Eagerness, tardiness and frustration twisted my insides like a bowl of spaghetti. As I began dashing toward Baldwin Co., just a few yards away, I yelled, "Hey, I live with my parents and their phone number's easy: eight, two, eight, one, eight, one, eight. Call me, okay?" I repeated, getting louder and faster as I distanced away, "Eight, two, eight, one,eight,one eight!"

I huffed and puffed up the stairs inside Baldwin whispering aloud, *Oh, that's just great. I wonder how many other shoppers memorized that number, too. Dad will kill me if we get kinky phone calls. Hope no student's parents witnessed my insane scene. They'll think I'm picking up some man in the mall. Now I need to focus. Help me, Lord.*

Each day I woke up thinking he would call for that coffee and pie date. Finally he did, but I didn't even recognize his voice. We both fished for eager, but proper, words.

"I'm so glad you called. It's..."

"Yeah, heh, heh..." he popped in nervously, "I didn't..."

"Oh, that's okay, my address is..."

"Oh, yeah, heh, heh, that's a good idea."

"It's 129 Harriett, close to San Pedro and Jackson-Keller."

"I know just where that is. My brother lives not far away on Pinewood. Pick you up at seven-thirty. See you then."

"Oh yes! Okay, bye now."

Whew, that was quick. I can't wait to tell the models he finally called.

I decided to wear my new fall outfit of tan turtleneck and brown pants under the latest style: long, below-the-knee-length, dark green, sleeveless vest with gold buttons from top to bottom and my new boots.

On November 11, 1969, in his old 1960, navy and white, Ford hardtop, Chris explained, "Ivan is staying a year in Europe. He bought a car to see the sights while working a little over there, but I only had a week off from Braniff."

Well, I guess I won't have to worry about dating Chris more than Ivan. It's only until January 24th, little over two months. Then I can go back to the convent.

Chris continued, "We're going to surprise some friends tonight. George and I rented rooms for about a year from Bohn in his new home to help pay the mortgage. When Bohn got married, Sue moved in, and we moved out. I want to see the house again and I want them to meet you."

I could not believe it. How would I tell him you don't just drop in on people? The excitement of my first date with Chris was oozing from my heart. Our family never did that. Dad would fume if someone just dropped in when he and Mom were not prepared, or when he was cleaning the pool or doing paper work. I was embarrassed, but glad he was not surprising any of *my* friends.

DING-A-LING-A-LING-A-LING—over and over. I rolled my eyeballs behind Chris' back with his itchy finger on the doorbell. My mind prayed, *Enough already. I hope they're not home.*

Someone fiddled with the latch a long time, and the door opened—just enough to peek. Bohn whispered, "Chris, good to see you. Come in." He opened the door wider.

My mind kept fluttering, *This is not happening! Poor Bohn. Slippers, sweats, unshaven, bed-head, eyelids half open. I knew we shouldn't have come. Chris should tell him we'll come another time.*

Chris eagerly bounded in with a hearty, "Hey, man. What's up? Haven't seen you in a long time. You still coaching? Wanted to see you guys again and see the house."

I thought, *Oh-h-h, yeah! Great time for an open-house tour. The place is dark, and somewhat disheveled—papers on tables, wilting blue bonnets and carnations in a vase. Pleasant smell, but I can't place it. Bohn's probably sick, or maybe Sue.*

A woman's faint voice called out slowly from the hallway, "Who is it, Bohn?"

Ignoring or not hearing, Bohn muttered, "Chris, we just got home from the hospital."

I knew it. I grit my teeth and I even grit my thoughts, *Chris, let's go. Can't you take a hint? Wish I could hide out in the car.*

"Hospital?" Chris asked.

"Oh, I thought you came because we had our first baby. It's a boy, Chris. Another football player. His name is Lance! Just think: coaching my own boy."

My mind pleaded, *Oh! Dear God, in heaven: Pa-leese. Can this get any worse? These poor people are so exhausted—they're like drunks in the middle of the night. I know what it's like: formulas, diapers, constant laundry, phone calls, visitors trying to be nice. In her free five minutes between all that, Mom had to decide whether to eat, take a bath, wash her hair, or return phone calls, when all she really wanted to do was melt into a mattress for a month. Now I recognize the nice smell—baby powder and baby oil.*

Tiny little Sue, with disheveled, brown hair, no makeup, looking like she was walking in her sleep, came shuffling into the family room, gripping her robe to her chest. The other hand clung to the edge of the couch "Chris, thanks for coming." She smiled sheepishly. "Give me your big hug." He bent down to her.

They looked past Chris at me, unsuccessfully hiding. One more thought, *Yes, Chris, remember, I'm here?*

"Oh, Chris, you're married?"

My body froze and defrosted in the same instant. I jumped in, quickly introduced myself and congratulated the sweet little couple. They offered us to sit, and Chris plopped on the *familiar couch* he recognized. I sat reluctantly, but declined the polite offer for coffee, hoping Chris would not respond, "Why not?"

I instantly assured them, "We're on our first date, and we're going for coffee and pie, but Chris had to stop by." They resumed breathing—a bit.

That poor lady. I felt we made them feel even more miserable, especially since we had dressed to make a good impression on each other for our first date. I was glad I had not worn all my stage makeup, especially those huge false eyelashes. That would have made a bigger wedge between them and us.

Chris exclaimed, "Mary Jo's a high fashion model for Frost Brothers and other places like Sears..."

What on earth? Surely my ears were deceiving me. I was numb. I don't know what Chris rattled on about. My brain cells angered, *Why not widen the gap between how we feel? Just what they needed to hear: I'm a high flutin' fashion model, and these poor darlings in this lovely house look like death warmed over— only they feel worse. Nothing like that first, good impression!* I assumed that was just him, a thirty-seven-year-old bachelor.

After visiting for what I thought was excessively too much time, I was eager to assure them, "I love little ones, being the oldest of six girls. And I understand how my own mother felt for weeks after coming home with another baby, but she had me to help her. The first one must be the hardest, learning how to care for the baby and take care of yourself."

I rose to give Sue a big hug. I knew she was at ease.

Finally, the excuse to excuse ourselves: "Chris, this happy couple needs to get to bed. They're in for long nights of short sleeps."

And that was my *impressive,* first date with Chris.

HOLIDAY DECISIONS

I donned my black turtleneck, my black tights and tall black boots. Then I slid a sleeveless lightweight, sliver, Mylar rectangle blouse with neck and arm openings over my head. A Mylar belt gathered the costume at my waist. This was the fashion for models doing promotions for men's British Sterling toiletries for seven days until Christmas in many stores across the nation.

My agent, Ms. Vincent said, "Mary Jo, in addition to your pay, you'll receive sets of cologne, aftershave and soap on a rope in retail packages attractively boxed as Christmas gifts, not samples."

I thought, *What a break! Maybe I'll get enough for Dad, both grandpas and Joe Lynch.*

We were at Wolff and Marx close to home at North Star Mall. "Mary Jo, be sure you ask the shoppers whether you may spray the wrist with British Sterling—and don't get it on their clothing."

I strolled around the men's department with my spray bottle, inviting clients to consider "the handsome boxes for men who are hard to please."

Each day was long and busy, but seeing the success of the sales, I was exuberated with the work. On Christmas Eve I instantly recognized a woman, despite the furrowed face of hard years of raising children as a military wife.

I froze. *I know that's Mrs. Donahue. I taught her oldest of four, John and Nelle, in Abilene during my first four years of teaching.* She tossed through men's shirts, ties, and other items before closing time. *I really want to talk with her, but I feel awkward—she doesn't know I left the convent, and I have all this stupid makeup on. She always saw me in the long, black and white religious garb. Lord, help me know what to do.*

I knew if I didn't approach her soon, she'd leave and I'd probably never see her again.

I questioned myself. *She's probably rushing to get home to celebrate. I wonder if they were transferred to San Antonio. I'm embarrassed. I have never had this situation happen and it won't be the last. Will she be ashamed of me?*

My hands trembled uncontrollably. *I've thought of her so often. She always reminded me of my caring mom, a lovely woman.*

I stepped close enough to talk so I did not advertise to the other customers what I thought would be an awkward conversation. "Mrs. Donahue?" She jerked up and looked me in the face.

Immediately I relieved her curiosity, "Do you remember me? I was Sister Mary Janet. I taught John and Nelle piano in Abilene."

She dropped her parcels onto the table and opened her arms for a hug. "Oh, Sister! I mean..." she stopped.

"Mary Jo Barbera." I gave her a twenty-second version of my leave of absence and my costume. "How are the children?"

She wiped her tears and rushed to a phone. In a few minutes, John and Nelle were visiting, also.

We were all sobbing with joy and laughing that their teacher-ex-nun's makeup was sliding off her face.

Mrs. Donahue broke in. "You Sisters worked so hard at St. Joseph Academy. We loved all of you."

"And we appreciated our military families. Air Force students were disciplined, dedicated students."

"We always remembered our fun at the piano," John remarked.

Nelle looked at me, "Sister—I mean, Mary Jo—you look the same, but so different. I don't even know how to put on that much makeup."

With a last round of laughter, we hugged good-byes. It was a moment in time to cherish. The very first students I had ever taught accepted me as a layperson. They actually remembered me, appreciated my work and were excited to see me; but all of us were eager to get home.

I studied the large brass clock across the men's department. I assumed Mom was already hosting the annual Christmas custom: grandchildren placing figurines in the elaborate crèche while someone read the familiar Christmas story, adults gripping lit candles, and all singing Silent Night. Cousins would be looking forward to exchanging the many gifts.

Chris was invited, but I wasn't sure he'd show up. Surely he had family or a date preplanned. I didn't know much about him, having known him for a short time and only *one* date. I wanted to be there with my family for the first time in many years, whether Chris attended or not. Besides, I was eager to get home with the dozen free sets of British Sterling for the men in my family and for Chris.

As I drove up at Mom's home, I smiled at the parked cars announcing that Barberas were having another huge family get-together; but I didn't see Chris' old navy and white Ford.

"Yeah! Mary Jo got off early! We haven't started yet!" Everyone welcomed me. I rushed to the back bedroom to change from my British Sterling outfit. Soon we heard DING-A-DING-A-DING-A-DING.

"I'll get it. It's Chris!" I called out as I pushed through about twenty adults and kids to greet him at the door. Not expecting him to remember names, I politely began to introduce him to all of my sisters and their families.

"Chris," Patti's husband, Joe Lynch, interrupted, "you're going to be quizzed. Be sure to take note."

I warned Chris, "You enter at your own risk with this gang."

"Oh no, I'm new here. This is be-kind-to-Chris day." He seemed to enjoy the frivolity.

The evening of ceremony, hearty snacks and excited confusion of gift paper, bows, tags, toys, new garments—all was in anticipation of a longer day after church tomorrow.

Chris obviously enjoyed the jabbing jokes and loud teasing in the living room. He yelled across the room to Dad, "Hey Joe, I know you're a fisherman. Have you caught the big one yet, or just *talk* about catching the big one?"

With a "gotcha-back" grin, Dad yelled back, "Hey, Chris, you said you played football as a Longhorn at UT, Austin. Did you really? What position did you play?"

Chris ping-ponged instantly, "I played tight end and I caught every pass I was thrown...both of them!"

You had a challenge knowing what to believe with the guys trying to up-one the last person who spoke.

Seeing the room was into their game of funs and puns, Mom snuck to the kitchen to begin cleaning up left over dips, chips and sandwich makings. I followed to pitch in and thank her for letting me invite Chris. She whispered, "Do you think he would like to come for Christmas dinner tomorrow?"

That was an unexpected question. I set the roll of wax paper down, thought, then said, "Mom, that's sweet of you, but I'm sure he has family. I don't know him that well yet. He would be embarrassed if he had to make up an excuse for not coming, especially if he has a date.

"That's how I feel. You can think about it, but he's invited to come."

My heart pounded. *What should I do? If I hurt Chris, he might not want to see me again. Maybe he'd be more hurt if I don't invite him.*

I measured my steps slowly back into the living room and pulled him aside, "Chris, Mom invited you for noon dinner tomorrow. If you have plans, we understand." I waited and hoped the family noise drowned the thud of my heart.

Chris raised his eye brows; his eyes danced around my face. "Oh, huh, eh, yeah? Well..." he shrugged his shoulders. "Sure. Fine. Thanks!"

I was overjoyed thinking, *No family? No date? Whoa! What kind of outgoing, handsome hunk, older guy has nowhere to go on Christmas? I really have to get to know what makes him tick, how he spends his life. Maybe he's lonesome. He seems outgoing, personable and witty.*

"Mom, I'm so glad I asked. He's coming!"

Her spatula picked up speed emptying a bowl of salad to a smaller container. "Great."

౿

The next day everyone arrived before Chris again. He entered with a heavy brown bag mounted on his right arm, gripped with his hand. "Joe Barbera, this is for you."

Dad jolted with surprise as Chris handed him a brand-new wallet in an unwrapped, expensive box.

"Joe Lynch, this is yours." He forked over a handsome, unwrapped manicure set.

Looking around the room, he spied Peggy's boyfriend, "This is yours, Clark." He continued around the room. Finally, he folded the empty bag.

We were like statues eyeing each other. Someone whispered, "How does he remember all the names he just heard last night, and have a gift for every man in the room?"

Being a bachelor for thirty-seven years, he probably got more wallets, pen and pencil sets, manicure sets, ties and handkerchiefs than he could use. So what? No one expected anything, especially to remember names.

I still dated my other friends, but only Chris seemed interested enough to interact with my family. I assumed that being single for so long, he probably wasn't looking for marriage. Neither was I. After all, I was going back to the convent in a few weeks. Why was I starting to feel queasy about the next few weeks?

That was my first all-day-Christmas at home in thirteen years, and that entire week of holidays offered an assortment of excitement, but also unusual—and important—decisions.

My Date
with the Rose

A predicament marinated my brain for days. Mom and Dad were allowing the Catholic Alumni Club (CAC) to use their home for our New Year's party. (CAC was our church social club to meet other single Catholic, college graduates at least 21 years old.) It was a little like dating in a fish bowl, but we enjoyed it and eventually attended some of their weddings.

I was dating six members of the club and had just started dating Chris, who didn't qualify for CAC since he was not Catholic or a college graduate. He had taken me to the children's play "The Magic Tent" one evening after I worked for British Sterling. We hardly had a chance to talk and I was glad I invited him to the party. After all, it was at my house.

Selecting recordings on vinyl 33.3 and 45-rpm for the party that night, I was at Mom's stereo in her large terrazzo den parallel with the same size living room.

The view of the lights around the 50x30 foot pool past the big covered patio, the high bar between the breakfast room and den—the place was perfect for parties! The lights among the little elf-faces strung over the bar, and the large Christmas crib in the living room took care of the main decorations. CAC members would bring all the foods, drinks, tableware, party hats and noisemakers. Actually, I had it easy, except...

The haunting thought of who my date at the party in ten hours would be kept stepping on my happy thoughts. Several liked me very much, especially Bob. And now—Chris! All of them would greet me with big smiles. Why did life have to be so complicated? Who should be my date?

I put down the record and sat sideways on the long, marble window seat next to the fish aquarium. My brain had sucked up too much energy. A glass of orange juice would give me strength.

I stared through the wall of window glass. The large patio walked my gaze to the large pool to think out things. Was I dating too many men? At the end of my dates I was embarrassed to reach for my calendar when they asked for another get-together. There were only seven nights in a week and too many dates! Do I wait for them to call and ask me to be their date? Girls didn't call guys anyway. (In the '60s it was not proper.)

DING.DING.DING. Saved by the doorbell. I put down my glass. I didn't like to think of things like that.

At the door, a florist handed me a long centerpiece, "Mary Jo Barbera? It needs water."

"Oh, yes! Thanks, this is perfect for the party tonight." I had never had flowers delivered to me in my life.

I walked slowly and placed it in the center of the open bar. The arrangement was heavy with yellow gladiolas spreading horizontal on the bottom a yard across. The white, yellow, and orange spider mums, greens, and long brown sprigs cascaded from top to bottom. In the center of the low triangular centerpiece stood an eight-inch, dark brown, antiqued hourglass, four inches in diameter.

A tiny card hid inside. I carefully opened the little envelope: *Happy New Year. See you tonight. Chris.*

I was touched. *Wow! This is too much.* I sat down. Got up. Sat down again. What should I do? I left well enough alone. I'd see him at nine tonight and be up late. I took a quick nap.

⌒⌒

What a great way to throw a party! Everyone started arriving at nine and placed their pots of luck on covered tables and on the bar with the lovely centerpiece. Dancing, high energy, clean, light drinking, and chitchat kept friends happy. My job of providing the place was over. I was free to introduce Chris and keep conversations with the other twenty-five people.

Mom's Grandfather Clock struck midnight—DING-DING-DING—the doorbell also rang in the New Year! Noises in the house dissipated as I went to the door with party guests close behind asking who would be showing up so late.

There he was—a faithful cab driver who announced he was "right on time" as he presented me with a long 20-inch floral box. Someone hired him to deliver the package wrapped around its middle with a wide, red satin bow. I thanked him and gently untied the sash.

The gang was edging in to get a view: "Who's it from? What is it? I can't see."

"How do I know?" I ceremoniously removed a slightly opened, perfectly shaped, light yellow *paper* rose with a long stem. It expelled a powerful, handsome and familiar aroma which I couldn't identify at that moment. Obviously, someone had doused it abundantly so it wouldn't lose its fragrance, at least not until midnight. A scroll of parchment paper tied with small ribbon lay next to the rose.

"Read it, Mary Jo. Read it."

Carefully, I laid down the box and unwound the scroll. The room was silent, patiently waiting. I read aloud what someone had typed in all caps:

TO MARY JO

SURELY – AS I HAVE

PLACED A KISS

UPON THIS ROSE

AT – THE STROKE OF MIDNIGHT

ITS FRAGRANT SECRET

WILL BE DISCLOSE

IF WITH YOUR LIPS

YOU PLACE YOUR KISS

AS I IMPOSE

THEN – YOU WILL

KNOW THE SECRET

THAT IT HOLDS

AND – IT WILL

HAVE SERVED THE

PURPOSE I HAVE CHOSE

THAT – TWO HEARTS MEET WITHIN A ROSE.

B. STERLING, THE SORCERER

NEW YEARS DAY. 1970.

My heart was thumping in sync with the crystal ball and count-down on TV in the middle of the Times Square crowd. The crowd of friends surrounding me was no help to the confusion I was experiencing as I tried to decipher just who the mystery man was. My mind spun shattering recollections.

That waft of fragrance was so thick and familiar, I could cut it with a knife. I wondered, *But what is that smell? I feel I'm on Jeopardy with a count-down to give the last name of my own father. Has Memory just fled with the last moments of 1969? Why did it abandon me? Too many questions—so little time—no answers. What am I to do? Think!*

I cancelled all distractions and concentrated, *The SORCERER? B Sterling?! Yes! I remember the sets of British Sterling cologne and aftershave I received as part pay for that Christmas promotion. But I gave several men here in this very room sets for Christmas. One of those tonight thinks he is the only man who received one. How do I handle that? My heart's pounding, but not out of joy and love, but because I'm shaking with awkwardness. And the SORCERER? Sounds so familiar, too! Who sent this rose and poem?*

Guests started picking up paper cups and decorations. Soon they left, except for Bob and Chris, who competed to be the last-man-standing, lingering on, keeping awkward conversation with each other—and with me.

I felt sorry for Bob. He was a fine person. I had dated him more often than I had dated Chris. His body spoke loudly—bewildered and nervous. However, I did invite Chris because he wasn't an automatically invited CAC member.

Bob killed time prancing back and forth, adjusting his tie and looking around, "That surely is a beautiful centerpiece—that big wooden hour glass and all!"

I blurted out, "Yes, isn't it beautiful? It's so different and appropriate!"

Chris interrupted, "I had it delivered to Mary Jo earlier today as a contribution to *our* party" while looking face to face with Bob. The two opponents wandered around the room, alternating with hands in pockets, or loosening a tie, or rubbing chin or forehead.

After about half an hour, Bob yawned, "Well, it sure is getting late."

Chris responded with his determined, but soft voice, "It looks like I'm going be here for breakfast." He had claimed a sympathetic victory.

Bob caved in and left, leaving Chris and me alone!

Fingering some left-over mints, I hovered disappointed thoughts, *Drats, Chris hasn't kissed me at any time yet since we've been dating. I had looked forward to midnight when everyone kisses everybody else. Oh, dear! No one kissed anyone at midnight! The taxi cab driver interrupted all of us.*

In the middle of the living room Chris explained he had a cold and knew he would not want to kiss me and *vice versa*. He clarified that he had sent the poem and paper rose, reeking with the British Sterling, since he wouldn't be able to kiss me.

The *SORCERER*? Ah, yes! That was the main character in the children's play he had taken me to see about two weeks earlier.

Impressing relief! I took out the powerfully fragrant rose and poem and read it aloud again. As we went to the door, I gave him a big smack—on the cheek! At least he could go home and know that now I was ready for him to give me his first kiss later, when he was over his cold!

I knew I'd cherish that rose—that the *hint* of British Sterling was destined to linger years to come, and that it would be a reminder of who my date with the yellow rose was in 1970.

RETURN OR NOT RETURN

I lay in bed tossing and turning. Sometime in the next twenty-three days, I must call the convent to let them know whether I am returning at the end of my year of leave. I've prayed fervently during the past year to know His will and I look forward to going back. I still love religious life—the community living, the vows of poverty, chastity and obedience, teaching music, and the Sisters who were a loving family. I treasure every mission I completed and got along with all of the Sisters. I thrived on the life. It's what got me up in the mornings.

Why do I feel edgy? I know I always did my part of the work; in fact, most of the time I did more than asked. I worked fast and hard and don't recall complaining. I had prayed before I informed the Sisters that I felt teaching high school choir was beyond what I was trained to do, even after two years of honest effort and prayer. I constantly heard, 'We think you can,' so I continued. Why am I hesitant?

I tossed onto my side again. Thoughts tossed more, but I smiled and I gazed at the stars in the clear night outside the window. Making tuition, music, science, kindergarten and other bills then balancing the books were challenging duties, but each month I managed to get it done. It gave me a feeling of accomplishment and I was doing it for Him. I cherished doing small things daily for His honor and glory. I felt I was fulfilling my purpose on my application to join the Sisters—to love God and make Him loved.

My thoughts turned on my side, too. *Maybe I wouldn't be fair to the Sisters if I returned. They've spent so much money paying my hospital bills and I don't remember how many times I was readmitted. They don't need more hospital bills.*

Lord, help me in this decision. I've been open and honest this entire year, doing all Dr. Bailey asked me to do. I certainly have dated enough men. It was fun dating, but I give that fun and experience back to Him. Men were respectful for the most part. I remember about four who wanted more from me on a date than I was willing to give; but I was firm, and never went on a date with them again. I've had four proposals, but I wasn't in love. Chris is nice, but he doesn't compare with religious life.

Yes, I was naïve in the convent taking on more than I could handle, but the Sisters taught us to say "no" only after praying and doing our best. I did that, took on more than my body and mind could handle, and I fell apart. If I return, will I be able to say no, or will I get sick again from overwork? That's what hurts. I do not want to be a burden to the Sisters.

I bawled in my pillow with those last thoughts. *I can't do that to the Sisters. Maybe they can help guide me.*

The receiver is too heavy—too hard to pick up to call the Sisters for assistance. I know they are busy. I don't know what to say—how to explain my difficulty of wanting to go back but being afraid of overwork. Why is it so hard for me to say no to requests? I should have called them by now. Should I ask for an appointment or just ask them over the phone? Who do I need to talk with? Reverend Mother should be the one for help. She always has much to do, but other Sisters used to make appointments and she was accommodating. Lord, I'm so confused. Help me know what to say and help me make that phone call.

Days passed without asking my approval. I'm definitely not a procrastinator with assignments—only when I need to ask for help for myself. Early one morning, RING.RING.RING. I stretched over, picked up the phone and answered through a yawn, "Hello-o-o."

"Mary Jo, this is Sister Florentine." (I worked with her in the convent office when I was in and out of hospital stays, recuperating from the overwork breakdown.)

I popped up, sat on the edge of my bed. *Oh God, help me know what to say! I know she's calling about my decision.* My brain cells were still asleep.

"Sister, I mean, Mary Jo, Reverend Mother asked me to call. Your year of leave is up on the twenty-fourth, just two weeks away. Have you decided whether you are coming back or going to get a dispensation from your vows?"

Wow, that was so direct. I swallowed, reached for the corner of the sheet, and wiped my tears. *What's my answer? I can't tell her my problem is that I'm not sure I will be able to say no to many requests from others.*

Sister Florentine never asked me to do more. She was always telling me to rest. She was a gem. I swallowed hard and put the receiver in my other hand. *I want to let her know I really do want to return, that I love community life and all it entails—vows and all. But I don't want to be an expense to them.*

The silence I heard was banging my ear, so I stuttered haphazardly, "You know, eh, I guess, I've met someone, and I'm, I'm afraid I'll miss him too much."

How did that nonsense come out of my mouth? I'm picturing Tim in my mind. We've gone out a lot and I know he likes me, but I wouldn't even miss him. It's just an excuse. How does she know?

Sister Florentine said, "Mary Jo, you know that we are canonically approved by Rome, so you need to get permission from the Pope to be relieved of your vows."

"Uh, yes, I know, Sister, but how do I do that?"

I grabbed a stubby pencil on the dresser and the back of an envelope from the trash can.

My hand shook as I stood to write on the dresser with the receiver propped on my shoulder, gripped under my left ear. She quoted an address and the exact words of only about four sentences.

"We should receive the response in about two weeks. We'll call to have you come to sign the forms."

I thanked her...BUZZ.BUZZ.BUZZ...and stared long and hard at the address written with the stubby pencil and the crumpled envelope from the trash can. It seemed sacrilegious.

What was I thinking—giving a lame excuse like that? Those comments had never entered my mind. It was not a reason. I used an excuse, so I would not hurt the Sisters' feelings.

That's all it would take? I'd been counting the days to return and I blew it with a few stupid words. Surely they will ask me to come for advice. Actually though, I didn't say I was confused or that I would like guidance. I tried to pick up the receiver, but it had gained more weight this time. *She's probably busy in the office. Why do I do this to myself?* I looked at the address again and searched for a tablet of stationery to get the letter off in the morning's mail.

In two weeks I had an appointment on January 24th, 1969, exactly one year to the day after I left the hospital and Mom brought me home for a year of rest. I had mixed emotions—extreme disappointment that I was about to say good-bye to my friends, my religious family, yet thrilled to be able to see them again on the 24th. I hadn't seen most of them in an entire year, but it seemed an eternity with my eagerness to return.

I am eager to see Reverend Mother and thank her for the thirteen years, for my increased love for God and for the opportunity to make Him loved through my life as a religious. I hope to see her council members and give sincere appreciation for the training I will cherish the rest of my life—prayer, meditation, spiritual reading, especially of Sacred Scripture.

I want to tell them how grateful I am for guiding me to be a music teacher, when I never wanted to be that mean old music teacher I had in elementary school. I realize I can teach children to enjoy, learn and make music with their God-given ability. How can I live without my music and the love of sharing it with others who, I pray, imagine His Beauty in the beauty of music? The Sisters were dedicated to training very fine teachers and I'm waiting to express my appreciation for the times that were hard, but made me considerate and patient as a teacher.

༄

My heart skipped beats of joy as I drove familiar Commerce Street and turned south onto 24th to the tall spires still poised in heavenly praise. I felt I was on the top of those spires reaching closer to heaven. BONG.BONG. BONG...ten times, as I pulled in front of the university building.

Seems strange we're meeting in Sister Providencia's office in the university. I think she was dean of students. I expected to be in the convent office. I suppose they are over here in the university waiting. I bet they are as excited to see me, as I am to see them.

I locked the car and skipped up the familiar stone steps to the arched entrance with filigreed Gothic double doors, similar to the convent entrance at the other end of the long row of buildings.

A student on door-duty greeted me, "Yes?"

"Oh, I know where to go, thank you." I headed forward, directly up the inside staircase close to the huge academy dining room and scullery where I'd come from the convent building hundreds of times to wash dishes, pots, pans, floors and tiles, sometimes three times a day with my fellow Sisters.

As I reached the second floor, Sister Teresa Joseph, secretary of the Sisters of Divine Providence, greeted me, "This way, Sister, I mean, Mary Jo." I followed her since I was not as familiar with offices in those buildings.

I smiled with anticipation, thinking, *Won't be long now. I'll see my Sisters.*

She opened the door. I was facing familiar Sister Providentia. She was sitting at her stately desk, which perched on the highly polished wooden floor. Shelves of books and curriculum catalogues lined the walls. Her back was to the large Gothic-filigreed bay window just above my car outside. I easily glanced over her shoulders and eyed the HemisFair tower of downtown San Antonio, the same skyline view from my former room off the sewing room a few attached buildings away. Sister's desk had a few neat layers of papers. She smiled. "Hello, Mary Jo, how are you?"

I was stunned, wanting to burst into tears. I looked around and wondered, *But where's Reverend Mother, her council, my friends? Maybe they're showing up in a minute.*

Sister Theresa Joseph rushed over to the big desk and asked me to sit in the shiny wooden chair in front. She remained standing, handed me a pen and slid the proper papers toward me, one at a time. She explained what each was saying. Sister Providentia was there as a witness, signing under my signatures.

Maybe they're going to ask me to go over to the convent to see my friends, maybe lunch?

However, when we were finished, we were finished. Business was business. They promised prayers which I appreciated.

"Oh, please give my prayers to the young Sisters, to Sister Florentine, to Sister Agnes Ann (my superior of the convent), and all of them. I miss them and think of you all every day." My feet stepped cautiously downstairs and past Door-Duty Student.

I felt crushed too much to drive. I sat in the car with a stack of tissues and questions. *Do I just go to the convent and ring the bell? Who would be there anyway? Young Sisters would be in classes, everyone would be doing what they do, cooking lunch, studying, cleaning or praying.*

Maybe I could go to the convent office and see Sister Florentine, but they are always busy and I'd be interrupting. They never catch up with work: books to balance, papers to file, bills to pay, paychecks to make, bank deposits to prepare. I know. I worked there, and I loved every minute. I looked forward down the campus's front road, past the high school, Main Chapel with the high steps and tower steeple, to the convent building. *I guess I just go home.*

I took a deep breath. The tower clock sang the sweet sound of the first quarter of the hour. We were finished in fifteen minutes. It was all over. I didn't know whether to celebrate or visit the cemetery behind the convent.

Oh, God, what do you have in store for me now? How many times have I asked You this in prayer? My life starts over again. I offer the rest of my life for Your honor and glory. Do with me what You will, and make Your will, my will.

I renewed my life motto I made when I was 16...to love God more and make Him loved. Time to get started—again.

⌒⌒

Life was never to be the same for me. Chris got over his cold and we began going together more often, even though I still enjoyed dating others in the Catholic Alumni Club.

He took me to movies, plays, concerts, Braniff Airline parties, etc. He surprised me for an evening at Trinity University to hear Ferranti and Teicher, the duo-piano performers. I learned he was clueless about piano and could not carry a tune in a bucket. He even confessed that when he was in third grade, the teacher told him before the Christmas concert to, "Stand in the back and just move your lips, Chris." That hurt my heart.

Although dating was fun, life's necessities were expanding. I needed income for health insurance, and maintenance, gas and insurance for the Plymouth Satellite Grandpa Barbera had purchased for me four months *before* the deadline of my year of leave from the convent. Furthermore, it had strings hanging on the fender: "You can have the car, but if you go back to the convent, you must return it to me."

Inside I snickered that he thought I'd give up the convent for a car. "Of course, Grandpa, I promise to give it back." He didn't know it wouldn't be mine anyway. I'd turn it in to the congregation for all of the Sisters' use, per our vow of poverty. I would not need a car. When I drove Sisters to doctor appointments or all over Texas and Louisiana for recruiting, or Reverend Mother and her council to our mission-schools, I used cars owned by the congregation.

I discovered another string hanging. He asked me to take Grandma Nona for hair appointments, shopping and to the tailor for alterations. "It would be nice if you could be with her while I'm at work, and stay overnight with her when I go hunting, now that you have a car."

True. I enjoyed seeing Nona more than just on special celebrations. She was lonely by herself all day and arthritis made her rub her knees continually.

I knew I'd be extremely busy with modeling assignments and piano teaching, since I desperately needed the income. I realized that eventually it was going to be impossible to have any time at all. We consolidated appointments. We would go upstairs in the *Vogue* to the beauty salon downtown. During Nona's appointment, I'd shop for her and my necessities at nearby stores. Afterward we'd drive to Lady Alteration, to the grocery store and drug store. We were tired, but I was glad she insisted to continue.

Back at her home at the end of one such day, she huffed and puffed as she balanced her walk grabbing doorframes, greeted back to her little yellow friend whistling in its cage, and began to rustle through her set-aside stack of newspapers. "Here are pictures of you and Patti I kept for ya'll," she plunged her broad bottom into one of the plush cushions of the bamboo lounge chair.

What a surprise! She carefully unfolded a newspaper article and pointed to a full page, color picture of me in a bridal gown of organza and simple lace. It was an A-line silhouette with batteau neckline, had long sleeves, a wide, long train and a tulle veil of the same lacey fabric. Pointing to the scenery, she quizzed, "That big lawn of yellow and brown bachelor buttons you're standing in and that large Texas mesquite tree—where were you in this picture? When did you get married? Why wasn't I invited?" She kicked off her shoes.

I laughed, "Nona, I'm just modeling the bridal dress for Sears." I showed her the headline for the annual section called Guide for Bride printed in the May 1969 Sunday *LIGHT*. She stared at the squared vinyl flooring under her arthritic, crooked feet.

"Nona, if I ever get married, you know you'll be invited." I wiggled my no-rings fingers in front of her eyes. "You know Italians love to wear wedding bands."

She looked at me sideways.

I read the long article under the picture aloud to convince her that I had not forgotten her from my wedding that did not happen.

"Well," she paused, "who is the man in this other picture?" She fingered the small stack of newspapers again to find a print with Chris and me on a fashion show runway.

"Nona, they needed a handsome tall man in that show, so my agent for Sears, Ms. Vincent, asked whether I knew anyone. I date Chris and he was in the show with us. Look, here's a picture of another fellow and me. They are models like Patti and me." I reached over and gave her a big hug.

"Do you believe me now, Nona?"

She smiled and hugged back, "That'll be some wedding when you get married—you, an ex-nun!"

She glanced at the newspapers spread on the floor with our pictures and asked, "Tell me about modeling. Do you have private dressing rooms? Did you have to practice? Tell me anything."

I hadn't realized I'd never spoken much to Nona about what we did. Our family went to her home for special occasions. We all exchanged Mother's Day, Father's Day, Christmas or birthday gifts. They seldom went to our homes— why, I never knew—but I hadn't talked one-on-one with either of them. I was delighted she wanted to know more about me.

"I'll tell you about my latest adventure when I went to table model for Sears in the new HemisFair tower downtown by the Alamo."

Her eyes perked up. She waited while I opened bottles of cold root beer.

"On Tuesday, I stayed overnight with you while Grandpa went fishing, remember? I brought my heavy, gray bag with makeup, combs, brushes, hairpieces and shoes—all kinds of modeling stuff. I went from here to get three changes of outfits from Sears to take to the tower to model while people ate lunch. When I arrived and parked below the tower, I didn't want to haul half of my belongings to the top, then ride the elevator down, go to the car and get the other half."

She bent forward, rubbed both knees with her palms, and turned her eyes on me—all as she did when she glued herself to the TV. Without distraction, she sipped more root beer, as if she needed energy to climb the tower herself, then put the drink on the side table.

"With all that stuff, I looked and felt like a bag lady who had spent every last dime on hair, makeup and clothes. I didn't know with whom to check in or where I was supposed to change. I darted past the lunch tables that were slowly rotating counter-clock wise while I tried to look over my arms-full of bulging, slippery bags. My arms were numb and my fingers felt welded to the metal loops on the coat hangers."

With force of habit from that recall, I stretched out my fingers, making Nona and me snicker.

"A young man with a baker's cap swung a kitchen door open. I explained my dilemma, waited for him to search for the day's *temporary* manager who said, 'You can use the linen room right here. I don't know where models usually dress.'

"With little time to think, I popped into to the room about the size of a large walk-in closet. I dropped my bag onto the floor, draped the three plastic-covered outfits onto a pile of neatly folded clothes lying on a long table and frantically began to undress in the short narrow aisle. I was ten minutes late already.

"Suddenly the door swung open. Being half-naked, I screamed, grabbed the Sears flowered pantsuit and clutched it in front of my in-undies-only body.

"I scared young Baker's Cap with my screech and he howled back."

Nona raised her arthritic knee and slapped it with her hand. I'd never seen her belly-laugh, and we amused each other to tears. "What happened? Hurry!" she demanded.

"Flabbergasted, Baker's Cap rattled, 'Lady, I'm so sorry. I will knock next time. I gotta get back to the kitchen.'

"I apologized, too. We understood each other's predicament. We had work to do, so we got back to urgent business. Naturally, we politely avoided each other throughout the lunch period.

"Nona, you asked me where we dress. Sometimes we never know."

MODELING MEXICO

Ten of us models met in an empty gathering area inside the airport entrance. Mr. Harris opened a large box. "Now ladies, instead of shipping these for the show, we'd like you to wear one on the plane. They're real furs—you know how to handle them. Wear them now to board and graciously again when we deplane in Mexico City. Girls closed in with facades of being nonchalant, but energetically grabbed their choice.

Girls aired as beauty queens. High-pitched chatter surrounded our first class leather seats on Braniff International Airlines. An announcement interrupted before take-off, "Mary Jo Barbera, would you please identify yourself."

I stiffened. *What did I do now? Am I in trouble?* I raised my fingers just enough to be noticed.

"This is from a secret admirer," the hostess said, bending over and handing me a lumpy 3"x 4" envelope. The outside read, "Miss Mary Jo Barbera, Flt 51 to MEX, 23 Feb." I stared at a one-inch, gold-metal hour-glass-shaped charm that fell outside, into my lap. That little thing was real. I flip flopped it to watch the sand. The inside card read,

> ...Thank you for letting me be with you, because I care! Mary – I thank you, I thank God! Love, Chris. P.S. boom, Boom, BOOM.

On the back was one large BOOM, the size of the card itself.

"Who's it from?" I asked her, and the girls quizzed me.

"Someone just handed it to me before I shut the cabin door." Hostess grinned and went back to the cabin.

It had to be Chris. I didn't know anyone else working for Braniff. Maybe

I mentioned our fashion show in Mexico City when he took me on our first real *date* to Hong Fong Restaurant. I reread the card several times throughout the flight, despite the non-stop, upper-classy, chitty-chatty.

Hours later we landed, taxied the tarmac and came to a stop. Jerri repeatedly tapped her window, "Look, there are the ladies waiting to greet us." An entourage of a dozen well-dressed, refined-looking women had formed a semi-circle around the tall, metal deplaning steps. Photographers aimed for good shots. We donned our Frost Bros. show-furs and gathered toward the open door at the top of the steps to descend dramatically for photographers.

Mr. Harris, Patti and I were behind the group at the top of the steps. Patti started teasing the crowd by *vamping* her fox fur with her right hand for fun. Mr. Harris whispered, "Patti, Patti," but she did not hear him and continued. The women chuckled—a wee bit.

A few girls rode in each woman's car. They drove us to a magnificent hotel where Patti and I shared a room.

Chris presented me with cloud nine by flying in on an airline non-revenue pass after work and checked-in a few doors down from our room.

Mr. Harris treated everyone for supper and itinerary. "Since it's a special show tomorrow, report to the dressing room by ten-thirty for set up and rehearsal. The show is at 1:00. Remember—*ten-thirty*. Be on time!"

My mind distracted, *Great! That will give Chris and me time to see some of Mexico City before ten-thirty.*

The next day, Chris and I set out for early breakfast—platter of eggs, sausage, refried beans, rice, large dollop of spicy guacamole and tortillas. We toured places I hardly recall. The filigrees, colors, old country carvings and local color were engulfing. We strolled for hours, hopped taxis, wandered in and out of stores with local crafts, and antique churches.

We ended up on the party-roof-top of an historical building alone. Leaning on the decoratively chiseled stone, four-foot ledge, watching the busy routines of cars and people three stories below, we chatted and asked questions about each other. I remarked, "This antique city makes me feel lost in time."

Instantly, I was horrified. My legs limped. "Time! Time! What time is it?" Chris jerked his watch to his face. "It's 12:30."

"Yieeks! Twelve-thirty? No way! Chris, I was supposed to be back at ten-thirty." We dashed across the roof top while I was yelling, "I've missed setting up for the show. It takes me forever to match items on my chart. And the important rehearsal—we hardly ever practice and this one's a *dress* rehearsal." I expected my thumping heart to jump up my throat.

We raced through the old wooden door of the higher floors of the building, tore down steps and out onto the street we had just viewed from up high. Vehicles were four abreast for blocks and no cab in sight.

We ran, trying to locate a taxi. "Chris, do you know the way back?"

"No, I just know we're far, far away from that hotel."

We craned our necks constantly, especially at the intersections, until Chris spied a taxi and waved his long, strong arms. Diving into the back seat, we begged the driver to speed fast.

"Lady, I no go fast. See? Too much cars. I weel try."

"Oh, Chris! Jerri's going to kill me and I don't blame her." I stumbled over my words.

"She's in charge of that entire show—the girls, the selection of garments, the jewelry, hats, scarves, shoes, hose—everything! Carmen and Mr. Harris are going to fire me for good."

We sat on the edge of the back seat, leaning forward and breathing down the back of Driver's sweaty, musty-smelling neck. Maybe we thought the taxi would go faster or at least our heads would arrive before the rest of our bodies.

Red or green lights made no difference. People drove with their horns, or fingers out the windows. Often we couldn't pass through intersections, waiting for the next green light. It seemed everyone was moving except us. My stomach trembled.

"What time is it now, Chris? I don't have a watch." Was I thinking that if I knew the time, we would get there sooner?

He tried to assure me, "It's noon."

I was puzzled, *Why so confident? Does he mean to say I'll be there before I know it? I'm not there, and I already know it!*

"Driver, how much longer before we get to the hotel? I am late already." I repeatedly asked.

We were going nowhere fast. The only fast thing moving was precious time and it was ahead of itself.

Driver banged on the horn, took his hands off the steering wheel and shook both clinched fists. "Lady, I do not know how much longer. I tell you, I no can go fast. What you want me to do? Today ees Friday. Many peoples go home early. Work ees finished. You no want to go with me? Okay, I stop. You pay. You get out. I take your husband to hotel."

I clenched my teeth and froze. *Whoa! My husband? We've hardly dated. No use to try to explain. Driver needs to concentrate on the traffic.*

"Oh, no, sir," I articulated clearly and slowly. "You do a good job. It is not your fault. I'm just nervous. I'm very sorry."

What was I thinking that morning, going so far away from our hotel, ignoring time? It was irresponsible. I was always dependable in the convent. I was a fish flapping out of water.

Another hour whooshed. We wriggled like a turtle.

Finally, there was a stretch of blocks with fewer cars. Driver sped. He veered a corner so fast, I knew we were driving on the right two wheels only—Chris slid over to my side. I tightened my eyes and prayed for the driver to slow down—it's better to be Mary Jo late, than the late Mary Jo. My pulse quickened. *Frost Bros. just paid a first-class trip, hotel and meals for this one occasion. I'm just here for the joy ride and I'm not enjoying that ride here. What if I have to pay Frost Bros. back? What about Jerri's job? What if they fire her?*

The taxi stopped suddenly. I panicked, "What happened? What now?"

"Theese ees your hotel, lady," Driver emphasized.

"Oh! I didn't know we were here already." My words seemed an oxymoron.

I darted inside while Chris paid Driver. The antique wall clock read one-fifteen. The show started fifteen minutes ago. What do I say? I missed the rehearsal. My stuff's not even set out. I headed to the concierge to direct me to the dressing room.

A blast from the past echoed through the reception area: "Mary Jo, where on earth? I could take your head off. What are you thinking?"

"Oh, Jerri, I..."

"I don't even want to hear it." She stood and yelled, her arm waving, papers flying on her clipboard, the other arm stretched out pointing at me. "Carmen's at the mic. She's supposed to be commentating the show. Instead, she's apologizing to the crowd of refined donors and dignitaries looking at their watches! She even told them you are my sister: late, late, late! I'm humiliated." She paused. "What are you waiting for? Get moving!"

I curled my face sheepishly, "Jerri, I don't know where to go."

"Ughh! I guess not!" she belted and motioned with that clipboard.

I ducked, thinking she was aiming Clipboard at me. I certainly deserved it. I shadowed her like a scampering, muddy puppy as we raced down one hall, into another wing. I began to unbutton and unzip. *It's going to take me another hour to sort out my clothing and tons of accessories and shoes, fix my hair and makeup and...*

Jerri opened a large, unbolted, double door. I stared at my verdict: Nine star-studded, tall, live mannequins in heels, with faces encrusted with superfluous paints and powders, curled, false eye lashes rising above their eyebrows, topped with fancy hairpieces of curls and tendrils—throwing mental daggers at my face of sweat and oil that blurred odd mixtures of color, street dust and taxi fumes. I knew they had been standing the entire time. Sitting in the garment was a model's mortal sin.

That was the longest two seconds my mind had ever stretched and I hoped it did not boomerang.

Jerri screeched, "Mary Jo," waving her pointy, painted fingernail to my station, "you can thank Patti and the others for using your dressing list, right there." She pounded it with Clipboard and persisted, "They untagged and lined up every costume, bag, scarf, hosiery, fur, hat, shoe and jewelry—every tiny earring. Fix that dang makeup and hair. You're on in a few minutes. BE ON TIME!"

She shrieked, hurling Clipboard with papers, to hail the girls behind stage.

I thought, "*I deserve every word and more. Wonder what the runway looks like, or the stage? This is surreal. If only I could get my heart to stop reminding me that it's thrashing. Where do I begin to get ready?*"

I began stripping my clothes and praying: "*Lord, I have a most earthly request. Please help me pull myself together. I don't want to ruin this important show. Help*

311

us sell the stuff we brought to benefit the Save the Children Program. Let the crowd have fun and everyone forgive my irresponsibility. How could I do this to Jerri and Patti—all of Frost Brothers?"

I continued with a fast powder puff, gripped with fluttering, fast, fingers, proper colors, false eyelashes, lip colors, hairpiece, hose, dress, scarf and jewelry—with an orderly layout by my colleagues.

Mariachi music, crowd applause, cheers and Carmen speaking in Spanish over the mic—the show had begun.

I grabbed my long white fur coat and stuck my arms in it, as I ran to Jerri behind stage. I wrapped the wide decorative belt around the coat and Jerri adjusted the bulk around my waist.

The ramp was another familiar runway, but extra-long. Patti was as understandably *livid,* as I was embarrassingly guilty. However, we both did our back-to-backs on the catwalk with professional grace, and the crowd was excited.

The show continued with Frost Bros.' uniqueness and perfection and ended on a high note. Immediately in another room, Carmen was translating and helping Mr. Harris sell every single item we had brought from the store. Save the Children would get a sizeable donation.

The situation needed my apology and their forgiveness at high peaks. How could I thank them enough?

After the sales event, Mr. Harris called us together with tickets fanned out in his hand, "Ladies, the women just presented me with these tickets to the Folkloric Show tonight and they're volunteering to take us in their automobiles."

Girls stiffened. I knew they had arrangements after supper. No one wanted to admit it.

Mr. Harris emphasized, "They bought these in gratitude for our work toward their cause—Save the Children." Dead silence hovered over the group. He tried again, "It's full of song and colorful costumes expressing stories through Mexican generations."

I was thinking, "*Chris flew down here to be with me and I want to go out with him. I don't know why anyone would pass up those wonderful tickets.*"

Patti spoke up for the group, "Mr. Harris, we're planning to go discotheque hopping after supper."

His smile faded. He nodded his head and looked down at the large colorful vouchers. Then he turned toward Chris and me and pleaded, "Mary Jo, would you and Chris like to go?"

In unison, Chris and I lit up, "We'd love it. We can't think of anything better! Thanks so much. What a great opportunity."

The girls were relieved we had gotten them off the hook. I felt they accepted it as well-deserved payback for setting up my stuff for the fashion show that morning. They broke in, overlapping comments like, "Yes, that would be great, Mary Jo." "You'll love the guitars and folklore." "You and Chris go and have a good time." They quickly disappeared.

Mr. Harris almost flew out of his shoes with gratitude. He grabbed Chris' hand for a firm shake and with a huge smile, "Chris, I really appreciate you for doing this for us. Mary Jo, I know you'll enjoy the cultural music and dancing rhythms. Carmen and I will be going, too. I'll arrange for two cars to take us."

I felt my morning's fiasco of delaying the show was overwhelmingly forgotten when we *volunteered* to use the tickets. What a break—a win-win! I was awarded two free show tickets for something we would have been willing to pay for in Mexico City. I wouldn't have felt bad if Mr. Harris had sent me to my hotel room as punishment.

We'd return to San Antonio with stories to tell and more catwalks to prance.

Parties, Proposals
and Wedding One-Liners

February 1970 brought excitement of Valentine's Day and Chris did his part to make mine special. Every day for about a week or two, he sent me another Valentine. Some were big and beautiful, but most were simple 10-cent ones. He attached four-inch, metal, gold-colored olive picks—in the shape of little arrows—to one of the hearts on each Valentine.

He never wrote the word *love*, but wrote *Chris + Mary Jo* on some of them. That was fine with me. Serious, steady dating did not make my list, soon anyway. I looked forward to seeing him often. We couldn't be out late, since we both worked early the next day.

Nevertheless, by March, Chris seemed more serious and I knew it—he hinted at going steady. I was not going to assume anything; he had to ask me directly!

The most obvious hint? Two little objects. One was a new, old-time, typewriter eraser—the kind that was terra cotta color, round, flattened thin, with a one-inch black brush attached to wipe away the eraser shavings. The other was a very small bracelet charm, similar to the large eraser, but was artificial and did *not* erase.

He stared into my eyes, held my hand and quietly whispered, "The big rubbery eraser is to erase the names of all the men in your pocket calendar." (He knew I was dating eight men with only seven days in the week). He explained further, "The tiny, wooden eraser is to erase *my* name in your calendar."

Stunned, I commented, "I have to admit I enjoy you more than I enjoy the others, but I have a line-up of commitments through Fiesta Week (fiesta is Spanish for party) a few weeks away. I'll not add any more dates; but I don't want to disappoint those I've promised."

His smile dissipated. "Not until after Fiesta Week? Remember, we have a date for the River Parade. Don't change that." I assured him I looked forward to that night.

In April, during Fiesta, the epicenter of the excitement was downtown and along the San Antonio River—the radius of about a mile around the Alamo. The glue that formed an automatic fiesta was the sound of mariachis playing lively or romantic songs on 12-string guitars, violins, and trumpets and singing.

Women in Mexican costumes kicked their black tap shoes, snapped castanets in their palms and swirled their full, colorful skirts, exposing layers of white petticoats.

You could close your eyes any time and smell your way to the Mexican rice, beans and enchiladas. Then be in Germany with the sausage on a stick resting in juicy sauerkraut, or sniff your way to Louisiana's Cajun red-peppered shrimp lined up like giant commas on long skewers.

I felt *initiated as an official member* to the fiesta when someone cracked a couple of cascarones on my head. (Cascarones are brightly painted, decorated eggshells filled with tiny confetti.) Partyers yelled and laughed while confetti burst into their hair, spilled into plates of food or glasses of margaritas and swirled in the breezes. This year I attended at least one, sometimes two, events each day with one of the eight men I dated.

Paul took me to Fiesta Monday for lunch. I'll never forget an embarrassing moment after leaving the famous, Casa Rio Mexican Restaurant along the San Antonio River Walk.

We were face-to-face with two white-haired religious Sisters I lived with on the mission. In their lay clothes, they blended with other tourists. I spontaneously reached out to hug and greet them. They squealed, "Sister Mary Janet, it's so good to see you," but caught themselves, "Oh, sorry..."

I interrupted to refresh their memory, "I'm Mary Jo and this is my friend, Paul. It's a perfect week for fiesta, isn't it? It's so good to see you. Give the Sisters my love. We're hurrying to the car now."

As we *rushed* slowly on our way, I uttered quickly to Paul, "Oh, I was in the convent a while with them," and changed the subject, hoping he thought I was there for a very short time a long time ago—not for thirteen years until only a year ago! Paul didn't know why I had to return home that afternoon. I had a date with Chris that same evening for the Texas Cavaliers' River Parade.

I should expect to see many former students and parents. Maybe some do recognize me and don't know whether to speak or not. I feel I'm on stage with people whispering and staring out of the corners of their eyes. Oh well, I have to get used to it forever, I supposed.

Tuesday, Peggy and Mae gathered a western hat and plaid blouse with red bandana for my first of three nights of *Night in Old San Antonio* on La Villita grounds and the daytime western parade. I folded up and climbed into a Volkswagen bug to go with Cynthia Vollmer, my best school-chum since sixth grade. She was one of the girls who formed the entourage that followed my family in cars when I entered the convent in 1955. I felt comfortable with Cynthia as she introduced me to many of her friends.

Tim invited me for the Fiesta Queen's crowning Wednesday afternoon and the beginning of three days of German Fest.

Fiesta Friday, all schools had a holiday, and most businesses closed for the biggest parade, which began in 1891, in honor of the fallen heroes at the Alamo. School bands, military bands and the organizational floats highlighted the week: the three-hour Queen and Her Court Battle of Flowers Parade.

By April I was exhausted from modeling, teaching more students and dating every night. I had had four proposals for marriage, and except for one, the men were very respectable—but I wasn't in love.

I realized I looked forward to dating Chris more than I looked forward to the other fine men. He stood out among my crowd. Life crowded in on me once again.

～

April brought more than rain showers. It was my own April with showers.

After a date to a circus the night before Easter, we sat in the car to elaborate about the evening's excitement. Chris started to kiss me, but whispered, "I am not going to *Chris* you anymore until you until you *Mary* me." He had finally asked me to *marry* him!

I sat taller, looked into his eyes and exclaimed, "Yes," and gave him a big hug. "I thought you never were going to ask. I was not going to let you get away with hints you've been giving me." He reacted with his *eh-eh-eh* while I laughed about his cleverness.

The next day, Easter Sunday, was bubbling at Mom's place with all the family and the engagement announcement. Remember Ivan, the confirmed bachelor whom Patti and Joe had introduced to me. Yes, he was the one who enjoyed the encounter with my floating falsies in the friend's pool. Ivan also introduced me to Chris between fashion shows in the mall. Ivan had been in Europe almost a year. Chris had flown and toured with him for two weeks. No one had heard from Ivan since he left on that trip—until the doorbell rang.

"I knew I'd find Patti and Joe and Mary Jo here today. Couldn't wait to come over. I got home from Europe two days ago," Ivan announced to Mom's wide eyes and lowered jaw.

She responded slowly, loud enough for Chris and me to hear, "Uhhh, gee—ah, happy Easter, Ivan. Good to see you. Come on in."

Ivan stepped inside and saw Chris and me. We relieved Mom's fluster.

"Hey, Ivan. Good to see you. You finally got home. How was Europe?" Chris said with today's enthusiasm still in his voice.

Poor Ivan. I felt sorry for him. He just didn't know *how* disappointed he'd be, until I cut in, "Great news! We just announced our engagement!" I should have expected the not-so-hearty response.

Mom came with a filled plate, conspicuously inconspicuous, to our rescue. "Here, Ivan, have some of my baked chicken, my famous potato salad and other goodies. And here's a beer. Sit right down." You could tell he was a hungry bachelor. The three of us chitchatted about Europe politely for about fifteen minutes. Then he disappeared to the restroom in the cabana. We figured he'd gone out to the pool to see Patti and Joe, but he had left. None of us heard from him again.

⸏⸎

Bob, whom I had dated often, called. He had purchased opera tickets for himself and me, not knowing of my engagement. He was the guest trying to outstay Chris after the New Year's party at our home.

His voice quivered after I told him our engagement news. "Mary Jo, I'm happy for you and Chris, but I'm sure he won't mind if I take you, since I didn't know you were engaged when I bought the tickets."

Reasoning didn't seem to help Bob. I knew he was hurt and I tried to be gentle, "Bob that's sweet of you to get the tickets. You know how much I love opera, but I don't feel right going out with anyone other than Chris."

After a quick prayer to the Holy Spirit, I said, "Bob, remember—engagement is a time to find out whether we really can give up dating others and be committed to the one we plan to wed. Several nice girls in the Catholic Alumni Club love music and would appreciate the offer to go with you."

Dead silence.

"And Bob, there's a lovely girl out there waiting for someone like you. Chris will be thirty-eight soon. You've got a long time to find that right girl."

"Oh, WOW. Chris doesn't look thirty-eight! I *do* have a long time."

I gazed up, *Whew, thank You, Lord. That was my first test with a happy decision to make, knowing I did it for Chris and me.*

Bob paused a short, long time. "Yeah, you're right, Mary Jo. I've enjoyed being with you. Chris is a lucky guy."

                                       ༀ

Spring forward to autumn:

"Mom, Chris and I are going to elope when you least expect it. We're going to come home already married." I teased seriously. Her kitchen table was scattered with old notes of photographers, florists, wedding cakes, bridal gown shops and invitations she'd used when planning my three sisters' weddings. The last one was just several months earlier. She and Dad had three more of our weddings.

"Elope? Oh, no, Honey. Why?"

I sat close to her and tried to be gentle. "Mom, Chris and I are older, neither of us has been married—we want to concentrate our time on the spiritual, the real reason of what we are about to do."

She sat back in her chair and thought a while. We both watched Dad from the large windows with a view overlooking the patio to the cool, blue waters of the fifty-foot long pool. Sweating under a large Mexican hat, he was pushing a long pool-broom back and forth in the section under the diving board.

"Well, you still want a cake, pictures, flowers, a gown and invitations, don't you?"

"I suppose we do, but we wouldn't need as big a cake or as many flowers or invitations. I don't mind wearing a simple white dress and short veil. I know we have an enormous family. Chris has just Charlie, Helen and the two children, and a few aunts and cousins."

She perked up, "Well, he could invite more of his friends."

"Mom, we talked about that. He says there's no end to his buddies. Besides, if we tell our relatives that we're having a close family wedding and they see many of his friends attending, that would be rather awkward."

Stunned, she shook her head. She flipped through her long list, naming her dear friends and relatives who had attended my sisters' weddings. "How can we have a small wedding with six of you girls and some with their families? We've always had all our girls in the weddings, except when you were a nun. And then each of them needed male escorts."

"Too bad you had six girls, Mom. You end up paying for all the brides' and bridesmaids' dresses and most of the wedding. You and Dad should have had the five boys you wanted."

Dad had come inside and shuffled to the refrigerator a few yards away, just in time for my last comment.

"What?"

We burst into laughter with his reaction to my teasing suggestion about having five boys.

Dad plunked a pitcher of lemonade and three glasses on the table. "Honey, it doesn't make me any difference whether I blow the money on two weddings close together or far apart. It's gone either way. Have your big wedding."

"Love you, Dad. Thanks, but we still want a small wedding and not the distraction of the commotion. I know we'll figure it out."

The next day, Mae *just happened* to drop by. "Mary Jo, you're welcome to wear my wedding dress. It's not fitted, just drapes straight down." She pointed to the large photo in Mom's dining room.

"Oh, Mae, it's more beautiful than what I expected to wear. It'll be my special *something borrowed*."

Later Patti took me to find a veil topper. The first one I saw was just what I liked, but she insisted we look around to be sure. I was sure. Mom had to stay in mother-of-the-bride-mode, so I let her make a finger-length, simple, tulle veil.

For my *something used,* I wore the same pair of white, low-heeled shoes I had worn for my confirmation, and 8th grade and high school graduations.

My five sisters hosted a festive homemade Mexican dinner-buffet in the apartment party-house where one of them lived. We invited family and friends. It was a fun, delicious opportunity to visit and explain our desire for a small chapel wedding with a home reception. Again, my sisters were there for me.

Since he was an airport employee, Chris could order from the airport caterer. He talked Mom into letting him do his part toward the reception. Mom was still apprehensive: trays of airline sandwiches for killer prices? She couldn't see pictures or have a selection? Not even taste them? What did Chris know about elegant presentation of wedding foods?

Chris and I spent most of our time choosing the perfect Bible selections for the Mass, ones that spoke what we wanted our lives to be together. As required by the Catholic Church, we attended the pre-Cana course in my parish for engaged couples. We learned so much those six weeks from the speakers, we signed up to attend at another parish with different presenters.

We memorized the new, updated wedding vows and practiced praying them aloud to each other every day and in the car before he walked me to the door after a date.

Big family, small wedding? How big is big, how small is small? It's a *relative* matter.

⌒

Wedding One-liners

Request by Monsignor William Martin:
"And now, who has the wedding bands?"

Purpose: marriage Mass covenant between
God, Chris Shaw and Mary Jo Barbera.

Date: November 11, 1970, a year after their first date.

Location: Our Lady of Grace Chapel, on
McCullough, in San Antonio, Texas.

Wedding attendants: Mary Jo's sister,
Patti. Chris's brother, Charlie.

Flower girl: Chris's niece Linda, six years old

Reader of Bible selections requested by couple:
Mary Jo's Uncle Pat Osborn.

Altar server: Mary Jo's cousin, Gerald Osborn.

Organist: Winnie's second cousin,
Martha Finto, college student.

Reception: home of Mary Jo's parents, Joe
and Winnie Barbera on Harriet Ave.

Attending: closest 60 relatives and friends,
including her maternal grandparents.

Unexpected: ornate wedding band Chris
designed to imitate their matching bands.

Surprise for Winnie: Exquisite trays of airline
sandwiches Chris ordered and delivered.

From Aunt Tantan: 100 delicate, handmade,
pastel, sugar flowers for the three-tier cake
and large yellow sugar rose on top tier.

Specific info Winnie needed last week for newspaper? "Denmark for sure, but we still don't know the other countries yet. Tell you when we get home! Bye, thanks, Mom and Dad, and everyone!"

Post Script: the wedding was exactly one year after their first date when Mary Jo found out Chris was surprising Bohn and Sue. Recall: they were just going to bed on their first day home with their first baby, and Chris did not know about the baby!

This was the beginning of two weeks of honeymoon with more dramatic surprises and quandaries.

WEDDING NIGHTMARE

Room 2006 in the Hilton Palacio del Rio was perfect. Chris opened the drapes, and with his hand at the back of my waist, led me onto our balcony. His cheek pressed against mine, as we overlooked the sights and sounds of Mariachis on the San Antonio River. We finally shared our first private kiss as a married couple, oblivious to the tourists vacationing twenty stories below on that Veterans' Day.

Soon we were holding hands, leaning on the wrought-iron railing, admiring the skyline. "Look, Chris." I pointed in the distant, due west. "We can see Our Lady of the Lake Convent campus and the spires on each side of Main Chapel."

"And it looks beautiful against the sunset," he said.

"A couple of years ago, I watched the top floors of this hotel rise from the ground, far from my convent window at OLL. Little did I know I'd be spending my wedding night here. Right now, the rings on my fingers are like ice cubes and they're making me cold," I teased.

"Would you like to call your Nona and Grandpa Barbera to thank them for the hundred-dollar bill he sent with your dad from work tonight? We won't talk long." We did.

Grandpa insisted, "Use it to buy a bottle of wine when you're in Rome, you hear?" It was a short and sweet call.

We admired the painting of abstract fiesta colors on the wall, hugged and kissed, until Chris asked, "Why don't we go down to the nightclub?"

I hesitated, "A nightclub? You're kiddin'?"

"I hear it's got a pretty good, little music combo."

"Darling, it's already late and we have to be at the airport so early."

"But we can have a drink and listen to a few songs."

I was confused. Was he shy, wondering what to do next? Maybe he thought because I had been a nun, I was shy. I knew he was looking forward to that night. We'd attended Pre Cana classes, read and spoke openly about the literature and books the doctors assigned at their classes.

I tried to put him at ease, speaking gently, "Chris, if it's okay with you, we've spent so much time in nightclubs dancing and drinking Coke. We've counted the days left until tonight, when you wouldn't have to take me home."

He didn't answer, but kept eyeing the door. I figured I had to be the one to break the ice. I hesitated, but picked up my gray bag, smiled and gave him a kiss. I used a happy, sing-song voice, "Well. I guess I'll go to the bathroom first."

I took my time at top speed. I stepped out of my handmade, pink pleated dress and slid into my new snow white, sleeveless lingerie gown. It had a simple lace yoke with a tiny pink ribbon rose. Gathered layers of thin nylon hit above my knees. *"Should I go out only in this, or wear its fluffy, long-sleeve negligee, too? It'd be more fun to have him remove it first."* It was more cute than seductive, but I knew we'd both like it. I brushed my teeth, scrubbed my tongue and was ready in less than ten minutes.

I wondered when to go out to the bedroom. *Maybe he's undressing. If I peek, the door might squeak.* I quit thinking so I could listen. My ear to the door didn't help. My fingers polished the inside door handle. I didn't hear anything and wondered what he was doing. My heart started to pounce.

I decided to take my bag with me for support. If I didn't know what to do, or he wasn't ready, I could fish around in it as if I were looking for something. I slowly opened the door. My eyebrows arched. My lips pursed a small smile. I peeked around and made my entrance.

My face went blah. He was sitting in the chair, tie still tight, jacket still buttoned, legs crossed. His elbow was on the table, with fingers supporting his face.

He dropped his hand to his lap. "Well. I'm going downstairs." He got up to leave.

"You are?" I gulped, dropped my bag on the floor and stared. My heart pounced more than just a tad. Blood went to my feet. What did I do? What did I say?

"I won't be long." He left.

I stared at the back of the door. How long was "long"? What should I do? Should I get dressed again? I thought he wanted to have lots of time with me. We had to get up in a few hours for the airport.

I flopped backward onto the top of the spread, glaring at the ceiling. *Oh, God, what did I do? Why does he want to spend our valuable short evening in a nightclub? I don't care if I never see another nightclub.*

I talked myself into holding back tears, thinking of how Mom, Dad and my sisters were so good to me. I pondered my wedding ring and smiled at all the symbolism Chris had put into it. When we'd be apart, we couldn't wait to see each other. He was the only one I dated who took me to church and he wasn't even a Catholic!

Reality wrapped tight around me again. I grabbed the hotel's tissue box from the side-table and put it next to me on the colorful spread.

I sat with my legs crossed in the middle of the king size bed. I considered getting dressed and going down to the night club. I'd feel embarrassed, especially if I said I was looking for my husband. I dared not say it's our wedding night! Would he be angry when he came to the room? What if he stayed down there all night?

I lay on the bed wiping tears away, not knowing whether to get some sleep so at least *I* wouldn't be drowsy in the morning. *Please, God, help me know what to do. Have I done the right thing, getting married? What's he doing in the night club?* My stomach jittered.

Time dragged its feet. I fought exhaustion and drained any fantasies of a dreamy honeymoon. It was becoming a nightmare. I lay staring at the ceiling while romantic violins playing on the river below became irritating noise.

CLICK. CLICK. CLICK. *Oh no, it must be the maid or?* I ran to the bathroom.

"Mary Jo?"

Oh, thank You, God! I ran over to him with open arms.

With two fingers, Chris handed me a single yellow rose in a vase with a yellow bow. I was so relieved, I sobbed uncontrollably. He hugged me and refreshed my memory of our reception at home. "You remember where the sign-in wedding book was on that little table by your Mom's front door?"

I looked into his happy eyes, "Yeah, where Taylor took a picture of my hand resting on yours on the closed book, presenting our new wedding bands. My bouquet was on the table, too. What about it?"

"I brought those *two* yellow roses when I delivered the sandwiches from the airport caterer this afternoon."

I beamed from ear-to-ear. "I didn't know *you* brought the roses by the book. My sisters were there and insisted it was bad luck to see you before the ceremony on our wedding day. That's silly, but I stayed in the bedroom until you left."

He continued, "Well, the little card was just like this one. But it had *two* printed roses, and I'd written: *For the 'two' of us! Love, Chris.* This is our *single* rose and there's one rose on the card. Read what it says."

Between my tears and quivering lips, I read, *Thank God for our 'oneness.' I love you. Chris.*

He cleared an area on the round table to display the little vase appropriately. We hugged a long time. "But where was this rose until now?"

He began removing his tie. "Early this morning, I came to the hotel to make our reservations and I wrote a note for the musicians to play Welcome to My World."

I jumped in, "Oh, I know why. After you dropped me off the night you proposed, you were driving home asking yourself, 'What did I just do? I'm thirty-seven and getting married!' I'll never forget that."

"Yeah, and when I turned on the car radio, it started playing *Welcome to My World.*"

I clasped him. "Chris, I didn't know you had that planned downstairs. I thought I'd done something to hurt you, or maybe you were uneasy about tonight. I would have gone with you. When I kept saying I'd rather stay in our room, I thought you were shy." I hoped he understood.

What I thought would be a wedding nightmare became a wedding night paradise. But I realized Paradise is for eternity.

While brushing my teeth in our hotel room the morning after our wedding, my stomach jiggled like Jell-O. I was recalling the *week* before our wedding. My sisters, so into high fashions, had gathered my wardrobe, each with lots of matching accessories for our honeymoon's two-week stay in Europe. I had wondered how I would haul all the stuff. Chris had come over to help.

He offered, "We-ll, I take only one suitcase, one that fits under the seat or in the overhead compartment. Sometimes a hang-up bag, too."

Surely he was teasing. My sisters insisted I take all those things for a two-week honeymoon. I couldn't fit even one outfit with its accessories and boots or shoes into a small suitcase.

Chris shook his head. "I've worked thirteen years for an airline and traveled each year somewhere, South America, Alaska, Europe. I know how luggage gets lost. You could arrive at your first destination, but your suitcases would not. When they did arrive, you had flown on to another country. When you got home, you hadn't seen your luggage the entire trip!"

We laughed at the horrific idea, but my heart skipped a few beats.

Chris continued, "I don't make reservations. I fly somewhere and stay if I like it. If I don't, I zip up my suitcase and fly somewhere else. I'm not locked into anyplace I stay."

What was I getting myself into? Maybe being a bachelor thirty-eight years was too long. I knew Mom would have a cat fit. She and Dad always had every minute planned. They would bend out of shape if their schedule had to change. She'd pack a pile of ties for Dad.

The convent was great. We wore our one, good habit for travel, and parts of it could be unsnapped to wash. One suitcase was plenty.

"But Chris, how will I go two weeks with so few clothes? My bathrobe, my makeup, hairdryer, boots and..."

"Oh, I take enough for several days and find a laundry-mat near my hotel when I need it. I sit, read a map, or travel book of the area and plan the next several days. Hair appointments are bargains in Europe."

My heart pumped a little easier.

"Besides," he raised his index finger, "when I go through customs with only a small carry on, I don't waste time waiting for luggage. I plop my little suitcase on the conveyor belt and it sails through customs. Sometimes they don't even open it and I'm outta there. They figure I can't have more than necessities, coming from so far, for so long, with so little."

I knew I could get used to that. If I took a few changes, I'd repeat outfits. If Chris didn't mind, I sure didn't, and I must explain to the family.

My sisters were appalled. "Two weeks to Europe with only a small suitcase and sharing a hanger bag? It is your honeymoon!! You'd be wearing an outfit more than once." They couldn't understand the practicality of our planning. I just let them line up my wardrobe in the long archway between Mom's living and dining rooms.

They didn't know I was packing my gray modeling bag with the intention of taking *only it* on the trip. We'd share the hang up bag.

I finished brushing my teeth in our hotel and ran a pick through my tousled hair. Chris tucked our airline passes into his coat pocket and zipped our two small bags. I begged: *Lord, please don't let my sisters notice I'll be taking only one suitcase.*

After a quick stop at Chris' duplex, we tore through the airport in time to carry on the Barbera Family's traditional send off. (Airports allowed anyone at the gates for last good-byes before 9-11.)

My sister grabbed my arm and alerted the others, "Hey, where are all your suitcases?" I froze.

Chris relieved me, "Oh, I'm with Braniff Airways, remember? I took care of 'em earlier." He *had* taken care of them: we had dropped them off in his apartment!

First class passes in hand, we pranced on the tarmac to the orange Braniff aircraft. Chris grinned over to me. "Your sisters thought I checked the bags at the ticket counter. Did I say that?"

"Nope! You didn't."

Honeymoon's Alpha Police

At Switzerland's airport in the dark of midnight, we boarded the small, rickety bus to shuttle us to the terminal. Exhausted, we stood and searched for seats. We balanced our suitcases in front of us to manage the narrow aisles and everyone crammed amongst bulky, winter overcoats and bulging luggage. We collapsed and wedged ourselves into the only remaining seats in the rear of the bus.

I exhaled until I was limp. My eyelids lowered, so did my head. You could tell the closed-in bus held many travelers who had not visited a hotel shower recently. I thanked God: soon we'd be freshened up and in a comfortable bed.

Instantly. Heads turned. Jerked. Everyone chatted or whispered mainly in Italian. Pointing fingers smeared foggy windows. Volume upped a few notches.

I nudged Chris, "What's the commotion all about?"

"We-ll, I'm not really sure." He shuffled in his seat. An airline employee, he knew something was brewing.

CLUNK. CLUNK. CLUNK. Boots pounded up the steps and onto our bus.

Lightening-flash silence. Eerie stillness.

"What's happening, Chris?" I grabbed his cold, sweaty hand and stared at what, I hoped, was just a horrible, traumatic nightmare.

In camouflage suits, two mustached men, one tall and muscular and his counterpart, short and thin, anchored themselves next to the driver's seat. Their machine guns waved frantically over the heads of front-seaters and at our helpless, jammed crowd.

Muscular Man growled in Italian. Italians gasped, shook heads, glared at each other. Men fumbled in pockets. Women agitated fingers around in bags.

My mouth locked open. I figured they were taking our money and were going to blow us to smidgeons. I didn't have any money. Chris had traveler checks and some foreign something. They were not going to take my new wedding bands Chris designed. Naively, I hid my hand under my bag.

Then the guy howled in broken English. "Two peoples on this bus should not be here. EEEverrrybody..." he pointed his gun again. Front seat passengers ducked. "Take out passports, NOW!!

Chris leaned toward my ear, "Oh, no. We should have stayed on our flight from Rome to Denmark."

We shuffled around for passports with little help from the tiny overhead light peering through the pitch purple of midnight. I prayed they didn't hear my heart pound. My passport slipped from my lap. I caused commotion and attracted more attention bending over to retrieve it. Certainly, they didn't think I was trying to hide in the stinky frump of junk.

Chris timidly swayed his passport from the back of the bus. "He-re we are." Military guns instantly pointed toward us, so did all tourist heads. I felt everyone was relieved, but their tension had osmosed into my skinny body.

Guns poking at us, they escorted us off the bus onto the tarmac.

Those people were still studying us head to foot. Watching Breaking News of international television networks the next day, they could say they had been first-hand witnesses! I hoped Mom did not see us on TV—she would have had a heart attack before we returned home.

The experience became a blur when Chris attempted to explain we wanted to spend a few days in Switzerland. We knew our Scandinavian Airline passes indicated we were to pivot out of Copenhagen like a *spoke* each time we flew to another country.

Before 9-11, Chris was accustomed to getting off planes to see the sights at stops before reaching his destination; then he would continue his trip on another day, using his pass. That was permissible in those years for airline personnel.

However, Switzerland did not allow those freedoms during the current turmoil and raised security. (There had been many bombings, including the Piazza Fontanne in Milan in 1969—border guards were still in high alert.)

With guns at our backs, we started marching back to the plane on the tarmac.

Chris kept looking over his shoulder. He opened and closed his mouth a couple of times.

Oh, God, zip his mouth, pa-lee-ase!

The power of my prayer was evident: he blurted, "He-e-y, put down those guns. We're getting on the plane. Leave us alone." Our pace picked up, so did the guns.

Alpha Police watched for everyone's safety. Soon we were in flight to Copenhagen, then on to London in the morning.

LONDON'S FIRST SHOWER

Our honeymoon's first five days in a quaint London bed-and-breakfast close to Hyde Park, provided one of the most embarrassing stories we were *not* eager to rush home to share with anyone, especially our family.

All of the three-story homes in the block of Vicarage Gate joined each other. Our third story room was one of them. The owner's family lived on the first floor and rented rooms on the other two. Since there were no elevators, we balanced ourselves carefully on each narrow wooden step, hauling our two small suitcases and shared hang-up bag.

We were delighted with the nice large bedroom with a hardwood floor, sink, and water closet (toilet). "You'll find the shower on the left, down the hallway," the owner said, as she handed Chris our room key and turned the knob to light the fireplace.

"Hmm, oka-ay," I side glanced Chris.

His eyes bulged. He shrugged his shoulders. The owner left.

I scurried over to the ornately framed window. Boutiques, tearooms, real estate and esquire offices lined the cobblestone streets below.

"Oh, Chris, let's start the day out there. It'll be like walking the picture pages in a story book." We felt intoxicated from the night trip when Swiss border security escorted us off the shuttle on the tarmac, but Chris was eager to go, too.

In bone-chilling, wet and cold months of November, daily I layered almost everything I had stuffed in that little suitcase. I planned it to last two weeks. Mismatched fashions weighted me down—and I was still cold.

After spending our first day at Speakers' Corner in Hyde Park listening to lectures from spontaneous orators on overturned boxes, observing people from various countries, and finding our way around the immediate area, we returned to the third floor late that night. Chris wanted to check out that *one-and-only* shower down the hallway before going to our room.

We tiptoed the approximately thirty-foot narrow, wood flooring that whined every time we moved. We hushed as we passed the unusually thin walls of a dozen guest rooms.

Chris whispered, "This must be the shower. It's the only metal door." He twisted the rickety handle.

My jaw dropped. "Chris! It's the size of a phone booth! How do you function in it?"

We studied the situation. When he opened the door and stepped in, he was directly under the showerhead, which permanently aimed down. I pictured my teased 1970s hairdo getting soaked. Only one coat-hook and it was *inside* on the shower door—no dressing area.

"Uh-huh." Chris shook his head. "It's definitely only a shower."

I shrieked, "Chris, where are we supposed to put our slippers, towel, soap and nightclothes so they don't get wet?"

"Shhh!" He put his finger to his lips. "We'll talk about it in our room. People can hear us through these walls." He contemplated our predicament with one last eye-sweep and tried to shut the creaky-hinged door quietly. We passed a knobby-legged, balding, man who, I hoped, wore something behind the folded towel over his bent arm. He looked up and tilted his head politely; his bare feet shuffled him forward, nose first.

We closed our door and stared at each other. To save space in our single suitcases, we had not packed robes. All I had were a few skimpy "nothing nighties."

I held up the short, white lingerie gown I had worn the last few nights and stared at it.

Chris huffed, "You are *not* going down the hall in that!"

I jumped in. "I'm not going down that hall by *myself*."

I thought, *Our overcoats can be shower robes, but where would we hang them? Mine is a big fake fur; his is huge, too. Chris had traveled the world in his 38 years of bachelorhood—this one is on him. I'm clueless.*

Chris studied, "I fiddled with the knob on the fireplace, but it wouldn't start. I didn't want to bring that up yet."

He continued, "Look, I have my long, thin nylon raincoat." He spread it open on the bed. "We can put toilet articles in these pockets. We'll hang it on that hook on the inside door. The coat will get wet, but we'll tuck the filled pockets in the folds."

"Great! I knew you'd figure something out." I froze. "But what about me? Chris, I really *don't* want to go down that hall by myself."

Instantly, he grinned and paused. He sang his words, "We can go together. You wear the raincoat and I'll wear my boxer shorts. They can hang under the raincoat on the hook."

Some part of my brain kicked in to overtime, *Oh, really! Did he say we're going to shower together? We've only been married a few days. This should be very interesting. M-o-m will have a fit, if she hears about it. I don't think I'd tell my family—maybe years later, if ever.*

There was no other way. We planned and prepared a long time for the shower. Take this, or that? No, this. Not that. Got to have that, and this. Eventually, we stuffed our belongings into the two pockets.

Chris peeked from our door and whispered, "The coast is clear. Stay close to me, but move fast."

THUD. THUD. THUD. I hoped my heart did not wake up anybody through these walls.

The trip from our bedroom to that tiny shower door was a marathon sprint. I felt like a thief, escaping with loaded pockets trying to jump into the nearest phone booth. Chris fiddled and yanked with the rickety handle. I stood guard. The rusty hinges had no mercy, either. Finally, we both squeezed in.

It was smaller than it looked!

Adrenalin dropped to our toes: we were inside. Laughter bounced off the metal walls encapsulating our bodies.

I gulped. "Chris, how do we turn around? How do I get out of this raincoat? This is impossible! I feel like we're stuffed in a coffin standing on its end." Hilarity bounced off the metal walls. Suddenly, "Shhh! Chris." His deep voice was howling so loudly, he drowned out my words. I softly yelled, "Shhh! Qu-i-i-e-t!"

Sharp silence.

This repetition of shattering laughter, sudden silence, laughter, silence was more overbearing and hard to control with each echoing outburst.

He managed to remove a washcloth and the tiny bar of soap from the raincoat pocket and replace them with slippers. However, what were we going to experience when that showerhead detonated water on top of our heads?

We mimicked solutions. Eventually, we bent our heads back as far as possible from the direct shot of an oncoming downpour. No worry about losing our balance in this stance: there was nowhere to fall. Let water do its normal routine, at least to wet our bodies. We were so mashed together, I wondered whether we even got entirely wet! We dabbed soap on each other—somewhere. At least we *faked* a shower.

Dry off? We were doing good to get back into the raincoat and boxer shorts. Somehow we mastered that one, too, and simply toweled down in our room.

Chris fingered and fidgeted with the fireplace knob. We had no option. Lady Owner climbed three flights in her long, thick, *dry* robe. Pounding her finger on a slot above the knob, she muttered, "You have to insert a sixpence every few hours." She turned to us with a pan face and heavy eyelids, stared a few seconds and then left as if she were a sleeping zombie.

I always wondered what lodgers on the third floor imagined. At least it was warm, free entertainment by some wacky couple enjoying first fun in that London shower in November of 1970.

MODELING MISHAPS

Mannequin modeling was just that: being a mannequin in ladies' better ready-to-wear, sometimes on a small platform in the department store. It demanded that we be perfectly still, staring pan face in the distance with extremely shallow breathing, striking a pose we could hold for long periods.

We were lucky to relax our stiff arms, wiggle our legs, or take several deep breaths when customers weren't looking, even from a distance. Most of the time we would find a few seconds to sneak a slight change of position or sniff a slightly larger whiff of air.

It was a challenge to ignore people looking at us, especially when we normally greeted them, identified the designer, the fabric and cost or answered questions.

I was watching the tired hands on the brass clock over the glass doors of the back entrance at Frost Bros. North, as were the employees with no clients on the floor. It was the last hour of a long Friday of mannequin modeling.

Two ladies walked in, strolled over to me and reached for the tag dangling from my wrist, "This is a lovely garment and..."

Forgetting I was a mannequin, I accidently broke in, "Yes, this is an Oscar de la..."

Alarmed and terrified, they vaulted back and screamed, "A-a-a-hhh!!!"

Startled, I shrilled even louder; my hands grabbed my cheeks.

Our piercing screech bounced from the four marble walls, columns and shiny floors. Managers and employees from all departments dashed toward us, while the two clients and I tried to outdo each other in apologies.

Warm hugs completed a mishap-day—one that I would have fun remembering.

Vogue Magazine editor, E. Groves, and eight Frost Bros. high fashion models gathered in the gardens and lush greens of the Lutcher Brown Estate. Lights and lanterns dangled from mature trees in the pitch black of night.

Blinded by spotlights, I posed and waited for Jerri's *go nudge* to begin the show. As I dashed out to the ramp, Patti immediately appeared and waited on the temporary stage to meet me for a back-to-back. Rows of golf ball–sized lights provided my only path on ramp. I could not see a single attendee sitting in the crowded area.

Large fast strides darted me straight ahead into the air, off the end of the ramp, almost into the lap of the closest guest.

Split second adrenalin shot me into a 180-turn. I sprung back up and onto the three-foot high runway!

Patti's eyes glared when we met center-ramp for our back to back.

Jerri rushed me to the dressing area repeating, "Are you okay? Are you okay?" She dotted tears of laughter as she painted the picture, "The ball of feathers bouncing on the end of that six-inch felt stick—standing on top your pill box hat—was the last I saw of you. Suddenly you surfaced back onto the ramp, cool as a cucumber. You still had the veil of the hat over your eyes, too."

Patti dashed into the dressing area, "I could hardly appear serious, Mary Jo. You were there, you disappeared and you reappeared, still with those crazy, decorative feathers poking from atop your hat. I saw them wiggle downward and pop up like Jack-in-the-box. How did you do it?"

No time, no explanation possible—we were frantically dressing into our next outfits. The show had to go on.

The closest guest at the end of the ramp whose lap I missed? My hubby, Chris, who did not have a second to help me. I had bounced back onto the runway!

Photos
Catwalk

All shows were held in San Antonio, TX,
newspapers, except the Mexico City event.

March 1969

Mary Jo poses newspaper ad for her first show—after only a one-month crash course in modeling. The big event hosted world renown designer Geoffrey Beene in the new Confluence Museum in downtown HemisFair Plaza. She poses against an example of elegance from another era...a red Duesenberg car of 1933, a part of the transportation collection of the museum.

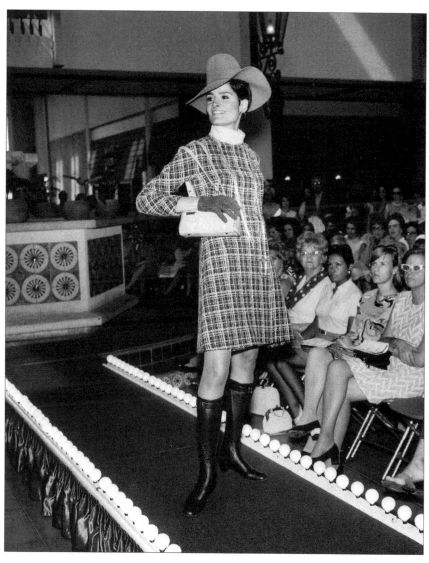

July 4, 1969

Mary Jo in an event including Miss America Judith Anne Ford in Frost's mall
fountain show. This was the day Mary Jo met Chris Shaw (future husband)
in nearby restaurant between shows.

Luncheon presentation in the Anacacho Room of the exclusive
St. Anthony Hotel, block away from Frost Bros.

Mary Jo in Frost's benefit show held in Mexico City in 1970.

Central Park ad for show with Military (later called Mannequin) Models
with Ms. Vincent, agent. Boots for women were the new fashion.

Brenner Couture Fashions ad for appearance at Oak Hills Country Club.

Mary Jo in Vogue winter pants and head-gear look.

Mary Jo wears a late-style pant suit at a
luncheon on a military base in 1970.

Asian attire worn by Mary Jo attracts Sears customers to
expensive woven rugs collection for three days.

Mary Jo models new fashion—
short pants worn with optional overskirt for Sears.

Caped pantsuit by Kimberly reflecting a new freedom of fashion in a Harper Bazaar film at Frost Bros. fashion show for the Decorators' Showcase Preview Champagne Party. Mary Jo downtown in 1970.

Mary Jo runs and jumps among busy downtown traffic for Frost Bros. ad. Exclusive St. Anthony Hotel is on far left (where she did many shows in the large Anacacho Room).

Former chief designer for Metro-Golden-Mayer during Hollywood's "golden years" Helen Rose (seated) twice won the coveted Oscar, was currently creating Debbie Reynolds' wardrobe for her upcoming television series. Mrs. Rose used this photo in her brochure with several models across the nation wearing her fashions. She asked Mary Jo to "turn and swish" the bright-colored gown with green, cinch, wide belting.

Mary Jo displays new fashion of long colorful scarfs in
St. Anthony Hotel's Anacacho Room.

Sears ad:
Men's department suit and new fashion for women pants. Chris Shaw and Mary Jo.

Junior League benefit gala full page color ad in San Antonio paper.

Ad for leather show and pants suit on Hemisphere Tower grounds.

Hippy years' fads –
Headbands, beads, bangles, rings, full-flowing pant sets: Mary Jo dons it all!

After army years, Chris
Shaw (age 23) starts his
football scholarship for the
University of Texas, Austin,
on September 4, 1955...the
same day Mary Jo enters
OLL Convent.

Mary Jo becomes
Mrs. Chris Shaw,
Nov. 11, 1970:
exactly a year later from
their first coffee and
pie date that followed
a surprise visit to Bohn
and Sue, parents of the
newborn.

Marriage engagement photo for Mary Jo Barbera and Chris Shaw.

Post Scripts

Bottle of Wine

Recall: Grandpa Barbera gave us a check as a wedding gift, "Use it to buy a bottle of wine while you're in Rome, you hear?"

We did, asking our young waiter to "select something appropriate—not too expensive, but tasty." Waiter returned, bowed low and announced emphatically with his rolled r's and Italian accent, "I barrrling you the finest in Rrrrome—Barbera wine!" (Barbera is my maiden name.)

For five minutes I blamed and teased Chris for setting it all up, until Waiter broke our laughter, "Look, Barbera is a famous name in Rome." (Only three Barberas were in the San Antonio phone book.) He lifted our coffee cup and saucer. "See, *Barbera* on the sides."

Eventually I was convinced; we toasted each other, and asked Waiter to sign the label so we could take it proudly to show Grandpa. Waiter pinned in Italian manuscript and presented it over to us:

Moreno Antonio
Roma 1970
16 Novembre

We enjoyed our laughter, from the quaint little restaurant in the basement of our hotel. Our small, one-suitcase-each was crammed. Chris had packed like an old bachelor—worn out undershorts and T-shirts—intending to discard them during our two-week honeymoon. "Why wash and carry them home?"

We had room to pack our empty, autographed bottle of Barbera wine for home.

BUT

When we visited Nona and Grandpa, he needled us, "Where is my bottle of wine I asked you to bring me from Rome?"

We froze. We were supposed to purchase the bottle to bring to Grandpa!

Chris saved the day, "Oh, we have the bottle at home."

We did. It was a small bottle labeled Barbera wine—empty!

Since we were kids, we had the challenge—what to give someone who has everything they need for gifting occasions? With no computers in the early '70s, we located a bottle of wine with Grandpa's name on it. That would top any gift he would receive! When he halfway opened our package for his birthday, he set it on the floor next to his recliner. "I buy Barbera wine by the *case* all the time."

The family sat motionless with dropped jaws. However, they purchased bottles for their own homes. Our Roman Honeymoon was far reaching!

London Pub Gang

Chris laughed, "I should have snapped a picture of your first experience in a pub. You shocked me when we stepped inside the doorway."

"Yeah! I had just told you how nice it was to travel half way around the world and go into a nightclub, or *anywhere* on a date, and not visit with someone who knows *you*.

Then we heard those people yell, 'Hi, Chris! What are you doing in London?'"

Chris had hesitated, so I started to announce, "Oh, we are on our..."

Instantly he grabbed my arm, spun around to leave and told the crowd, "Uh, we're in the wrong place to meet someone." He almost shoved me out the door.

Why? They were Braniff Airline employees using a promotional free tour, as Chris often got which included trips, hotels, meals and shows. He explained, "If that gang knew we were on our honeymoon, they'd track us down and tease us no matter what country we visited!" I had learned fast.

Secret Revealed

Aunt Tantan wrapped her love around my day of birth as a treasure and kept it in a special niche in her heart. She telephoned yearly for at least fifty-five years to sing *Happy Birthday* and recount details of those first cherished days.

Tantan would begin, "I remember the day you entered my life. You were deep blue; your lungs wouldn't open properly. The doctors had no hope you'd live—they didn't have the medical help we have today.

"Your Uncle Pat (Mom's and Tantan's younger brother) and I spent the day at the hospital praying. Father came immediately to baptize you in your hospital crib. That's how Pat and I became your godparents. The family began *three* days of storming Heaven with prayer.

"Your mother had been one of Santa Rosa's finest nurses. The entire staff knew Winnie's baby was ill and stayed overtime to watch you, and to comfort and pray with all of us. When the doctor came to your mother's room, he said, 'We don't know how your precious baby is still alive and we don't expect her to live through the night. Joe, I'll take you to her crib so you can touch her and talk to her, if you like.'"

Tantan took a deep breath and continued, "I watched from the glass show-window of the baby ward. Joe's tired, shaking palms wrapped around the crib's top rung for support as he knelt down for a closer gaze. With a choke in his throat, his voice cracked and he blurted out, 'Daddy's baby!'

"WAAAAA...WAAAAAAA! Mary Jo, your scream was one of the best sounds I'd heard in years!

"Nurses in the ward clapped silently. They scoot over to Joe. Everyone was crying with joy. I buried my face in my handkerchief and told God I'd firmly keep *the promise* I made to Him during the last three days of deep prayers for your recovery.

"I made a pledge that night: 'Someday I will tell Mary Jo what I promised to God when we prayed three days for her recovery.'"

⌒⌒

I always knew that, besides my Heavenly Father, Tantan had her eye and influence on me in special ways: her dedicated interest in my prayer life, her guiding my great love for music, her volunteering in Sunday school and at church, and her wanting me to learn to make the delicate sugar flowers as she made for her many beautiful cakes.

However, I didn't yet know about her secret prayer.

Before dementia caught up with her in her late 80s, I called Tantan. As she sang for my birthday, I smiled into the telephone. Then she spoke in a different tone. Her voice was weak, but firm, selecting her slow words carefully.

"Mary Jo, I always wanted you to remember your first three days, and now I want to tell you about a *secret promise* I made to God. I prayed that if He let you live, I would dedicate myself to seeing that your life would be one of loving Him and serving Him to the best of your ability with His help and grace."

I wiped teardrops from the phone's receiver. We were living so far apart (we had moved to Las Vegas, NV), but we were the closest during those moments.

The next year or so, she moved into the retirement center with the Sisters of Divine Providence, where Aunt Sister Clair (Tantan and Mom's sister) was living. What a blessing—to spend her last years with friends she had loved and who loved her all of her life. She had loved her God and she had made Him loved.

Her influence is still His instrument in helping me to treasure my Catholic faith and to live my motto (typed in my convent application): to love God more and make Him loved.

Convent to Catwalk Glossary

Family and Convent Terms

Mary Jo's family names often used

Parents: Joe & Winnie (Osborn) Barbera

Five younger sisters: Jerri, Patti, Candy, Mae, Peggy

Maternal grandparents: Ahmama (Mary Josephine Finto) & Danny (Phillip Giles) Osborn, Sr.

Tantan & Sister Clair Osborn: aunts (Winnie's sisters)

Paternal grandparents: Nona (Mary Giovannazzi) & Pawpaw (Charles Frederick) Barbera, Sr.

Kayo Osborn: cousin

CDP—Congregation of Sisters of Divine Providence

John Martin Moye—founded CDP congregation in Alsace Lorraine in France. His Sisters arrived in Texas in 1866.

Nun—used in this book as same as religious Sister which is capitalized to distinguish from blood sister.

Our Lady of the Lake (OLL)—blocks of campus housing large conventual Chapel, convent, high school, university, St. Joseph Hall for ill &recuperation, and short &long term retirement, demonstration teaching school (St. Martin Hall), social work, etc. in San Antonio, TX.

Office—1.Office Book often chanted prayer: includes morning Matins, Lauds, & evening Vespers, Compline. 2. assigned chores e.g., mopping, washing dishes. 3. room for business.

Habit—full religious garb with white or black veil.

Mistress—title of Sister in charge of women in various steps of training, e.g., Mistress of Postulants, etc.

Investiture—ceremony when after 6 months, a postulant dressed as a bride and became a novice for one year, received the habit with white veil & religious name. Novices DO NOT take vows. Investiture was the step after being a postulant for 6 months.

Vestibule—gathering space in the back of the church, often closed off by doors, separating the gathering space from the large seating/pews area in the body of the chapel/church.

Steps in Training in 1955 to Become a Sister

Aspirancy—aspirant–in high school. Wore beige & brown skirt, shoes, socks.

Candidacy—candidate–1.5 years attended college 2 years. Wore black blouse (with wide, white starched collar), long skirt, hose, shoes.

Postulancy—postulant–six months. Wore same as candidate, but received waist length black cape of the religious habit (with small white starched stand up collar) black skirt, shoes & hose.

Novitiate—novice–one year of longer quiet prayer, intense religious study of Scripture (Bible), the Holy Rule of the Congregation, preparing to make vows at investiture ceremony.

Obedience—1. mission/work assignment for the year. 2.one of the vowed contracts with the CDP's.

Professed Sisters—make vowed (promise) contract with the Congregation of poverty, chastity, obedience.

One—Junior Sister–first year with annual vows, had 1 year of study to earn college degree.

Two—Perpetual Professed–(vowed) for life, after the 5 years of annual vows.

Mission Sister—most with final vows, on mission assignment to schools or hospitals run by the Sisters or parish.

Psalms—song-prayers in Bible.

Sister Blanda—music mentor, in Abilene, first mission.

Sister Blandina—helped Sister Janet teach English, spelling, religion in Abilene.

Modeling Terms

Catwalk—(ramp, runway)–T-shaped with the top extending out into an audience, for models to show fashions.

Frost Bros.—high end, exclusive fashion dept. store. One downtown, other at North Star Mall.

Ms.Vincent & Ms. Staples—modeling agent & assistant.

Geoffrey Beene—a top designer in USA. Studied in New York and Paris.

Henry Ginsberg—Geoffrey Beene's assistant.

Carmen—couture buyer for Frost Bros.

Mr. Harris—VP & merchandise mgr. for Frost Bros.

Ramp or Runway—see catwalk.

Back-to-back—routine on ramp when one model meets another model coming from opposite end of ramp—turning back-to-back, then passing to continue walking in original direction.

DID YOU ENJOY CONVENT TO CATWALK?

*My best friend is a person who will give me
a BOOK I have not read.*

—Abraham Lincoln

Good, clean *family* books are great for all ages—
as gift-giving for men, women, and teens—
for birthdays, Christmas, thank-you, and anytime.

Crossroads to Convent and ***Convent to Catwalk***
are ideal for book clubs, church groups,
the bedridden, the hospitalized, and for those
who just love or *don't love* to read!

Book rates make shipping easy to send anywhere.

How can I help you with my free, fun, book reads/signings, and/or
with easy at-your-event fundraising, at luncheons, bazaars,
schools, or with bulk orders or purchasing?

Contact me, the author, directly:
Maryjoshaw3@gmail.com